A COMMENTARY

ON THE

New Testament Epistles

BY

DAVID LIPSCOMB

EDITED, WITH ADDITIONAL NOTES,

BY

J. W. SHEPHERD

Ephesians
Philippians
AND
Colossians

GOSPEL ADVOCATE COMPANY
Nashville, Tenn.

COPYRIGHT BY
GOSPEL ADVOCATE COMPANY
NASHVILLE, TENNESSEE
1989

Complete Set ISBN 0-89225-000-3
This Volume ISBN 0-89225-009-7
Paperback ISBN 0-89225-441-6

COMMENTARY ON THE EPISTLE
TO THE EPHESIANS

TO

JULIA NEELY SHEPHERD

MY WIFE

WHO WITH GENTLENESS OF AFFECTION, AND
PATIENCE OF LOVE, HAS BEEN FOR FIFTY-
TWO YEARS A FAITHFUL COWORKER
WITH ME IN THE LORD, I MOST
AFFECTIONATELY DEDICATE
THIS VOLUME

*"How strong our scores of wedded years
Has wrought our union, true and sweet?
These fleeting days have been replete
With purest joys, and few their tears.*

*"Our work has been our common task;
Our victories a common store;
And which has helped the other more,
We do not know and do not ask.*

*"Thy presence has been unto me
An inspiration passing wine;
And as thy life has mated mine;
I dedicate this book to thee."*

CONTENTS

                                                                                   Page

INTRODUCTION 9

PART FIRST

THE CHURCH IS CHOSEN, REDEEMED, AND UNITED IN CHRIST (1: 1 to 3: 23).. 15

    Section one. Ascription of praise to God for blessings in Christ Jesus (1: 1 to 2: 21).. 15

    1. Apostolic address and greeting (1: 1, 2)...................... 15

    2. Praise to God for spiritual blessings in Christ (1: 3-14)........ 17

    3. Thanksgiving and supplication for the church as the body of Christ who is the Head (1: 15-23).......................... 29

    Section two. The church redeemed in Christ (2: 1-22)............ 38

    1. Redemption in Christ is deliverance from death through a new creation (2: 1-10)... 38

    2. Redemption in Christ as reconciliation between Jew and Gentile, because both are reconciled in the one body in Christ unto God (2: 11-22) 46

    Section three. The apostle's office and prayer in view of the mystery of the universal church in Christ (3: 1-21).................... 55

    1. Paul's office in the church as an apostle to the Gentiles (3: 1-13). 55

    2. Paul's prayer for the church (3: 14-19)...................... 62

    3. Paul magnifies the gracious power of God which works all for us and within us (3: 20, 21)................................... 68

PART SECOND

PRACTICAL EXHORTATIONS (4: 1 to 6: 24).................. 70

    Section one. The principles necessary to the development and growth of the church (4: 1-24)...................................... 70

    1. The unity of the church of Christ (4: 1-6).................... 70

    2. Diversity of gifts in the glorified Christ and the purpose of all (4: 7-16) 74

    3. An exhortation to a holy life, from the fact that they differed from other Gentiles (4: 17-24)..................................... 83

CONTENTS

	Page
Section two. Sundry precepts (4: 25 to 5: 21)	88
1. Exhortation against special sins (4: 25-30)	88
2. Exhortation to take the love of God in Christ as a pattern for imitation (4: 31 to 5: 2)	95
3. Special warnings against sins of uncleanness (5: 3-14)	98
4. Exhortation to Christians to regulate their conduct with wisdom, to make good use of opportunities, and instead of indulging in riotous pleasures to express their joy and thankfulness in spiritual songs (5: 15-21)	104
Section three. Special duties in household relations (5: 22 to 6: 9)	111
1. Relation of husbands and wives consecrated as a type of the union of Christ and his church (5: 22-33)	111
2. The relation of parents and children (6: 1-4)	117
3. The relation of masters and servants made a brotherhood of service to one Master (6: 5-9)	121
Section four. Final exhortation and conclusion (6: 10-24)	125
1. The armor of God and the fight against the powers of evil (6: 10-20)	125
2. Commendation of Tychicus (6: 21, 22)	137
3. Benediction and blessing (6: 23, 24)	138
PHILIPPIANS	141
COLOSSIANS	239
INDEX	321

INTRODUCTION TO EPHESIANS

I. EPHESUS

The city of Ephesus was in the first century the capital of the Roman province of Asia. It stood on the south side of a plain about five miles long from east to west, and three miles broad, with mountains on three sides, and the sea on the west. It was very early brought into intimate relations with Greece. It was famous for its trade, art, and science, but it was even more celebrated for the presence of the Temple of Diana, reckoned one of the Seven Wonders of the world. This was a building of the Ionic order of architecture, which had been burnt by Herostratus to gain immortality for himself, on the night of the birth of Alexander the Great (335 B.C.), but rebuilt in the course of the centuries at great cost. Contributions to its restoration were made throughout all Greece and western Asia. It was four hundred and twenty-five feet long and two hundred and twenty feet wide, and supported by one hundred and twenty-seven marble columns, sixty feet high, of which thirty-two were beautifully carved. It is now in utter ruin, and so is the city itself, not a living soul resides within its walls.

That Ephesus was admirably adapted as a center for evangelistic work becomes apparent when we learn its great advantages of location. It was on the line of communication between Rome and the East in general. It was one of the places where many side roads converged to feed the main route. From the north and the south coasting vessels brought travelers to the city on their way to Rome, or carried away travelers and officials who were going from Rome to their parts of the province. (Acts 19: 21; 20: 1, 17; 1 Tim. 1: 3; 2 Tim. 4: 12.) Thus it was a regulation that the Roman governors under the Empire must land at Ephesus; and the system of roads was such as to make the city the most easily accessible from all quarters of Asia. Hence it was naturally marked out as the center where Paul should station himself in order to affect the great province; and thence Christianity radiated over the whole of the province (Acts 19: 10), partly through the fact that the great number of provincials came to Ephesus for various purposes, and heard the word, and carried it back to their homes, partly through special missions, on which doubtless Paul's helpers, like Timothy and others, were sent by him.

II. ORIGIN OF THE CHURCH AT EPHESUS

From Acts (16: 6) we learn that on Paul's second missionary journey he was hindered by the Holy Spirit from speaking in Asia. This indicates that his purpose was, after passing through Phrygia and Galatia, to carry the gospel at once to the great continent of Europe. On his return journey he paid a flying visit to Ephesus (Acts 18: 19), in company with his faithful helpers, Aquila and Priscilla, who remained there, apparently several years. At that time there was no church there. But as usual Paul went to the synagogue of the Jews, by whom he was well received, and invited to remain. This he could not do, but promised to return. (Acts 18: 21.) Some time after Paul's departure, there arrived at Ephesus Apollos, who presented eagerly, as he imperfectly understood them, the claims of Jesus, and while doing so, he learned from Aquila and Priscilla the real significance of the gospel he endeavored to proclaim. Shortly afterward he went to Achaia and continued his earnest work for Christ.

In the spring of 54, Paul returned to Ephesus and joined Aquila and Priscilla. At that time he "found certain disciples: and he said unto them, Did ye receive the Holy Spirit when ye believed? And they said unto him, Nay, we did not so much as hear whether the Holy Spirit was given. And he said, Into what then were ye baptized? And they said, Into John's baptism. And Paul said, John baptized with the baptism of repentance, saying unto the people that they should believe on him that should come after him, that is, on Jesus. And when they heard this, they were baptized into the name of the Lord Jesus. And when Paul had laid his hands upon them, the Holy Spirit came on them; and they spake with tongues, and prophesied. And they were in all about twelve men." (Acts 19: 1-7.) Their baptism was doubtless an important era in the history of the young church. As at Corinth, Paul began his work at Ephesus, in the synagogue. After three months strong opposition arose, but during that time he had gathered around him a band of faithful men and women. These he now separated from the synagogue, and secured a place of meeting in the school of Tyrannus. In this place he continued to preach without molestation for three years, a longer time than he had before spent in one place; and with great success. With Ephesus as a center, the gospel was proclaimed throughout the whole province. Asiatic superstition was confronted by the most wonderful miracles wrought by Paul. Certain Jews who attempted to use as a charm the name of Jesus were utterly confounded by the evil spirits they tried to exorcise. And many believers, convicted by the manifested power of God, "brought their books together and burned them in the sight of all. . . . So mightily grew the word of the Lord and prevailed." (Acts 19: 18-20.)

III. TIME AND PLACE OF WRITING

The place was undoubtedy Rome, and it was written during the two years' captivity which we find recorded in Acts (28: 30), which would make the date about 62.

IV. OCCASION OF WRITING

It does not seem to have been called out by any special circumstances, no event to have involved any distinctly precautionary teaching, but to have been suggested by deep love which Paul felt for the church at Ephesus, and which the mission of Tychicus, with an epistle to the Colossian church, afforded him a convenient opportunity to impress upon the Gentile Christians a just appreciation of the plan of redemption, as a scheme devised from eternity by God, for the manifestation of the glory of his grace; to make them sensible of the greatness of the blessing which they enjoyed in being partakers of its benefits; to lead them into the spirit of the gospel as a system which ignored the distinction between Jews and Gentiles, and united all the members of the church into one living body destined to be brought into full conformity to the image of Christ; to induce them to live as it became the gospel which had delivered them from the degradation of their condition as heathen, and exalted them to the dignity of the sons of God.

He therefore calls upon them to contrast their former condition as heathen with their present state. Formerly they were without Christ, aliens from the commonwealth of Israel without God, and without hope. But by the blood of Christ a twofold reconciliation had been effected—the Jews and Gentiles are united in one body, and both are reconciled to God, and have equally free access to his presence. The Gentiles, therefore, are now fellow citizens of the saints, members of the family of God, and living stones in the temple in which God dwells by his Spirit. (2: 11-22.)

The Gentiles, therefore, are bound to enter into the spirit of this scheme—to remember that the church, composed of Jews and Gentiles, bond and free, wise and unwise, is one body, filled by one Spirit, subject to the same Lord, having one faith, one baptism, and one God and Father, who is in, and through, and over all. They should also bear in mind that diversity in gifts and office was not inconsistent with this unity of the church, but essential to its edification. For the ascended Savior had constituted some apostles, some prophets, some evangelists, some pastors and teachers, for the very purpose of building up the church, through them as the channels of the truth and grace of Christ, the church was to be brought to the end of its high calling. (4: 1-16.)

They should not therefore live as did the other Gentiles who, being in a state of darkness and alienation from God, gave themselves up to uncleanness and avarice. On the contrary having been taught by Christ, they should put off the old man and be renewed after the image of God. Avoiding all falsehood, all dishonesty, all improper language, all malice, all impurity and covetousness, they should walk as the children of the light, reproving evil, striving to do good, and expressing their joy by singing hymns to Christ, and giving thanks to God. (4: 17 to 5: 20.)

He impresses upon his readers reverence for the Lord Jesus Christ as the great principle of Christian obedience. He applies this principle to the binding obligations of husband and wife. The marriage relation is illustrated by a reference to the union between Christ and the church. Marriage is shown to be not merely a civil contract, not simply a voluntary compact between the parties, but a vital union producing a sacred identity. The violation of the marriage relation is, therefore, one of the greatest of crimes, and one of the greatest evils. Parents and children are bound together not only by natural ties, but also by spiritual bands; and, therefore, the obedience on the part of the child, and nurture on the part of the parent, should be as unto God. Masters and slaves, however different their condition before men, stand on the same level before God; a consideration which exalts the servant, and humbles and restrains the master. Finally, he teaches his readers the nature of that great spiritual conflict on which they have entered, a conflict, not with men but with the powers of darkness. He tells them what armor they need, and how it is to be used, and whence strength is to be obtained to bring them off victorious. (5: 21 to 6: 20.)

COMMENTARY ON THE EPISTLE TO THE EPHESIANS

PART FIRST
THE CHURCH IS CHOSEN, REDEEMED, AND UNITED IN CHRIST
1: 1 to 3: 23

SECTION ONE
ASCRIPTION OF PRAISE TO GOD FOR BLESSINGS IN CHRIST JESUS
1: 1 to 2: 21

1. APOSTOLIC ADDRESS AND GREETING
1: 1, 2

1 Paul, an apostle of Christ Jesus through the will of God, to the saints

---

1 **Paul, an apostle of Christ Jesus through the will of God,**—This phrase was Paul's ordinary designation of his apostolic mission and authority; used whenever there was nothing peculiar in the occasion of the epistle, or the circumstances of the church to which it was addressed. It may be contrasted, on the one hand, with the more formal enunciation of his commission, addressed to the Roman church (Rom. 1: 1-5), and the emphatic abruptness of the opening of the Galatian Epistle—"an apostle (not from men, neither through man, but through Jesus Christ, and God the Father, who raised him from the dead)." (Gal. 1: 1.) On the other hand to the Thessalonian church, in the epistles written shortly after their conversion, he uses no description of himself whatever (1 Thess. 1: 1; 2 Thess. 1: 1); in the epistles to the Philippians and to Titus he simply describes himself as the "servant of Christ Jesus" (Phil. 1: 1), to Titus, he says: "an apostle of Jesus Christ" (1: 1), and to Philemon: "Paul, a prisoner of Christ Jesus" (1).

to the saints that are at Ephesus,—All Christians are called saints in the scriptures. They are so called more frequently than Christians or any other name in the scriptures. The term is ap-

that are ¹at Ephesus, and the faithful in Christ Jesus: 2 Grace to you and peace from God our Father and the Lord Jesus Christ.

¹Some very ancient authorities omit *at Ephesus*.

---

plied to all who claim to be Christians, regardless of their degree of consecration or perfection of character. Some are more faithful than others. Paul prayed for the Thessalonians that God would sanctify them "wholly." (1 Thess. 5: 23.) To grow in faithful obedience to the will of God is to become more sanctified. There is a gradual growth in sanctification, as there is in obeying the truth of God.

and the faithful in Christ Jesus:—The faithful are not a different people from the saints, but another descriptive term applied to them. [Faithfulness is faith in action, the relation in which fidelity is exercised and shown; trusting and trustworthy.]

2 **Grace to you**—This is a prayer that God would give them all the blessings they were capable of receiving and enjoying.

and peace—Peace is a state of freedom from war. As war conveys the idea of discord and numberless calamities and dangers, so peace is the opposite, and conveys the idea of concord, safety, and prosperity. Thus to wish one peace is the same as to wish him safety and prosperity. The word peace is used in contrast with that state of agitation and conflict which a sinner has with his conscience. The sinner is like the troubled sea which cannot rest. (Isa. 57: 20.) The Christian is at peace with God through our Lord Jesus Christ. (Rom. 5: 1.)

from God our Father—God is the Father of all Christians, as they have been begotten by him "unto a living hope by the resurrection of Jesus Christ from the dead" (1 Pet. 1: 3), have been adopted into his family, and are like him. (Matt. 5: 45; 1 John 3: 1, 2.) The expression here is equivalent to a prayer that God the Father would bestow grace and peace on them.

and the Lord Jesus Christ.—The two graces are here in their due order; for there is no peace without grace. They cover the whole space of the believer's life; for it begins in grace, its latter end is peace. [There is a certain intensity of bright suggestion in the asserted origin of these blessings. The Father is "the God of all grace" (1 Pet. 5: 10) and "the God of peace" (Heb. 13:

20); and equally so "grace and truth came through Jesus Christ" (John 1: 17), and "he is our peace" (2: 14). But the Father is the original fountain of all blessings, and Jesus Christ is the dispenser of the blessings to the faithful believer.]

2. PRAISE TO GOD FOR SPIRITUAL BLESSINGS IN CHRIST
1: 3-14

3 Blessed *be* ªthe God and Father of our Lord Jesus Christ, who hath blessed us with every spiritual blessing in the heavenly *places* in Christ: 4

ªOr, *God and the Father* See Rom. 15. 6 marg.

---

3 Blessed be the God and Father of our Lord Jesus Christ, —Glory and honor and praise and thanksgiving to be God for the gift of his Son and for the blessings that have come through him to the world.

who hath blessed us with every spiritual blessing—Jesus Christ had bestowed upon them spiritual blessings that built up and strengthened the spirit of man. These blessings were such as were bestowed by the Spirit of God. "God is a Spirit: and they that worship him must worship in spirit and truth." (John 4: 24.)

in the heavenly places—This must refer to the church of Christ and the exalted spiritual relations into which God had brought them in Christ.

in Christ:—The idea of fellowship is the prominent thought; every spiritual blessing we have received, the heavenly places in which they are received, are ours only through our fellowship with Christ. It seems to qualify all that precedes, rather than any one phrase. In this section especially, these words form the center and heartbeat of the apostle's mind. In this verse is suggested what is afterwards unfolded, that Father, Son, and Holy Spirit are concerned in the one blessing we receive.

Before proceeding further in the study of this epistle, it is very important to get firmly fixed in the mind the use of the words *we* and *us,* and *ye* and *you,* as used in the first, second, and third chapters. *We* and *us* are used down to and through the twelfth verse, and refer to the Jewish Christians; beginning with the thirteenth verse, *ye* and *you* are used, and refer to the Gentile Christians. By reading the first, second, and third chapters with these

even as he chose us in him before the foundation of the world, that we should be holy and without blemish before ³him in love: 5 having foreor-

---

³Or, *him: having in love foreordained us*

---

facts in mind, this becomes evident and explains much of the foreordination of chapter one having taken place in the selection of the Jews for the reception of the Messiah.

4 **even as he chose us in him before the foundation of the world,**—From this we learn that certain persons were chosen in Christ before the foundation of the world, but there is not a word said as to whether this choosing was conditional or unconditional.

that we should be holy and without blemish before him in love:—This is the character to be worn by the persons chosen, and it clearly shows that Paul was speaking of a class, and not of individuals as such. This in no way intimates that God by any direct power made them holy and without blemish; but he had chosen that class as his beloved, and left it to every man to make himself one of the class. It is said of that class that they were the elect "according to the foreknowledge of God the Father, in sanctification of the Spirit, unto obedience." (1 Pet. 1: 1, 2.) One who does not first show his election by obeying God may be sure that he will never be elected to anything beyond obedience. So obedience is the prerequisite to all other and higher election. There is not a word in this to discourage a man from seeking to make his calling and election sure, nor to give him assurance of salvation, save to obedience to the will of God.

5 **having foreordained us**—There is no doubt but there is a certain foreordination taught in the Bible. In the passage before us it is clearly taught, as well as in some others. Jesus said: "And other sheep I have, which are not of this fold: them also I must bring, and they shall hear my voice; and they shall become one flock, one shepherd." (John 10: 16.) In this he recognizes that he had a flock that were not then following him as the Shepherd. At Corinth the Lord said unto Paul: "Be not afraid, but speak and hold not thy peace: for I am with thee, and no man shall set on thee to harm thee: for I have much people in this city." (Acts 18: 9, 10.) They had not yet believed, but God calls them his people. The meaning of both passages is that there were a num-

dained us in adoption as sons through Jesus Christ unto himself, according to the good pleasure of his will, 6 to the praise of the glory of his grace,

---

ber of persons of that frame of mind and disposition of heart that when they heard the gospel they would believe and obey it.

unto adoption as sons—[Adoption is a term of relation, expressing sonship in respect of standing. It was taken from the Roman custody, that was made for the taking of a child who was not one's child by birth to be his son, and legal heir, the transference of a son who was independent, as by the death of his natural father, to another father. Thus among the Romans a citizen might receive a child who was not his own by birth into his family and give him his name, but could do so only by a formal act, attested by witnesses, and the son thus adopted had in all its entirety the position of a child by birth, with all the rights and all the obligations pertaining to that relation. By adoption, therefore, Paul does not mean the bestowal of the full privileges of the family on those who are sons by nature, but the acceptance into the family of those who do not by nature belong to it, and the placing of those who are not sons originally and by right in the relation proper to those who are sons by birth. So Paul regards our sonship not as lying in the natural relation in which men stand to God as his children, but as implying a new relation of grace, founded on a covenant relation to God and on the work of Christ. (Gal. 4: 5-7.)]

through Jesus Christ unto himself—It is through the mediation of Christ that the adoption of men is realized. (Gal. 3: 26 to 4: 7). He not only brings men into relation as sons, but makes them sons in inward reality and character, giving them the filial mind, leading them by his Spirit (Rom. 8: 12-14; Gal. 4: 6; 5: 18), translating them into the liberty of the glory of his children. The final object of God's foreordination of men to the standing as sons is to bring them to himself, into perfect fellowship with himself as the true end and object of their being.

according to the good pleasure of his will,—God foreordained the provisions of salvation, the characters that should be saved, and the conditions and tests by which they would be saved. He left every man free to choose or reject the terms and provisions of sal-

⁴which he freely bestowed on us in the Beloved: 7 in whom we have our redemption through his blood, the forgiveness of our trespasses, according to

⁴Or, *wherewith he endured us*

---

vation and in so doing to refuse to form the character God has foreordained to be his children and so predestined to everlasting life.

6 to the praise of the glory of his grace,—Those adopted as sons are to bring praise and honor to the glory of his grace. The riches of grace manifested in the blessings brought to man by Jesus Christ are entitled to praise, honor, and glory to God on earth and in heaven.

which he freely bestowed on us in the Beloved:—In or by that grace we are accepted in Christ, the beloved of God. This all teaches that all those in Christ are blessed.

7 in whom we have our redemption—Jesus redeemed all who would trust him, follow him, become his servants. To redeem is to rescue or relieve from enthrallment. Man was enthralled in sin, Jesus suffered, shed his blood, and died to redeem from bondage to the evil one. Through sin man had become enthralled to the devil. Jesus subjected himself to death to rescue man from the bondage of death. Only those who accept the redemption on the terms offered can appropriate it, or be its beneficiaries. Only those who are in Christ are redeemed, purchased, ransomed.

through his blood, the forgiveness of our trespasses,—Jesus shed his blood to secure for man the remission of sins. "For this is my blood of the covenant, which is poured out for many unto remission of sins." (Matt. 26: 28.) "Being justified freely by his grace through the redemption that is in Christ Jesus: whom God set forth to be a propitiation, through faith, in his blood, to show his righteousness because of the passing over of the sins done aforetime, in the forbearance of God; for the showing, I say, of his righteousness at this present season: that he might himself be just, and the justifier of him that hath faith in Jesus." (Rom. 3: 24-26.) This shows that the redemption was provided in Christ, and that it was such that enabled God to be just while justifying him that believes in Christ. To the Ephesian elders Paul said: "Take heed unto yourselves, and all the flock, in which the Holy Spirit hath made you bishops, to feed the church of the Lord which he

the riches of his grace, 8 ⁵which he made to abound toward us in all wisdom

⁵Or, *wherewith he abounded*

purchased with his own blood." (Acts 20: 28.) The statement that "he purchased with his own blood" is doubtless equivalent to "he laid down his life for us." "The blood is the life." (Deut. 12: 23.) The shedding of his blood is giving up his life. He gave his life for our lives.

according to the riches of his grace,—The great word *grace,* which has been used twice already in these opening verses, touches the sentiment of all Paul's teaching on the redemption of sinful men. It has a large place in all his epistles, and not least in this one. For here it meets us at every turning point in the great statement of the divine counsel, the securities of the forgiveness of sin. The way of salvation. It has the particular sense of free gift, undeserved bounty, and is used specially of the goodness of God which bestows favor on those who have no claim or merit in themselves. That our redemption cost so great a price—*the blood of Christ*—is the supreme evidence of the riches of the divine grace. And the measure of what God does for us is nothing less than the limitless wealth of his loving favor.

8 which he made to abound toward us in all wisdom and prudence,—In that grace he provided that the apostles and spiritually endowed teachers should have wisdom and prudence abundantly in carrying forward the provisions of his grace.

[Of the two gifts, wisdom clearly is the higher gift, signifying the knowledge of the true end of life, which can only come from some knowledge of the wisdom of God—divine purpose of his dispensation. Such knowledge is revealed to us through the "mind of Christ," who is himself the true wisdom of God (1 Cor. 1: 24, 30; 2: 6-10, 16), hence wisdom is spoken of with various other gifts, which are but partial manifestations of it. Here with *prudence*— wisdom in action; in Colossians (1: 9), with *understanding*— wisdom in judgment; in 1 Corinthians (12: 8) and Colossians (2: 3), with *knowledge*—wisdom in perception; in Ephesians (1: 17), with *revelation*—the means by which wisdom is gained.]

and prudence, 9 making known unto us the mystery of his will, according to

9 making known unto us the mystery of his will,—To Paul was committed the revelation of the great mystery. Ten times is this mystery named in his epistles. When in prison in Rome, he besought his brethren to pray: "That utterance may be given unto me in opening my mouth, to make known with boldness the mystery of the gospel, for which I am an ambassador in chains; that in it I may speak boldly, as I ought to speak." (6: 19, 20.) It was a revealed mystery, which had "been hid for ages and generations" (Col. 1: 26)—indeed, "hid from the foundation of the world"; a matter, not unknowable, but simply unknown until it came to light through the revelation made known through Paul.

[Not only the types and prophecies of the Mosaic dispensation, but the whole history of the world, with all the marvelously intricate movements of providence, had a certain Christward tendency and leaning as if to prepare the way for him who was the end of the law, the turning point between the old and the new, "the pivot on which the entire plan of God moves." Thus we find the coming of the Messiah into the world in human flesh to be the center of gravity of the world's great movements. The mystery of the gospel which Paul made known was a very large and inclusive thing, embracing Jews and Gentiles, heaven and earth, in its full and gradual development. Sometimes it appears as if it meant only Christ "to whom God was pleased to make known what is the riches of the glory of this mystery among the Gentiles, which is Christ in you, the hope of glory." (Col. 1: 27.) Sometimes it appears as if it included nothing but the reception of the Gentiles into the church upon conditions of perfect equality with the Jews: "Whereby, when ye read, ye can perceive my understanding in the mystery of Christ; which in other generations was not made known unto the sons of men, as it hath now been revealed unto his holy apostles and prophets in the Spirit; to wit, that the Gentiles are fellow-heirs, and fellow-members of the body, and fellow-partakers of the promise in Christ Jesus through the gospel." (Eph. 3: 4-6.) It was never revealed till after the day of Pentecost following the resurrection of Jesus Christ from the dead that the law of Moses was abolished. Sometimes it is as if it meant a divine

his good pleasure which he purposed in him 10 unto a dispensation of the

purpose or plan, with Christ for the center, stretching out over the whole length of the Christian dispensation, and finally re-collecting into one "the things in the heavens, and the things upon the earth." (1: 9, 19.) In fact it means all three things; for the divine plan "to sum up all things in Christ, the things in the heavens, and the things upon the earth," included, as one of its earliest and most momentous facts, the inclusion of the Gentiles in the church, and Jesus Christ as the very center of the whole divine dispensation, and "unto him shall the obedience of the peoples be" (Gen. 49: 10) in all ages of the world. This is the mystery of the gospel—not the church, for it was by the church that the mystery was to be made known: "To the intent that now unto the principalities and the powers in the heavenly places might be made known through the church the manifold wisdom of God." (3: 10.) Yet the church was included in this glorious mystery of God, as the form in which there should be the final summing up of all things in the heavens and upon the earth.]

according to his good pleasure which he purposed in him—God's mystery would be made known on his own terms, as he in Christ had proposed or determined. [God formed in Christ the purpose, by which the dispensation of his grace, in due time was to reunite the universe under the leadership of Christ. This mysterious design, hitherto kept secret, he has made "known unto us." Its manifestation imparts a wisdom that surpasses all the wisdom of former ages. (3: 4, 5; Comp. 1 Cor. 2: 6-9; Col. 2: 2, 3.)]

10 **unto a dispensation**—That at the time when he would consider it most favorable he would gather together all things in Christ. [This marks the period during which the summing of all things is to be accomplished—the period of the dispensation of grace. The term suggests the idea or system not consisting of mere fragmentary parts, but a thoroughly compact and organized system, in which the individual parts have their due places in the working out of a destined result. Just as in creation there is unity of plan with certain typical ideas and regulative members lying at its base, so there is in God's dispensation a certain succession of times and seasons working out the purpose of his will. The God

fulness of the ⁶times, to sum up all things in Christ, the things ⁷in the heav-

⁶Gr. *seasons.*
⁷Gr. *upon.*

---

who "made of one every nation of men to dwell on all the face of the earth, having determined their appointed seasons, and the bounds of their habitation." (Acts 17: 26.) The coming of Christ into the world marks the new era in history, dividing it into two parts. The appearance of Christ marking the turning point between them.]

of the fulness of the times,—The epoch in question is the best time in the divine calendar. For it is God's time, and he is the Lord of all time. The age that saw the advent of the Savior was ripe for the event. It was "the day appointed of the father." (Gal. 4: 2.) The Roman Government had opened the highways for the gospel in every land by its mighty conquests and its large toleration, while Greece gave the world the richest of languages to become the New Testament inspiration. Meanwhile man-made religion had outlived itself, and skepticism mocked at the decaying superstition of the people. "In the wisdom of God the world through its wisdom knew not God." (1 Cor. 1: 21.) All Gentile experiments in living had been tried, but with the unvarying results of disappointment. Meanwhile there was at the heart of heathenism a mysterious longing for some change in the world's destinies, and the eyes of men turned instinctively to the East. It was God's will that the Gentiles should, with a conscious need of redemption, feel after him for themselves, "if haply they might . . . find him." (Acts 17: 27.) Among the Jews, likewise, there was a significant "looking for the consolation of Israel." (Luke 2: 25.) Idolatry among them had entirely disappeared and many hearts were prepared to welcome the desire of all nations. (Hag. 2: 7.) The full age had come, "when the heir would enter on his inheritance." Thus the advent was in every sense "the fulness of time." It was the due time "when Christ died for the ungodly." The world had long waited for it. The purpose of God had only to receive its fulfilment by the coming of Christ.]

to sum up all things in Christ,—These words strike the keynote of the whole epistle—the unity of all in Christ. "To sum up

ens, and the things upon the earth; in him, *I say,* 11 in whom also we were

all things" is the same expression used where all commandments are said to be "summed up in this word, namely, Thou shalt love thy neighbor as thyself." (Rom. 13: 9.) The full meaning of the expression in the passage before us is to gather again under one head the things that had been originally one, but had since been separated. The best comment upon the truth here briefly summed up is found in the following: "In him were all things created, in the heavens and upon the earth, things visible and things invisible, whether throne or dominions or principalities or powers; all things have been created through him, and unto him; and he is before all things, and in him all things consist. And he is the head of the body, the church: who is the beginning, the firstborn from the dead; that in all things he might have the preeminence. For it was the good pleasure of the Father that in him should all the fulness dwell; and through him to reconcile all things unto himself, having made peace through the blood of his cross; through him, I say, whether things upon the earth, or things in the heavens." (Col. 1: 16-20.)

the things in the heavens, and the things upon the earth;— All things in heaven as well as in earth are reconciled in him. The apostle says: "Wherefore also God highly exalted him, and gave unto him the name which is above every name; that in the name of Jesus every knee should bow, of things in heaven and things on earth and things under the earth." (Phil. 2: 9, 10.) That is, everything in heaven and on earth shall be united under the rule of Christ. The government of Christ on earth is the kingdom or rule of heaven extended to earth. In the beginning the earth was an outer court of heaven, in which God dwelt, and over which he ruled supreme, but his rule has been subverted and destroyed by the rebellion of man.

in him, I say,—[He is not speaking of Christ in the abstract, considered in his person or as he dwells in heaven, but in his relation to men and to time. The Christ manifest in Jesus (4: 20, 21), the Christ of prophets and apostles, the Messiah of the ages,

made a heritage, having been foreordained according to the purpose of him who worketh all things after the counsel of his will; 12 to the end that we should be unto the praise of his glory, we who ⁸had before hoped in Christ:

---
⁸Or, *have*

---

the husband of the church (5: 23), the author and finisher of this grand restoration.]

11 in whom also we were made a heritage,—[This is to be closely connected with *in him,* and here has the full sense of *in Christ.* All Christians are God's heritage; but the succeeding verse limits it to the original Jewish believers. The word used is derived from one meaning *lot* or *portion.* The idea is that of such passages as: "Jehovah's portion is his people; Jacob is the lot of his inheritance" (Deut. 32: 9), transferred into the spiritual conception of the New Testament. This is a strong way of expressing the value put upon the fruit of the Lord's redeeming work.]

having been foreordained according to the purpose of him who worketh all things—Those who enter Christ are foreordained in accordance with the provision of God's will.

after the counsel of his will;—This is not only the deliberate exercise of God's will, but also the guidance of that will by wisdom to the fulfillment of the law of his righteous dispensation.

12 to the end that we should be unto the praise of his glory,—The apostles were appointed to a work that brought praise to the glory of God. This was done by preaching what God had done for man, to save him from sin, to eradicate the spirit of rebellion from the world and to restore man, and through man, the world to harmonious relations with God and the universe.

we who had before hoped in Christ:—[This unmistakably refers to Israelitish saints who had the promise before the coming of the Messiah, and hoped accordingly. Such were Simeon, Anna the prophetess, and others up to the birth of the Lord. (Luke 2: 34-38.) Among those who had been looking for the redemption of Israel were the early disciples, the obedient on the day of Pentecost, and thousands of other Jews, including Paul himself. The Jewish people generally had been expecting his appearing. But only the true spiritual Israel could be said to have hoped in the Messiah, and these also included only those Jewish converts who

13 in whom ye also, having heard the word of the truth, the ⁰gospel of your salvation,—in whom, having also believed, ye were sealed with the Holy

⁰Gr. *good tidings.* See marginal note on Mt. 4. 23.

---

hoped in him him upon his coming. As God's own people, as his heritage, confidently hoping in Christ, who was to come, they contributed to the glory of God. Praise in respect to them and by them would redound to the glory of God.]

13 in whom ye also, having heard the word of the truth,— Here the Gentile Christians, as distinguished from the Jewish nation, are clearly meant. "In whom" is repeated before the close of the sentence, which remains incomplete till near the end of the verse. So far as the Ephesians were concerned, they had heard the word of truth from Paul.

the gospel of your salvation,—This, the word of truth meant this good news of salvation which, through faith, they were enabled to appropriate to their own salvation.

—in whom, having also believed,—The repetition of "in whom" keeps the attention fixed upon the main thought in the verse, that all this benefit so received is in Christ. We should notice how constantly the apostle keeps in view the faith which accompanies and conditions all these great benefits. Faith in God enables the humblest to trust and be guided by the wisdom of God. Jesus Christ and his teachings are the perfect wisdom of God, and the simple child of mortality through faith can walk in the light of that wisdom.

ye were sealed with the Holy Spirit of promise,—These Ephesians received this gift of the Spirit by the laying on of the hands of Paul. (Acts 19: 1-7.) They received this gift of the Spirit in its miraculous manifestation. We do not; but we receive it in our hearts, by receiving the word of God into our hearts and bring them into subjection to it. The Spirit becomes the controlling element in the heart and dwells there. We do not recognize it by our senses as did those who received the miraculous gifts, but it is nonetheless a real controlling element in the heart and life, bearing fruit of the Spirit. And this Spirit of Christ in the heart is a seal that we have been accepted by God.

Spirit of promise, 14 which is an earnest of our inheritance, unto the redemption of *God's* own possession, unto the praise of his glory.

---

14 which is an earnest of our inheritance,—An earnest is money given in advance, as a pledge or security that the full amount promised shall be paid. In its use here, it means that assurance that the believer has of the work of the Holy Spirit in his heart that the ultimate blessing, of which he has now a foretaste, shall not fail. The following is illustrative of the meaning here: "The Spirit himself beareth witness with our spirit, that we are children of God: and if children, then heirs; heirs of God, and joint-heirs with Christ." (Rom. 8: 16, 17.) It should be observed that the earnest of the Spirit in the passage before us and the witness of the Spirit is not some vague, mysterious experience of which no rational account can be given. It is rather the very work of the Spirit himself. The Spirit gives the directions as to the kind of life the believer is to live, and his own spirit bears testimony as to whether he conforms his life to these instructions. But the Holy Spirit, through this testimony or witness, moulds the human spirit into his own likeness, dwells with the spirit of the believers; so that the same Spirit that was in Jesus Christ dwells in him. He is led by the Spirit, and through the Spirit of God acts and works, because his spirit is imbued with the purposes, thoughts, temper, and being of the divine Spirit (Gal. 5: 22, 23) there is a happy and harmonious union of the Holy Spirit with his spirit that brings confidence and assurance to his heart and enables him to cry: "Behold what manner of love the Father hath bestowed upon us, that we should be called children of God." (1 John 3: 1.) [The inheritance thus acquires a significance which should be noticed. As earnest money is part of the full amount which is ultimately to be made complete, so what a Christian experiences now is, while an earnest of the inheritance to be finally his in its fullness, a part of that very inheritance, and in so far makes him know what the inheritance as finally enjoyed shall be. So much of real spiritual blessing as he now enjoys is heaven already in his heart; what he has in the work and fruits of the Spirit is for him alike pledge and foretaste.]

unto the redemption of God's own possession,—The redemption is the raising them from the grave to immortality. [For this we wait till the time appointed of the Father—the time when he will reclaim his heritage in us, and give us full possession of our heritage in Christ. We do not wait as did the saints of former ages, ignorant of the Father's purpose for our future lot. Life and immortality are brought to light through the gospel. By faith we see beyond the chasm of death. We enjoy through the gracious promise: "That the sufferings of this present time are not worthy to be compared with the glory which shall be revealed to us-ward. For the earnest expectation of the creation waiteth for the revealing of the sons of God. For the creation was subjected to vanity, not of its own will, but by reason of him who subjected it, in hope that the creation itself also shall be delivered from the bondage of corruption into the liberty of the glory of the children of God. For we know that the whole creation groaneth and travaileth in pain together until now. And not only so, but ourselves also, who have the first-fruits of the Spirit, even we ourselves groan within ourselves, waiting for our adoption, to wit, the redemption of our body." (Rom. 8: 18-23.)]

unto the praise of his glory.—[His grace having done its work, all issues to the praise of his glory. This paragraph began with an ascription of *blessing,* it ends with this refrain which makes *praise* the ultimate end of the entire scheme of redemption. Our free ascription of praise is for what he has done and for what he is.]

3. THANKSGIVING AND SUPPLICATION FOR THE CHURCH
AS THE BODY OF CHRIST WHO IS THE HEAD
1: 15-23

15 For this cause I also, having heard of the faith in the Lord Jesus

15 **For this cause I also, having heard of the faith in the Lord Jesus which is among you,**—This does not imply that he had only heard of their conversion, but refers to the report he had heard, since being with them four or five years previously. Perhaps he had heard nothing after the time when he bade farewell to the Ephesian elders at Miletus (Acts 20: 36-38), until the time to which the reference is here made. It certainly was, therefore, a

which is ¹⁰among you, and ¹¹the love which *ye show* toward all the saints, 16 cease not to give thanks for you, making mention *of you* in my prayers; 17 that the God of our Lord Jesus Christ, the Father of glory, may give unto

---

¹⁰Or, *in*
¹¹Many ancient authorities omit *the love*.

---

matter of great interest to hear from them; and that they were growing in piety and devotion to the Lord. The expression "faith among you" indicates that it was of a marked degree.

and the love which ye show toward all the saints,—[This love is founded upon the character and relations of its objects as the people of God, and therefore it embraces all the saints. The word *all* permits no distinction as respects condition, rank, possessions, or internal endowments either mental or spiritual. But the community of faith precedes and produces the community of feeling. The order is always faith and love.]

16 **cease not to give thanks for you,**—A remarkable feature of Paul's life was the frequency of his thanksgiving, indicating the prevalence in him of a bright, joyous state of mind, and tending to increase and perpetuate the same. Constantly to recognize God's goodness in the past begets a larger expectation of him in the future.

making mention of you in my prayers;—[While thankful for them his heart was not satisfied regarding them—he wished them to forget the things behind, and reach forth to those before. His prayers for the saints are always remarkable. They are very short, but wonderfully deep and comprehensive; very rich and sublime in aspiration; powerful in their pleas, whether expressed or implied; and exhaustive in their range of blessings which they implore.]

17 **that the God of our Lord Jesus Christ,**—This brings out the dependence of the Lord Jesus upon the Father, and sets forth the prominence of the divine sovereignty so conspicuous in the foregoing act of praise. Christ's constant attitude towards the Father was that of his cry of anguish on the cross, "My God, my God" (Mark 15: 34), and after the resurrection, he said: "I ascend unto my Father and your Father, and my God and your God" (John 20: 17). Yet he never speaks to men of *our* God. To us God is "the God of our Lord Jesus Christ," as he was to the Israelites of

1: 17, 18.]   EPHESIANS   31

you a spirit of wisdom and revelation in the knowledge of him; 18 having the eyes of your heart enlightened, that ye may know what is the hope of his

---

old time "the God of Abraham, and the God of Isaac, and the God of Jacob."

the Father of glory,—The key to this is found in "Christ was raised from the dead through the glory of the Father." (Rom. 6: 4.) In the light of this august manifestation of God's power to save the lost in Christ, they were called to see light. (Verses 19, 20.) Its glory shines already about the blessed name of Father, thrice glorified in the apostle's praise. (Verses 3-14.)

may give unto you a spirit of wisdom and revelation in the knowledge of him;—The prayer was that God would give them a spirit of wisdom that they might understand the revelation, that they might acknowledge him as Lord. The same thought is expressed in the following words: "For this cause we also, since the day we heard it, do not cease to pray and make request for you, that ye may be filled with the knowledge of his will in all spiritual wisdom and understanding" (Col. 1: 9); or, understanding the spiritual truths revealed in him. [The spirit here is neither exclusively the Holy Spirit nor the spirit of man, but the complex idea of the spirit of man dwelt in and moved by the Spirit of God, through the word of truth. Wisdom seems to denote the general gift of illumination; revelation, capacity of apprehending the revealed—perceiving the drift and meaning of what God makes known, so that it may be a real revelation to us. (Matt. 13: 11.) In seeking to know Christ more, we are in the true way to get more insight into all that is divine. (John 14: 9.) The importance of seeking more knowledge, after we have believed and been sealed by the Holy Spirit, is here apparent; a growing knowledge is a most healthful feature of the Christian life. (2 Pet. 3: 18.)]

18 having the eyes of your heart enlightened,—The heart is the innermost center of man. It is the seat of the understanding and the source of thoughts, desires, emotions, words, and actions. It is the motive power of human life. Whatever is in the heart rules the conduct. *The eyes of the heart* enable one to look out on the world and shape his course. This is a figure of speech that is common in all languages. What the eye is to the natural body the mind is to the soul of man. When the Lord Jesus appeared unto Saul on the way to Damascus, he said unto him: "To this end have I appeared unto thee, to appoint thee a minister and a witness both of the things wherein thou hast seen me, and of the things wherein I will appear unto thee; delivering thee from the people, and from the Gentiles, unto whom I send thee, to open their eyes, that they may turn from darkness to light and from the power of Satan unto God, that they may receive remission of sins and an inheritance among them that are sanctified by faith in me." (Acts 26: 16-18.)

[In pursuance of his duties under this commission, Paul prays that through this inspired wisdom his readers might have the eyes of their hearts opened so as to see the grandeur and wealth of their blessings in Christ. To illustrate the point: Two men sit side by side in the assembly of the saints, at the same gate of heaven. The one sees heaven opened; he hears the song of praise, his spirit is a temple filled with the glory of God. The other sees the place and the aspect of his fellow worshipers; he hears the songs of praise, the voice of those who read the scriptures and offers the prayers. But for anything besides, any influence from the heavenly world, it is no more to him at that moment than are the most beautiful strains of music to the ox that eats the grass. It is not necessarily strangeness and distance of divine things alone that cause insensibility; their familiarity has the same effect. He knows the gospel so well, he has read it, gone over its points of doctrines many times; it is as familiar to him as the alphabet. He discusses without a tremor of emotion truths the first whisper and dim promise of which once lifted men's souls into ecstasy, or cast them down into shame and bewilderment so that they forgot to either eat or sleep. The awe of things eternal, the Spirit of glory, and God rest on him no longer. So there come to be *gospel-hardened preachers* and *gospel-hardened hearers*. The eyes see and see not; the ears hear and hear not; the lips speak but without feeling; the heart is *waxen fat*. (Deut. 32: 15.) This is the retributive justice of grace abused. It is the result that follows by an invincible psychological law where outward contact with spiritual truth is not

calling, what the riches of the glory of his inheritance in the saints, 19 and

attended with an inward apprehension and response. We certainly need to pray, in handling these dread themes, for a true sense and savor of divine things—that there may be given, and ever given afresh to us, "a spirit of wisdom and revelation in the knowledge of him."]

that ye may know what is the hope of his calling,—What is the ideal of our faith, the purpose for which God called us into the fellowship of his Son, and what is he going to do for us and make of us? He will deliver us from the present evil world, and richly supply unto us "the entrance into the eternal kingdom of our Lord and Saviour Jesus Christ." (2 Pet. 1: 11.) This hope is an "anchor of the soul, a hope both sure and stedfast and entering into that which is within the veil." (Heb. 6: 19.) But is this the hope of our calling which Paul here chiefly signifies? It certainly is not. But with many it is the one thing which stands for the hope of the gospel. They say: "We trust that our sins are forgiven and we hope we shall get to heaven." The experiences of many begin and end there. They make it an anchor of refuge, a soothing of the conscience, and an escape from the anguish of guilt and fear of death, not a life vocation, a grand pursuit. [This may suffice for the beginning and the end; but we need something to give body and substance, meaning and movement to the life of faith. Of himself Paul said: "I count all things to be loss for the excellency of the knowledge of Christ Jesus my Lord: for whom I suffered the loss of all things, and do count them but refuse, that I may gain Christ, and be found in him, . . . that I may know him, and the power of his resurrection, and the fellowship of his sufferings, becoming conformed unto his death; if by any means I may attain unto the resurrection from the dead. . . . I count not myself yet to have laid hold: but one thing I do, forgetting the things which are behind, and stretching forward to the things which are before, I press on toward the goal unto the prize of the high calling of God in Christ Jesus." (Phil. 3: 8-14.) Certainly Paul hoped for heaven; but he hoped for something else first, and most. It was through Christ that he saw heaven. To know Christ, to fol-

what the exceeding greatness of his power to us-ward who believe, according

low him, and be with him forever was the thing for which Paul lived, and can we hope to be eternally blessed if we fail to cherish a like devotion?]

what the riches of the glory of his inheritance in the saints, —[God cares immensely about men, about the character and destiny of men. He said unto Satan: "Hast thou considered my servant Job? for there is none like him in the earth, a perfect and an upright man, one that feareth God, and turneth away from evil." (Job 2: 3.) God holds a man like that in high esteem. Who can tell the value that the Father of glory sets upon the tried fidelity of his humblest servant here on earth; the intensity with which he reciprocates the confidence of one trembling heart. "Jehovah taketh pleasure in them that fear him." (Psalm 147: 11.) "To this man will I look, even to him that is poor and of a contrite spirit, and that trembleth at my word." (Isa. 66: 2.) Thus we learn that Jehovah is deeply concerned about his children, in the character of his saints. It should be noted that the *inheritance* is spoken of as *his* and that it is an inheritance *in* the saints, not *for* them. The language is much like that of verses 11 and 14 which makes the meaning to be that *inheritance* unto the redemption unto God's own possession which God is spoken of as having in his redeemed people—his *heritage*.

The riches of the church lie not in the moneyed resources, but in the men and women who compose it, in their godlike attributes of mind, in their knowledge of the word of God, their zeal, their love of God and man, in purity, gentleness, truthfulness, courage, and fidelity manifested before God and man.]

19 and what the exceeding greatness of his power to us-ward who believe,—Paul is here speaking of the glorious state of believers, the exceeding greatness of God's power which surpasses all difficulties, being omnipotent, is to be understood of that might which is manifested, both in present redemption and future glorification, not in the latter alone, which, however, is included. There is thus a kind of climax—the hope which the calling awakens—the exhaustless and inexpressible glory of that inheri-

1: 19, 20.] EPHESIANS 35

to that working of the strength of his might 20 which he wrought in Christ, when he raised him from the dead, and made him to sit at his right hand in the heavenly *places,* 21 far above all rule, and authority, and power, and do-

---

tance to which hope is directed—the limitless power that bestows it.

according to that working of the strength of his might—[The power of God is not latent; it actually works "according to," that is, up to the full measure "of the strength of his might"—of the strength which is a part of his nature. The whole phrase forms a glorious climax, in which the apostle accumulates words even stronger and stronger to approach the omnipotence of the Spirit. It is a force of exceeding greatness; its only measure is the immeasurable might of the divine nature.] This power is the Spirit that raised Jesus from the dead, for "if the Spirit of him that raised up Jesus from the dead dwelleth in you, he that raised up Christ Jesus from the dead shall give life also to your mortal bodies through his Spirit that dwelleth in you." (Rom. 8: 11.)

20 **which he wrought in Christ, when he raised him from the dead,**—This was the act of almighty power, the wonders at once of a triumph over the physical mystery of death, and the manifestation of an "eternal redemption" from condemnation and sin. The power which raises those dead in trespasses and sins is the same as that which raised Christ from the dead, and there is a striking analogy between these events and an intimate connection between them. The one was not only the symbol, but the pledge and the procuring cause of the other. [From another point of view the resurrection was the act of the Savior's own will; he said: "I lay down my life, that I may take it again. No one taketh it away from me, but I lay it down of myself. I have power to lay it down and I have power to take it again. This commandment received I from my Father." (John 10: 17, 18.) But where it is viewed as the Father's acceptance of the work of the Son, or as the Father's testimony to the Son, it is attributed to the Father as his act. (Acts 2: 24; 3: 15.)]

and made him to sit at his right hand in the heavenly places, —[This does not mean any particular place, but the power which the Father bestowed on Christ, that he may administer in his name the government of heaven and earth. The expression does not

minion, and every name that is named, not only in this ¹world, but also in that which is to come: 22 and he put all things in subjection under his feet, and gave him to be head over all things to the church, 23 which is his body, the fulness of him that filleth all in all.

¹Or, *age*

refer to any bodily posture, but denotes the highest royal power with which Christ has been invested. God has raised Christ to his right hand, because he has made him to share in his government, because by him he exerts his power; the metaphor is borrowed from earthly princes who confer the honor of sitting along with themselves on those whom they have clothed with the highest authority. As the right hand of God fills heaven and earth, it follows that the kingdom and power of Christ are equally extensive.]

21 **far above all rule, and authority, and power, and dominion, and every name that is named,**—The power that raised Jesus from the dead set him at the right hand of God in heaven, far above all principalities and powers and dominions of heaven and of earth. Separate shades of meaning may doubtless be found for these expressions, but the main object of the accumulation is to expand and deepen the idea of Christ's universal lordship.

not only in this world,—[The pre-eminence of his name is to be eternal. It shall never be eclipsed by any other name, nor shall there be any name worthy to be coupled with his name. In all the history of humanity we find no name that can be fitly coupled with his.]

but also in that which is to come:—[This takes in all the duration after that event. Thus Christ is raised far above all created powers in heaven, all that are recognized in the present dispensation, and all that may exist in the future beyond. All this is said to exalt our sense of the divine power that so raised up and exalted Christ Jesus—the same power that still works in believers.]

22, 23 **and he put all things in subjection under his feet,**—That same power had put all things pertaining to the church under the authority and rule of Jesus Christ.

and gave him to be head over all things to the church, which is his body.—The church is the body of Christ on earth of which Christ is the head. Among animals the head is the center and source of life. Jesus stands as the head of the body, whence it receives instruction and life and vigor. The bodies of men controlled by the Spirit of God are the only manifestations of the church visible to men in the flesh. This relation of the church to Christ, represented by the body to the head is a spiritual one and is regulated by the Spirit of the head permeating all the members of the body. But the Spirit does this through the word of truth he presents. Spiritual influences are directed to the spirit of man that thinks, considers, wills, purposes, and acts in accordance with that will.

the fulness of him that filleth all in all.—In Christ all the fullness of the Godhead dwells. In him is manifested to the world the fullness of the power, the wisdom, and the love of God. Of him the apostle says: "But of him are ye in Christ Jesus, who was made unto us wisdom from God, and righteousness and sanctification, and redemption." (1 Cor. 1: 30.) Jesus filled with all the fullness of God bestows the fullness of his blessings on his body, the church.

SECTION TWO

THE CHURCH REDEEMED IN CHRIST
2: 1-22

1. REDEMPTION IN CHRIST IS DELIVERANCE FROM DEATH THROUGH A NEW CREATION
2: 1-10

1 And you *did he make alive,* when ye were dead through your trespasses and sins, 2 wherein ye once walked according to the ²course of this world,

---
²Gr. *age.*

---

1 **And you did he make alive,**—The apostle makes a sudden transition from the thought of that which God wrought in Christ himself to that which he wrought through Christ in men who were dead through trespasses and sins but now believe in Jesus Christ. So God raised, exalted, and glorified his Son Jesus Christ—and *"you."* The same almighty power that was laid upon the body of the dead Christ and raised him from the dead to the highest seat at the right hand of God is now laid upon those who were dead in trespasses and sins to share by faith the glories of eternal life.

when ye were dead through your trespasses and sins,—They had been dead in sin, wholly separated from God, given over to idolatry. This associates the change that takes place in those dead through trespasses and sins with the stupendous power that raised Christ from the dead. There is a re-enactment in the dead sinner of the crucifixion, burial, resurrection, and ascension, when we realize through the power of faith that which was done for mankind in him. It is "the power of God unto salvation" (Rom. 1: 16) that summons men to faith, challenging their confidence wherever this message goes and awakening the spiritual possibilities dominant in their nature. It is a supernatural force, then, which is at work within us through the word of God. It is a resurrection power, that turns death into life. It is the power of love which went out towards the slain and buried Jesus when the Father raised him from the dead, exerted over us as we lay dead in sin, and exerted itself with a might no less powerful to raise us from spiritual death to sit with him in the heavenly places.

2 **wherein ye once walked**—The Gentiles had walked in this rebellion and sin after the practices common to the people of this

according to the prince of the ³powers of the air, of the spirit that now wor-

---
³Gr. *power.*

---

world, before they became Christians. [The idea of dead creatures walking is not altogether incongruous. It implies that a kind of life remained sufficient for walking; but not the true, full spiritual life.]

according to the course of this world,—This was the way marked out by the world. They thought it brought true good. The course was the gratification of the lusts and appetites of the flesh as a means of happiness. [The course of this world denotes the present system of things, as conducted by those who have regard only to things seen and temporal, and no regard to God or to the future life. When there is spiritual death there is insensibility to these things.]

according to the prince of the powers of the air,—The earth and the surrounding atmosphere constitute the world. Earth, air, water are the trinity of substances essential to the development and ministration of life—vegetable and animal. The evil spirits were supposed to inhabit the air and the devil who ruled over them was called the prince of the powers of the air. In this sense of the term the heavens and the earth were equally corrupted and perverted by man. Hence they must both be purged or purified by fire—pass away and give place to a new heaven and a new earth in which dwelleth righteousness. Hence it is said: "The day of the Lord will come as a thief; in the which the heavens shall pass away with a great noise, and the elements shall be dissolved with fervent heat, and the earth and the works that are therein shall be burned up. Seeing that these things are thus all to be dissolved, what manner of persons ought ye to be in all holy living and godliness, looking for and earnestly desiring the coming of the day of God, by reason of which the heavens being on fire shall be dissolved, and the elements shall melt with fervent heat? But, according to his promise, we look for new heavens and a new earth, wherein dwelleth righteousness." (2 Pet. 3: 10-13.) This refers only to the firmament—the atmosphere. It is all sin-polluted and must be purified by fire. Purified, it will be a new heaven and a new earth in which no sin will enter. In that purified temple God will dwell.

keth in the sons of disobedience; 3 among whom we also all once lived in the lusts of our flesh, doing the desires of the flesh and of the ⁴mind, and were

---
⁴Gr. *thoughts.*

---

of the spirit that now worketh in the sons of disobedience;—[That particular spirit, whose domain and work are in evil men. Sons of disobedience are those to whom disobedience is their very nature and essential character, who belong wholly to it. Once that spirit worked in all those addressed; now it works not in them indeed, but in those given over to disobedience to God's will. So the lordship belonging to the prince of evil extends not only over all those malign powers whose seat is in the air, but also and more particularly over that spirit who operates as an energy of wickedness in the hearts of men opposed to God.]

3 **among whom we also all once lived in the lusts of our flesh,**—The *we* refers to the Jews. They among others had their course of life previously to becoming Christians. Notwithstanding they had the law of Moses, it did not prevent their following the rule of fleshly lusts. [The apostle here brings Jews and Gentiles together. "We also," as well as you—we were all in the same condition, all in a miserable plight, not merely occasionally dipping into sin, but spending our very lives in the lusts or desires of our flesh, living for noble ends, but in an end of carnal desire, as if there were nothing higher than to please the carnal nature.]

doing the desires of the flesh and of the mind,—[These two clauses illustrate very clearly the extended sense in which the word *flesh* is used by Paul, as may be seen by the following catalogue of the works of the flesh: "Now the works of the flesh are manifest, which are these: fornication, uncleanness, lasciviousness, idolatry, sorcery, enmities, strife, jealousies, wraths, factions, divisions, parties, envyings, drunkenness, revellings, and such like." (Gal. 5: 19-21.) In the text before us, "the flesh," in the first clause, includes both "the flesh and the mind" of the second; that is, it includes both the appetites and the passions of our fleshly nature, and also the thoughts of the mind itself, so far as it is devoted to this visible world of sense, alienation from God, and therefore under the power of evil. In fact, in scriptural use the sins of "the flesh," "the world," and "the devil" are not different classes of

by nature children of wrath, even as the rest:—4 but God, being rich in mercy, for his great love wherewith he loved us, 5 even when we were dead through our trespasses, made us alive together ⁵with Christ (by grace have

⁵Some ancient authorities read *in Christ*.

---

sins, but different aspects of sin, and any one of the three great enemies is made at times to represent all.]

and were by nature children of wrath, even as the rest:— Paul distinctly states that those who had become Christians were by nature formerly children of wrath, as well as those not Christians. [The Jewish Christians were once, when in a state of nature, the objects of God's wrath, because they were in sin, just as the Gentiles were. The state of nature is the unconverted state.]

4 but God, being rich in mercy,—The preceding verses convey the idea of a rushing towards inevitable ruin, when all hope from man is hopeless. The *but* is very emphatic, and wonderfully reverses the picture. The sovereignty is very apparent on its gracious side. It interposes to rescue those who would otherwise plunge irretrievably into ruin. God, who is wroth with sin, is also a God of grace. His disposition towards those who are dead by trespasses and sins is one of mercy, and this no stinted mercy, but a mercy that is rich, exhaustless.

for his great love wherewith he loved us,—If mercy is God's attitude to sinful men, love is his motive in all that he does with them; and as the mercy is rich, so the love is great. With this great love God loved us when he chose us, and it is on account of that love that he acts with us as he does.

5 even when we were dead through our trespasses,—This is a repetition for vivid contrast with the foregoing description of God and his love; a close parallel with Rom. 3: 23, where for a similar contrast we have a like summary of foregoing teaching.

made us alive together with Christ—As in Colossians where the same word is explained by "having forgiven us all our trespasses" (2: 13), it reverses all that is implied in the words "dead through our trespasses." We were once in consequence of our sins a spiritual corpse, given up to corruption utter and helpless, from which nothing could save us except the life-giving power of God.

ye been saved), 6 and raised us up with him, and made us to sit with him in the heavenly *places,* in Christ Jesus: 7 that in the ages to come he might show the exceeding riches of his grace in kindness toward us in Christ Jesus: 8 for by grace have ye been saved through faith; and that not of your-

---

(by grace have ye been saved),—Paul adds this by way of explanation, lest they should think God partial in the love he showed for the Jews. By the favor or mercy of God provided through Jesus Christ, who is called the grace of God, he saved the Gentiles. [We are already saved from our past sins, but we must continue faithful till the end, for the Savior says: "Be thou faithful unto death, and I will give thee the crown of life." (Rev. 2: 10.)]

6 and raised us up with him, and made us to sit with him—He united all believing Jews and Gentiles in one body in Christ Jesus.

in the heavenly places, in Christ Jesus:—He calls the church, its principles, services, promises, all of which are enjoyed in Christ, heavenly places. The church of God is the reign of heaven on earth. The truth, services, and hopes are all heavenly. The temper to be cultivated is heavenly.

7 that in the ages to come he might show the exceeding riches of his grace in kindness toward us—That in the future state he may show us what rich blessings his grace has provided for us.

in Christ Jesus:—All the blessings and joys of heaven come to us through Christ Jesus our Savior. Without his intervention, and without the help he gives the Christian in his struggle for a higher and better life, he could never be fitted to enjoy the heavenly home. Through all the eternal years of God, the redeemed in heaven will give thanks and glory to his name.

8 for by grace have ye been saved through faith;—The Gentiles as well as the Jews are saved by grace, the favor and mercy of God. God puts no difference between Jew and Gentile, saving both by grace through faith in Jesus Christ. Faith is the medium through which all accept his salvation. On the part of God salvation is by grace; on the part of man it is through faith. God gives man the capacity to believe, reveals to him the things to believe, and ample testimony to produce the faith required. (John 20: 30,

selves, *it is* the gift of God; 9 not of works, that no man should glory. 10

31; Mark 16: 15, 16; Rom. 1: 16; Acts 11: 14; 16: 14, 15, 30-33; 18: 8.)

and that not of yourselves,—The salvation is not of man, neither was it prepared or earnèd by man.

if is the gift of God;—It was prepared and bestowed on man by God. It is obtained by entering into Christ according to the appointed directions.

9 not of works,—Not of the works of the Jewish law, or by any works of man's invention or device.

that no man should glory.—The works that do not save are such as allow glorying. The works of man's device allow glorying, but salvation does not come through such works. The term *works* is used in two senses. It is used to denote the inventions of men or devices of men and to denote the appointments of God. God appoints certain things to be done. Man must do them, but they are God's works. When he does the things appointed by God, he does not do his own works, but God's. Man is saved by walking in the way appointed by God, by doing the things commanded of God. He is saved in doing the works of God. He is not saved because of the merits of the works, but because he proves his faith by doing the things commanded by God. The works of the Jewish law, after that law was fulfilled and taken out of the way, ceased to be the works and appointments of God, and became man's works. This does not teach that man cannot be saved by walking in the works of God.

Then the whole drift of Paul's argument is to cut man off from all works and inventions devised by man, that allow glorying, and that produce only human righteousness, and tie him down as a lost and ruined sinner, dependent upon the works of God provided in the gospel and sealed by the blood of Jesus Christ for salvation. To these he must come by faith in Jesus Christ. He is not dissuading or discouraging men from doing in faith all that God through Christ has provided and commanded and sealed with his blood. He cuts him off from everything save these, and leaves him to walk in "the law of the Spirit of life in Christ Jesus" as his only hope. In this walk he comes to the blood-sealed appointments of

For we are his workmanship, created in Christ Jesus for good works, which God afore prepared that we should walk in them.

God, and is washed and cleansed by the blood of the Son of God. He did not discourage them from walking in that law. By so walking he does the works of God. He does the works without which faith is dead and by which James says (2: 14-20) it is made perfect and by which we may be justified before God. The works of God, the works of faith, are included in the law of faith that makes faith perfect, excludes all glorying, and justifies man. Paul and James, so far from disagreeing, agree perfectly. Paul cuts man off from everything except the works contained in the law of faith, and James warns that no faith can justify that is not made perfect by works, included in the law of faith, and to which faith leads.

10 **For we are his workmanship, created in Christ Jesus for good works,**—Christians are the workmanship of God, begotten by him, perfected by his direction and guidance, and are created in order to perform the good works in which God has ordained us to walk. The things he has commanded us to do are those embraced in his commands to us. But is this a slavish system? This depends wholly on the spirit in which his commands are obeyed. If wholly from a sense of fear it is slavish, and becomes mechanical. But if it is done from a joyful trusting love of God and a desire to please him, it is not slavish. Christ's service to God was not slavish. It was the joyful, loving service that a child renders to his father that he loves supremely—and the joy he found in doing the commandments of God was the measure of his love for him. To substitute anything else than obedience to God's commandments for service is to displace the fear of God with the love of self—the wisdom of God with man's sensual wisdom.

which God afore prepared—God prepared works in which his children should walk before he created them in Christ Jesus. He who fails to live that life fails to fulfill the ends for which he was created in Christ Jesus, and must fail of the rewards that are prepared for him in the world to come.

that we should walk in them.—The works in which Christians are called to walk were prepared of God, not invented by man. So they are saved by the works of God, not of man, when sinners and after they become Christians. [God's purpose in the place which he gave to good works in his decree was that they should actually and habitually be done by Christians. His final object was to make good works the very element of their life, the domain in which their action should move. That this should be the nature of their walk is implied in their being his handiwork, made anew by him in Christ; that the good works which form the divine aim in their life shall be realized is implied in their being designed and made ready for them in God's decree; and that they are of God's originating, and not of their own action and merit, is implied in the fact that Christians themselves had to be made a new creation in Christ with a view to good works. The term *walk* here denotes the habitual tenor of life; it is to be spent in an atmosphere of good works. Here is one of the divine safeguards against the abuse of the doctrine of salvation by grace. When men hear of salvation irrespective of works, they are apt to fancy that works are of little use, and do not need to be carefully done. On the contrary, they are part of the divine decree, and if professed believers, are not living a life of good works, they have no reason to believe that they have been saved by grace. Beyond a doubt, all efforts to outgrow the necessity of carefully and watchfully obeying all the commandments of God, and of doing service to him because commanded by him, and seeking to do the things commanded by him because well-pleasing to him, have degenerated into low types of earthly sensualism and must continue to do so. The highest degree of spirituality possible to man can be found only in learning submission to his will and as his children doing from the heart his commandments, with a desire to please, honor, and obey him. To seek to go beyond this is presumption, is to be wiser than God, and is sin and folly of the darkest hue.]

2. REDEMPTION IN CHRIST AS RECONCILIATION BETWEEN JEW AND GENTILE, BECAUSE BOTH ARE RECONCILED IN ONE BODY IN CHRIST UNTO GOD
2: 11-22

11 Wherefore remember, that once ye, the Gentiles in the flesh, who are called Uncircumcision by that which is called Circumcision, in the flesh, made by hands; 12 that ye were at that time separate from Christ, alienated

---

11 **Wherefore remember, that once ye, the Gentiles in the flesh,**—He again addresses the Gentile converts in Christ and reminds them of their former condition. [They were to remember the change between the past and the present—what they were by nature, and what they had become by grace. The contrast is indicated in various particulars, both of outward condition and of inward privilege and character. The great things done for them by God's grace should incline them to think of the past from which they had been delivered, which would make them more thankful for their present privilege, and more careful to walk in the good works which God had in view for them.]

who are called Uncircumcision—[A further definition of what they were, suggestive of the regard in which they were held as members of that class. A name of contempt which was flung at them.]

by that which is called Circumcision,—[This is a description of those who were Jews outwardly, but who were destitute of the true circumcision, which was of the heart. They were "the concision." (Phil. 3: 2.) The Jews were a striking illustration of the effect of ascribing to external rites objective power, and regarding them as conveying grace and securing the favor of God, irrespective of the subject state of the recipient. This doctrine rendered them proud, self-righteous, malignant, and contemptuous, and led them to regard religion as an external service compatible of unholiness of heart and life. This doctrine the apostle everywhere repudiates and denounces as fatal.]

in the flesh, made by hands;—This intimates that their circumcision was only of the flesh, not of the heart, and that they were no better than those they called "Uncircumcision."

12 **that ye were at that time separate from Christ,**—The condition of the Gentiles was deplorable. They had no knowledge of Christ, no interest in him, no life or blessing from him.

from the commonwealth of Israel, and strangers from the covenants of the promise, having no hope and without God in the world. 13 But now in Christ Jesus ye that once were far off are made nigh in the blood of Christ. 14 For he is our peace, who made both one, and brake down the middle wall

alienated from the commonwealth of Israel,—The Jews when out of Christ, before he came, were the citizens of the commonwealth of Israel.

and strangers from the covenants of the promise,—The Gentiles were separated from God, aliens, foreigners from the commonwealth, strangers to the promises and covenants made with Abraham. (Gen. 12: 2, 3.)

having no hope—The Gentiles could look forward with no hope beyond afflictions, sorrows, and sufferings of this present world, because they knew not God, and did not trust or honor him.

and without God in the world.—[They were unconnected with God; without any friendly and beneficial relation to him that would bring into their souls the fullness of God. The five-fold negative description of this verse has a cumulative effect; the situation becomes graver and more terrible, and the last clause is the climax.]

13 But now in Christ Jesus ye that once were far off are made nigh in the blood of Christ.—But since the gospel of Jesus Christ was preached to them, and they had believed it, these Gentiles who were far from God, far from the people of God, have been made nigh by the blood of Christ. [Jesus Christ came to break down the middle wall of partition between Jew and Gentile and to make peace between them. He came to bring all nigh to God and to one another. The way to unite people to one another is to unite them all to God. Jesus brought them to God by shedding his blood for them to reconcile them to God.] Jesus said: "I lay down my life for the sheep. And other sheep I have, which are not of this fold: them also I must bring, and they shall hear my voice; and they shall become one flock, one shepherd." (John 10: 15, 16.) There were those among both Jews and Gentiles who would hear his voice, these he would call into the one fold by his bloodshed, his life laid down for them, that they might be one fold.

14 For he is our peace,—The personal Christ, whose blood was shed is our Peace, not simply our peacemaker; for in his per-

of partition, 15 having abolished in his flesh the enmity, *even* the law of commandments *contained* in ordinances; that he might create in himself of the two one new man, *so* making peace; 16 and might reconcile them both in one

---

son as God-man, the reconciliation took place. His own nature being the only tie of unity between God and mankind, and between Jews and Gentiles. Through the whole passage thus introduced there runs a double meaning, a declaration of peace between Jew and Gentile, and between both and God. The latter is based upon the former, and the apostle gives prominence now to the one, and again to the other, but here necessarily includes both in the phrase, "our peace."

who made both one,—[So there is no ground for separating between a Jewish element and a Gentile; in Christ they are unified. If all were really in Christ, war would disappear.]

and brake down the middle wall of partition,—The wall of partition was circumcision and the ordinances and observances of the Jewish law on the one side; on the other side were the worship of idols, the fleshly sins, and pollutions that accompany idolatry, and the lack of faith in God. Jesus removed these separating causes.

15 **having abolished in his flesh the enmity, even the law of commandments contained in ordinances;**—Christ by his death abolished the law. This is the great truth Paul had to teach. We are "not under law, but under grace." (Rom. 6: 14.) We are not required to seek salvation on the ground of obedience to the law which says: "Cursed is every one who continueth not in all things that are written in the book of the law, to do them." (Gal. 3: 10.) Christ has freed us from the law as a covenant of works, by himself being made subject to it (Gal. 4: 5); by bearing its penalty (Gal. 3: 13), "in the body of his flesh through death" (Col. 1: 22), "to the cross" (Col. 2: 14). The teaching of the passage, therefore, is that the middle wall of partition between Jews and Gentiles consisting of their mutual enmity has been removed by Christ's having through his death abolished the law in all its forms, as a rule of justification, and thus opening one new and living way of access to God, common to all Jews and Gentiles.

that he might create in himself of the two one new man, so making peace;—Christ took them out of the way so that he

body unto God through the cross, having slain the enmity thereby: 17 and he came and ⁰preached peace to you that were far off, and peace to them that

⁰Gr. *brought good tidings of peace.* Comp. Mt. 11. 5.

---

could bring both into himself through faith, and of the two—Jew and Gentile—make one new man in Christ, so making peace. [The union or peace which flows from the abrogation of the law by the death of Christ is progressive so far as it is inward or subjective. The outward work is done. The long feud in the human family is healed. The distinction between Jew and Gentile is abolished. All the exclusive privileges of the former are abrogated. The wall which had so long shut out the Gentiles is removed. There is now one fold and one shepherd. Since the abrogation of the law, "there can be neither Jew nor Greek, there can be neither bond nor free, there can be no male and female; for ye all are one man in Christ Jesus. And if ye are Christ's, then are ye Abraham's seed, heirs according to promise." (Gal. 3: 28, 29.)]

16 and might reconcile them both in one body unto God through the cross,—Jesus died on the cross to reconcile man to God, to redeem him, to rescue him from his sinful course and bring him back to God, "that he might himself be just, and the justifier of him that hath faith in Jesus." (Rom. 3: 26.) He through the cross brought both Jew and Gentile into one body, into Christ, as Paul said: "God was in Christ reconciling the world unto himself, not reckoning unto them their trespasses, and having committed unto us the word of reconciliation." (2 Cor. 5: 19.) Man brought into Christ was brought into reconciliation with God.

having slain the enmity thereby:—Having slain the enmity between God and man, he slew the enmity between all that come to God. No man can be in union with God without being in union and fellowship with every other being in the universe in union with him. The Psalmist said: "I am a companion of all them that fear thee, and of them that observe thy precepts." (Psalm 119: 63.) Again, "if we walk in the light, as he is in the light, we have fellowship one with another, and the blood of Jesus his Son cleanseth us from all sin." (1 John 1: 7.)

17 and he came and preached peace to you that were far off, and peace to them that were nigh:—He proclaimed the same

were nigh: 18 for through him we both have our access in one Spirit unto

terms of peace both to the Gentiles who were far off and to the Jews who were nigh. Of the Gentiles, Peter said: "Brethren, ye know that a good while ago God made choice among you, that by my mouth the Gentiles should hear the word of the gospel, and believe. And God, who knoweth the heart, bare them witness, giving them the Holy Spirit, even as he did unto us; and he made no distinction between us and them, cleansing their hearts by faith." (Acts 15: 7-9.) [The coming was subsequent to the transactions of the cross. It cannot denote what Christ did personally, but what he did by sending the Holy Spirit to the apostles and other early preachers of the gospel. It was only after the cross and after the resurrection that peace could be proclaimed on the footing of faith in a Savior who had died and that God had raised him from the dead. And only in the sense of having sent Paul and other proclaimers of the gospel could Jesus be said to have preached to the Ephesians.]

18 **for through him we both have our access**—The proof that peace has thus been obtained for Jew and Gentile is that both have equally free access to God through Christ and since Gentiles have as free access to God as Jews, and upon the same terms and in the same way, it follows that the peace procured by the death of Christ was designed for the Gentiles as well as for the Jews.

in one Spirit—The word of God is the seed of the kingdom. (Luke 8: 11.) The Spirit of God dwells in the word, as the germinal principle dwells within the seed. The epistles contain the teaching that the Holy Spirit gave, through the apostles, to Christians, teaching them how they should conduct themselves as individuals and as worshipping assemblies. All the teaching that the Holy Spirit gave is found in the word of God. It is the ministry of the Spirit to the church and the world; the word of God is the only teaching of the Spirit that the church has. When we follow the word of God, we are led by the Spirit of God; when we turn from the word of God, we refuse to be led by the Spirit; when we take the word of God into the heart, we receive the Spirit into our hearts, just as we place the germinal principle of the wheat in the soil. The Spirit of God never dwells in the heart that

the Father. 19 So then ye are no more strangers and sojourners, but ye are fellow-citizens with the saints, and of the houseold of God, 20 being built

---

does not receive and cherish the word of God. When the word is cherished in the heart, the Spirit of God dwells there, spreads his influence abroad, and molds all the feelings, desires, and purposes of the heart in accordance with the will of God. When one reaches this stage he is in the one Spirit.

unto the Father.—[As the right is theirs only through Christ, so it is made theirs in actual experience in the one Spirit, and they have it alike because it is one and the same Spirit that works in both Jew and Gentile. So both have continuous access to God from whom once the Gentiles were far removed, to him, in the benign character of the Father whom they can approach without fear.]

19 so then ye are no more strangers and sojourners, but ye are fellow-citizens—Since the Spirit had guided them through Christ to God, and they had become partakers of the blessings of the children of God in Christ Jesus, they were no more strangers and sojourners, but fellow citizens with the saints.

with the saints,—This is a comprehensive name for Christians; the whole community of believers in Christ, without distinction of Jew and Gentile, are citizens of the kingdom of heaven. They were brought into the enjoyment of all the honors and privileges of the most honored sons of God.

and of the household of God,—Members of God's family. The idea is that of a child at home. In the deepest sense the Gentile believer, once "far off" in both position and condition, is now at home with his loving Father. [The prominent characteristic of a family is mutual affection. A family is held together by love. There is the love of the father for each and all and there is the love for him and for each other. And so it is in the divine family. "God is love"; pure, infinite, and eternal love. This, as it is the glorious summary of his perfections, is the characteristic of every individual member of his spiritual family. "We love, because he first loved us. . . . And this commandment have we from him, that he who loveth God love his brother also." (1 John 4: 19-21.)

upon the foundation of the apostles and prophets, Christ Jesus himself being

That, however, which the apostle seems to have more particularly in view is the high privilege which attaches to this divine relationship.]

20 being built upon the foundation of the apostles—The Gentiles were builded as stones—living stones—into the temple of God resting upon the foundation of the apostles and prophets. "Ye also, as living stones, are built up a spiritual house, to be a holy priesthood, to offer up spiritual sacrifices, acceptable to God through Jesus Christ." (1 Pet. 2: 5.) The gospel as preached by Paul and the other apostles is the foundation on which their converts were built into the spiritual temple—the church. Some expositors object to this interpretation, saying that those who are parts of the building could not act as agents in laying the foundation; but they rested on it even while they laid it.

and prophets,—The New Testament prophets were a distinct class of inspired teachers to make known the will of God after it had been revealed through the apostles.

[It is fitting that the following should be said in reference to the apostles, as exercising authority, and entitled to be received in that representative character with which the Lord had endowed them. The promises of the Lord unto Peter certainly imply an apostolic office and function: "I will give unto thee the keys of the kingdom of heaven: and whatsoever thou shalt bind on earth shall be bound in heaven; and whatsoever thou shalt loose on earth shall be loosed in heaven" (Matt. 16: 19); and later on to the whole group of apostles, he said: "These things have I spoken unto you, while yet abiding with you. But the Comforter, even the Holy Spirit, whom the Father will send in my name, he shall teach you all things, and bring to your remembrance all that I said unto you" (John 14: 25, 26); on the day he ascended to heaven, he said: "Behold, I send forth the promise of my Father upon you: but tarry ye in the city, until ye be clothed with power from on high" (Luke 24: 49); and the power came upon them on the day of Pentecost, following his resurrection when "they were all filled with the Holy Spirit, and began to speak with other tongues, as the Spirit gave them utterance." It is, therefore, but the recognition of what had been thus

the chief corner stone; 21 in whom ⁷each several building, fitly framed together, growth into a holy ⁸temple in the Lord; 22 in whom ye also are builded together ⁹for a habitation of God in the Spirit.

⁷Gr. *every building.*
⁸Or, *sanctuary*
⁹Gr. *into.*

---

appointed when for the apostles as a body, and for the prophets whose service bore such an intimate relation with their own, a place and function so fundamental is indicated.]

Christ Jesus himself being the chief corner stone;—[The cornerstone is a massive stone in which the two lines of the wall at their foundation meet, by which they were bonded together, and on the perfect squareness of which the true direction of the whole walls depended, since the slightest imperfection in the cornerstone would be indefinitely multiplied along the course of the walls.]

21 in whom each several building, fitly framed together,— In Jesus Christ all the buildings formed of both Jews and Gentiles who enter Christ are builded or fitly framed or fitted together, not separated and divided. [This represents an action still going on, namely, that of fitting together the different parts. The growth is both outward and inward, extensive and intensive, in number and in grace.]

groweth into a holy temple in the Lord;—The church is *one*, the manifestations of it are many—the local bodies of Christ. The local bodies are manifestations of the Spirit dwelling in and controlling men in the flesh. They are the holy temples of God on earth; they are the dwelling places of God. They are the most sacred bodies on earth. More precious and sacred with God than with the fleshly body of his Son. It is the greatest of sacrilege to change, modify, or mutilate that body—strip it of its God-given functions and bestow them upon another body of human make. It is the highest of crimes to make it subserve human-made bodies.

22 in whom ye also are builded together for a habitation of God in the Spirit.—Christians are builded together in Christ, for a habitation, a dwelling place of God on earth. He dwells in his holy habitation in the person of the Spirit. The church is a spiritual body, embracing all the spirits in harmony with God in heaven and on earth. It manifests on earth as the souls of men inhabiting earthly bodies are brought into spiritual oneness with

God, and so separate their bodies from the corrupt ways and organizations of men into bodies controlled by the Spirit of God.

The New Testament clearly recognizes each separate congregation as the body of Christ. So that God through his Spirit dwells in each distinct and separate church. The church is the body of Christ in the community in which it is situated. It is not a foot in Corinth, an arm in Ephesus, an eye in Philippi, an ear in Antioch. But each was a complete integral body of Christ composed of all the different members needed to make up his body. Take the church at Jerusalem. It was in existence before any other church. Was it not the body of Christ when it was the only church on earth? Did the planting of another church take from it any of its parts, any of its functions, despoil it of its integralism and completeness as a body of Christ? Certainly not. What about the church? My conviction is that he possessed within himself all the elements of a church of Christ when no other churches were in reach of him, and the multiplication of the seed or the word of God in him would produce a church of God wherever he went, and the same is true of every child of God. A child of God in a strange land has only to worship God himself, multiply the word of God in the hearts of others and the result is a church of the living God, complete in itself without reference to any other organization in the world. If you should ask: "Would it not be a monstrosity for Christ to be the head of so many different bodies?" Not more so than for God to be present in all places at one time.

SECTION THREE

THE APOSTLE'S OFFICE AND PRAYER IN VIEW OF THE MYSTERY OF THE UNIVERSAL CHURCH IN CHRIST
3: 1-21

1. PAUL'S OFFICE IN THE CHURCH AS AN APOSTLE TO THE GENTILES
3: 1-13

1 For this cause I Paul, the prisoner of Christ Jesus in behalf of you

---

1 **For this cause I Paul,**—[Paul having finished his portraiture of the church, consisting of Jews and Gentiles, built up harmoniously in Christ and constituting the habitation of the indwelling Spirit, offers a prayer that they may arise to a full apprehension of the blessed privileges of which they have been made partakers. Accordingly he begins, "For this cause I Paul"—but having gone so far, he enters on a digression, relating to himself and his office as an apostle, which continues through thirteen verses, at the conclusion of which he resumes with the same words —"For this cause I"—and concludes the sentence with "I bow my knees unto the Father." (Verse 14.)]

the prisoner of Christ Jesus—The phrase is dwelt upon with an emphasis, explained by Paul's conviction that his bonds tended "unto the progress of the gospel," by showing the victorious power of God's word and grace to triumph over captivity and the danger of death. When he calls himself the prisoner of Christ Jesus, he represents the Lord's own will, as ordaining his captivity and for his own transcendent purpose of good, making him "an ambassador in chains" (6: 20) and these "the bonds of the gospel" (Phile. 13); and "for because of the hope of Israel I am bound with this chain" (Acts 28: 20). Hence in the passage before us Paul speaks of his captivity as a special proof of the reality of his mission, and a new step in its progress; and appeals to it accordingly, just as he closes one of his epistles: "Remember my bonds." (Col. 4: 18.) The whole idea is a striking instance of faith turning all things to good to them that love God. (Rom. 8: 28.)

Gentiles,—2 if so be that ye have heard of the ¹⁰dispensation of that grace of God which was given me to you-ward; 3 how that by revelation was made known unto me the mystery, as I wrote before in few words, 4 whereby, when ye read, ye can perceive my understanding in the mystery of Christ; 5

---

¹⁰Or, *stewardship*

in behalf of you Gentiles,—This was literally true of the origin of his captivity, proceeding as it did from the jealousy of the Jews, excited by the admission of the Gentiles into the church without requiring them to be circumcised and keep the law. But the reference is not to be limited to this. Paul regards the captivity as only one incident in a mission sending him entirely to the Gentiles. (Acts 21: 21; Rom. 11: 13; Gal. 2: 9.) And he did not forget that the suspicion of his having taken an Ephesian named Trophimus into the temple with him created the popular disturbance that led to his capture and his final appeal to Caesar, his journey to Rome, and his imprisonment in that city.

2 if so be that ye have heard—This does not express a doubt whether they heard it or not, for he takes it for granted that they had. He had informed them and it would not be inconsistent with usage to say, "if so be that ye have heard," as alluding to a well-known fact, and as referring to it in the way of calling them to self-scrutiny as to the time when they heard it and the person from whom they heard it.

of the dispensation of that grace of God which was given me to you-ward;—The Lord had called Paul to preach the gospel to the Gentiles. (Acts 9: 15.) This he called the dispensation to you-ward. God had committed the work of preaching to the Gentiles to Paul as the chief worker and teacher, as he had that of preaching to the Jews to Peter. (Gal. 2: 9.) [By grace is meant the favor whereby Paul was constituted the apostle of the Gentiles. Deeply though he felt his being sent away from preaching to his countrymen (Acts 22: 18), he took kindly to the new sphere allotted to him, and magnified his ministry (Rom. 11: 13).]

3 how that by revelation was made known unto me the mystery, as I wrote before in few words,—Christ revealed the purpose to Paul when he first called him, saying: "To this end have I appeared unto thee, to appoint thee a minister and a witness both of the things wherein thou hast seen me, and of the things wherein I

which in other generations was not made known unto the sons of men, as it hath now been revealed unto his holy apostles and prophets in the Spirit; 6

will appear unto thee; delivering thee from the people, and from the Gentiles, unto whom I send thee, to open their eyes, that they may turn from darkness to light and from the power of Satan unto God, that they may receive remission of sins and an inheritance among them that are sanctified by faith in me." (Acts 26: 16-18.) [Of this Paul had already told them "in few words." (1: 9, 10; 2: 18.) He was not indebted for his knowledge of the gospel to the instruction of others. Hence he says: "For I make known to you, brethren, as touching the gospel which was preached by me, that it is not after man. For neither did I receive it from man, or was I taught it, but it came to me through revelation of Jesus Christ." (Gal. 1: 11, 12.) As the apostles were witnesses, their knowledge must be direct and not founded on hearsay. This was one of the indispensable qualifications for the apostleship.]

4 whereby, when ye read, ye can perceive my understanding in the mystery of Christ;—The reception of the Gentiles on an equality with the Jews is the mystery of Christ. A mystery was something unrevealed. When they read what he had told them in this epistle, they had his knowledge concerning the mystery. When it was once revealed, it was no longer a mystery. The term mystery as here used does not mean something difficult to be understood or incomprehensible, but something unrevealed, however simple it might be. [What Paul had written respecting the calling of the Gentiles in the preceding chapter was an indication of his knowledge of the whole plan of salvation, here designated as "the mystery of Christ," which includes far more than the truth that the Gentiles were "fellow-partakers of the promise in Christ Jesus through the gospel."]

5 which in other generations was not made known unto the sons of men,—This truth of the reception of the Gentiles had not been known unto the sons of men, through the ages from Abraham to the coming of Jesus Christ. It had been foretold to Abraham and to various prophets that the blessings in the seed of Abraham should be to all nations, but always in a way that they did not understand.

to wit, that the Gentiles are fellow-heirs, and fellow-members of the body, and fellow-partakers of the promise in Christ Jesus through the ¹gospel, 7

---

¹Gr. *good tidings*. See Mt. 4. 23 marg.

---

as it hath now been revealed unto his holy apostles and prophets—It has now been revealed to them, as plainly and fully as it was to the apostles and prophets by the Holy Spirit who guided them. They were directed to go forward and preach to the Gentiles and receive them in such manner that they could not fail to see and understand what was meant. This direction and revelation was given to Peter at the house of Cornelius (Acts 10: 34, 35; 11: 18), and to Paul and Barnabas (Acts 15: 12), and has been made known to the whole church at the apostolic council at Jerusalem (Acts 15: 12-29).

in the Spirit;—[The source of the revelation is here indicated. Jesus promised to send the Spirit to guide the apostles into all the truth. (John 16: 13.) The things of Christ, pre-eminently such things are here in question, he should declare unto them. It is precisely of this that Paul is now speaking.]

6 **to wit, that the Gentiles are fellow-heirs,**—Fellow heirs with the Jews as saints, and belonging to the family of God. They have the same right to the inheritance as the Jews. The inheritance is all the benefits of the covenant of grace; the knowledge of the truth, justification, adoption, and sanctification; the indwelling of the Spirit, and life everlasting.

and fellow-members of the body,—[They are constituent portions of the body—the church; as nearly related to him, and as much partakers of his life as their Jewish brethren.]

and fellow-partakers of the promise—They were members of the same body, incorporated in it as believers; they shared the same privileges, summed up in the phrase "the promise."

in Christ Jesus—They do not get this blessing by becoming Jews, but directly as Gentiles; and they became fellow heirs, fellow members, and fellow partakers in Christ Jesus, enjoying all privileges in him, in a state of union and fellowship with him.

through the gospel,—To this state they were invited and admitted through the gospel; by receiving the glad tidings they entered on the blessings. (Rom. 10: 15-18.) This statement of reli-

3: 6-8.] EPHESIANS 59

whereof I was made a minister, according to the gift of that grace of God which was given me according to the working of his power. 8 Unto me, who am less than the least of all saints, was this grace given, to ²preach unto the Gentiles the unsearchable riches of Christ; 9 and to ³make all men see

²Gr. *bring good tidings of the &c.* Comp. ch. 2. 17.
³Some ancient authorities read *bring to light what is.*

---

gious equality between Jews and Gentiles is strong, clear, and complete. Hence the apostle enlarges on the dignity and importance of preaching the gospel.

7 whereof I was made a minister,—He did not gradually grow up to the office, but became, at a given time and place, a minister. This is his service; the work for which he is engaged and to which he is bound to devote himself.

according to the gift of that grace of God which was given me according to the working of his power.—[The working of God's power is described as the measure of the gift of his grace. In fact, what is a gift in its source is "the working of his power" in its actual nature. In the whole of this passage, however, the chief emphasis is laid not on the spiritual power, but on the freedom of God's gift to Paul of his high privilege of preaching the mystery of the gospel to the Gentiles.]

8 Unto me, who am less than the least of all saints,—Paul felt his unworthiness because he had persecuted the church. He says: "For I am the least of the apostles, that am not meet to be called an apostle, because I persecuted the church of God." (1 Cor. 15: 9), and "Though I was before a blasphemer, and a persecutor, and injurious: howbeit I obtained mercy, because I did it ignorantly in unbelief." (1 Tim. 1: 13.) So he felt his unworthiness as the least of all the saints on account of the course he had pursued.

was this grace given, to preach unto the Gentiles the unsearchable riches of Christ;—He felt that it was a matter of special grace that he was permitted to preach the gospel with its blessings that were past finding out, through labor and toil and suffering, for which favor he was always grateful. [The thought of his having such riches to offer to all made him regard his office as most glorious, raised him far above the point of view from which the world would despise it, and filled him with adoring gratitude to God for having conferred it on him.]

what is the dispensation of the mystery which for ages hath been hid in God who created all things; 10 to the intent that now unto the principalities and the powers in the heavenly *places* might be made known through the church

9 and to make all men see what is the dispensation of the mystery—The reception of the Gentiles carried with it the revelation of the glorious purpose God had always of redeeming man from sin and rescuing the world from the rule of the evil one and the ruin brought upon it; of purging it of all evil, and bringing it back to more than its pristine relations to God and the universe. The redemption of the Gentiles was the significant step in the work. The mystery had been entrusted to Paul that he might make it known.

which for ages hath been hid in God who created all things;—[In these words is a recognition of that sovereignty in God based upon the fact that all things owe their origin to him, by virtue of which he not only of right appoints events "according to the good pleasure of his will" (1: 5), but times their fulfillment as his infinite wisdom sees in all respects fitting and right, and appoints the agent through whom the proclamation of a truth of such magnitude requires.]

10 to the intent that now unto the principalities and the powers—By principalities and powers is meant the angelic being in their several orders of beings. The *now* of the passage suggests the fact that what had once "been hid in God has now," the time for its revelation having arrived, "been revealed."

in the heavenly places—The heavenly places are those occupied by angels. But as angels not only dwell in heaven, are "all ministering spirits, sent forth to do service for the sake of them that shall inherit salvation" (Heb. 1: 14), the places from which they are being taught the manifold wisdom of God are partly in heaven and partly in the regions of our atmosphere. Whatever their places are, their places are heavenly, and one thing that makes them so is the fact that they are learning through the church which they serve the manifold wisdom of God.

might be made known—[In this Paul passes on to consider the manifestation of God in Christ brought to the knowledge of angels who are described as desiring "to look into" (1 Pet. 1: 12) the consummation of the gospel mystery. In the same sense the

the manifold wisdom of God, 11 according to the ⁴eternal purpose which he purposed in Christ Jesus our Lord: 12 in whom we have boldness and access in confidence through ⁵our faith in him. 13 Wherefore I ask that ⁶ye may not faint at my tribulations for you, which ⁷are your glory.

⁴Gr, *purpose of the ages.*
⁵Or, *the faith of him*
⁶Or, *I*
⁷Or, *is*

---

apostles, in their ministration of the gospel, are said to be "made a spectacle unto the world, both to angels and men" (1 Cor. 4: 9), and Christians are encouraged in their warfare against sin by knowing that they "are come unto mount Zion, and unto the city of the living God, the heavenly Jerusalem, and to innumerable hosts of angels" (Heb. 12: 22). The angels are, therefore, represented to us as not only ministering to the church of Christ, but learning from its existence and fortune more and more of the wisdom of God. Hence we gain a glimpse of a more than world-wide purpose in the supreme manifestation of God's mercy in Christ fulfilled towards higher orders of God's rational creatures, aiding even them in progress towards the knowledge of God in Christ Jesus, which is life eternal. This view of angels as our fellow learners in the school of Christ accords well with the wide sweep of thought characteristic of this epistle, literally gathering up all things in Christ.]

through the church the manifold wisdom of God,—To the extent that through the church with its blessings to both Jews and Gentiles, the manifold, or many-sided, wisdom of God might be made known, as it is unfolded in the working of his church on earth.

11 according to the eternal purpose which he purposed in Christ Jesus our Lord:—These things were all developed in the church, according to the purpose of God. He proposed to bring them about in and through Christ from the beginning of the world, when Christ was a lamb slain from the foundation of the world, but manifested in these last days.

12 in whom we have boldness and access in confidence through our faith in him.—Faith in Christ secures the access and gives the boldness to come to God as his children; because we have such a high priest, it is said: "Let us therefore draw near with boldness unto the throne of grace, that we may receive mercy, and may find grace to help us in time of need." (Heb. 4: 16.) Faith in Christ gives boldness to come to God.

13 Wherefore I ask that ye may not faint at my tribulations for you, which are your glory.—Because of the boldness that faith gives he desired that they faint not—be not discouraged and cast down on account of the imprisonment, persecutions, and sufferings that he endured for their sake. [His confidence in Christ emboldened him to make this request, for he is sure that Christ is able to make them also brave.]

2. PAUL'S PRAYER FOR THE CHURCH
3: 14-19

14 For this cause I bow my knees unto the Father, 15 from whom every ⁸family in heaven and on earth is named, 16 that he would grant you, accord-

---
⁸Gr. *fatherhood.*

---

14 **For this cause**—[The sentence begins in 3: 1 and interrupted at verse 2 is now taken up again. The ideas which came to expression, which were expressed in 2-13, are no doubt in view in some measure. The thought of the new relations into which the Ephesians had been brought by grace toward God and toward the Jews—the reconciliation of the cross, peace effected where once there was only enmity, the peace given in the household of God—gave Paul cause for prayer in their behalf.]

I bow my knees unto the Father,—He prays the Father of our Lord Jesus Christ that they faint not, be not cast down, and give up their faith in Christ. The bowing of the knees was so universally the accompaniment of prayer that to bow the knees meant to pray. [This was an emphatic way of denoting prayer; but not incidental, occasional prayer, inspired by some passing feeling; the attitude, "bow my knees," denotes deliberate prayer (Dan. 6: 10), making a business of approaching God with reverence and godly fear.]

15 **from whom every family in heaven and on earth is named,**—The whole family—servants, angels, the spirits of just men made perfect in heaven, and Christians on the earth—are one family named from the head and Father, God, as the human family takes its name from the head and father of the family.

ing to the riches of his glory, that ye may be strengthened with power through his Spirit in the inward man; 17 that Christ may dwell in your

16 that he would grant you, according to the riches of his glory,—[It is not his power to the exclusion of his mercy, nor his mercy to the exclusion of his power, but it is everything in God that renders him glorious, the proper object of adoration. The apostle prays that God would deal with his people according to the plentitude of his grace and power, which constitutes his glory and makes him to his creatures the source of all good.]

that ye may be strengthened with power—[To be powerfully strengthened so as to bear trials; to perform duties, to glorify his name.]

through his Spirit in the inward man;—The inner man is the spiritual man as distinguished from the outer or fleshly man. This is strengthened by the Spirit of God, that it may be able to stand in the trials and temptations, to which it is subjected. The Spirit increases their strength by their feeding on the sincere milk of the word, or on the pure teachings of the Holy Spirit. "We all, with unveiled face beholding as in a mirror the glory of the Lord, are transformed into the same image from glory to glory, even as from the Lord the Spirit." (2 Cor. 3: 18.) The Spirit gives strength and growth to the spiritual man, after he has entered into the body of Christ, or the church of God. Again, Paul says: "Not by works done in righteousness, which we did ourselves, but according to his mercy he saved us, through the washing of regeneration and renewing of the Holy Spirit, which he poured out upon us richly, through Jesus Christ our Saviour." (Tit. 3: 5, 6.) They were washed from their past sins; then in their Christian life they were continually renewed, made stronger by the Holy Spirit giving strength at every step they take in the way marked out by the Holy Spirit through the word given to guide them, and so they were saved. It is very hurtful for one to think that he can receive the help of the Spirit without taking the word of the Spirit into the heart. The Spirit gave the law, dwells in the law, and imparts his blessings through the law.

17 that Christ may dwell in your hearts through faith;—The Spirit strengthens the inner man by causing Christ to dwell in the

hearts through faith; to the end that ye, being rooted and grounded in love,

---

heart through faith. Christ is the bread of life, the manna that came down from heaven. He is food to the heart, or spiritual man, as bread is food and brings strength to the outward or fleshly man. The great truths concerning Jesus—his spirit, his life, his self-denial—are taken into the soul through faith. On this spiritual food the soul feeds, and is made strong. Paul states the thought in other words: "For this cause we also, since the day we heard it, do not cease to pray and make request for you, that ye may be filled with the knowledge of his will in all spiritual wisdom and understanding, to walk worthily of the Lord unto all pleasing, bearing fruit in every good work, and increasing in the knowledge of God; strengthened with all power, according to the might of his glory, unto all patience and longsuffering with joy." (Col. 1: 9-11.) Every Christian's heart is a temple in which Jesus dwells by faith. When Christ dwells in our hearts he in his works, teachings, sufferings, and character, is in our thoughts, feelings, shapes the life, directs the purposes of our hearts and moulds the character.

[The indwelling of Christ in us is not like that of a man who, dwelling in a house, is nevertheless in no sense identified with it. No; his indwelling is a possession of our hearts that is truly divine, quickening and penetrating their innermost being with his life. The Father strengthens us inwardly with might by his Spirit, so that the Spirit animates our will and brings it, like the will of Jesus, into entire sympathy with his own. The result is that our heart then, like the heart of Jesus, bows before him in humility and surrender; our life seeks only his honor; and our whole soul thrills with desire and love for Jesus Christ. The inward renewal makes the heart fit to be a dwelling place of the Lord.]

to the end that ye, being rooted—The result of taking Christ into the heart is that he becomes rooted and grounded in love and in the faith of the Lord Jesus Christ. [Rooted and grounded are two conceptions—one borrowed from the process of nature, and the other from architectural art. A tree and a house are the material objects which are used to express a spiritual thought. The idea implied in *rooted* is of striking down deeper and spread-

18 may be strong to apprehend with all the saints what is the breadth and

ing wider into the soul. We cast our affections down into the character and the being of God; we wind them about his attributes; we strike them into his promises; we drive them deep into his faithfulness. Thus the roots of our affections lie. They take up, they drink in the nature of the love of God in which they live; to it they are always assimilating themselves.]

and grounded—By grounded is meant the firm basis on which the children of God ultimately rest.

in love,—[This is not itself the root or foundation (for this is Jesus Christ himself), but the condition under which growth takes place. The roots of a man's faith and hope must penetrate, not inward into the love which he exercises, but outward into the love which is exercised toward him. The roots of a tree grow, not upward into the tree itself, but into an independent soil which at once supports its weight and nourishes its life. In like manner a Christian's faith does not lean and live upon anything within himself; it goes out and draws all its support from God's love to sinners in the gospel of his Son.]

18 **may be strong to apprehend**—He prays that they might apprehend that which is beyond the apprehension of men, and to know that which is past knowledge, that the love of Christ has shown to the world to lift up and redeem man. [It takes strong faith to apprehend the love of God. The spiritual realities are "things which eye saw not, and ear heard not, and which entered not into the heart of man." (1 Cor. 2: 9.) The exercise of faith is for him of similar quality to the vigorous use of the mind, when he is striving with all his force to master some difficult problem that confronts him. He recognizes that the love of God is hidden and elusive, that it can be "laid hold of" only by strenuous effort. The condition of the vigorous exercise of faith is for him to remember that the Lord said it is the pure in heart who see (Matt. 5: 8); the eye that is single is full of light (Matt. 6: 22); and that it is the doing the will of God that yields knowledge of the teaching (John 7: 17). If we are to know the love that is above us, it will be through the experience of love within us.]

length and height and depth, 19 and to know the love of Christ which passeth knowledge, that ye may be filled unto all the fulness of God.

with all the saints—[A saint, as here used, is one whose mental conception, whose capacity for thought, has become so quickened and enlarged as to enable him to realize that holiness is necessary to link him to all saints. The knowledge of the love of Jesus Christ depends on our purity of thought and life. God does not allow us to be satisfied with anything less than perfect holiness, so we continue our efforts in spite of failure. The word of God is severe in its demands; but though it is a sharp sword, that cuts down and lays bare the deepest motives hidden in the heart, it is with the deepest motive of love.]

what is the breadth—[The love of Christ is as broad as the necessities of the world and as the expanse of the nations of earth. It embraces all men—both Jews and Gentiles—and of all ages of the world. "Jesus, because of the suffering of death crowned with glory and honor, that by the grace of God he should taste of death for every man." (Heb. 2: 9.) The great salvation is as free as the air and the sunlight. Jesus unfolded the breadth and comprehensiveness of his love when he told the people of Nazareth that he had been sent to preach the good tidings to the poor, proclaim release to the captives, and recovering of sight to the blind, to set at liberty them that are bruised, and proclaim the acceptable year of the Lord. (Luke 4: 18.)]

and length—[To what length will the love of Christ go? "Jesus knowing that his hour was come that he should depart out of this world unto the Father, having loved his own that were in the world, he loved them unto the end." (John 13: 1.) "Greater love hath no man than this, that a man lay down his life for his friends. Ye are my friends, if ye do the things which I command you." (John 15: 13, 14.) Paul, in giving encouragement to the brethren, said: "Being confident of this very thing, that he who began a good work in you will perfect it until the day of Jesus Christ." (Phil. 1: 6.) Whenever the love of the Lord Jesus Christ begins a work he never lays it down till he can say, "It is finished."]

and height—[Love's aim always determines its height. The height of the Lord's love was: "Father, I desire that they also whom thou hast given me be with me where I am, that they may behold my glory, which thou hast given me." (John 17: 24.) It is the supreme desire of his love that his disciples should share his glory, and sit with him "in heavenly places," and partake with him in all the fullness of grace.]

and depth,—[The love of Christ is as profound as the uttermost of human sin and wretchedness. It is vast and measureless, it has gone down far deeper than the lowest depths of human sin. The vilest wretch who crawls the earth today, if in faith and repentance he turns away from his sin and wickedness, may have the everlasting arms beneath him.]

19 and to know the love of Christ which passeth knowledge, —Man's knowing, in the sense of taking into the heart, and letting the love of Christ rest and rule in him, helps to fill the soul with the fullness of God.

that ye may be filled unto all the fulness of God.—To be filled with the fulness of God is to take him into our hearts, as the temple of God that he may make his abode there, and mould and control our whole being. [This clause should be taken as dependent, not merely on the clause immediately preceding, but on the whole sentence. It describes the final and glorious consequence of the indwelling of Christ in the heart—being filled with grace "unto all the fulness of God." The meaning is more clearly seen in the fuller expression: "Till we all attain unto the unity of the faith, and of the knowledge of the Son of God, unto a fullgrown man, unto the measure of the stature of the fulness of Christ." (4: 13.) It is simply perfect conformation to the image of him in whom "dwelleth all the fulness of the Godhead bodily" (Col. 2: 9), and whose fullness is therefore "the fulness of God," manifesting all the attributes of the divine nature. The process is thus described: "But we all, with unveiled face beholding as in a mirror the glory of the Lord, are transformed into the same image from glory to glory" (2 Cor. 3: 18), its consummation in: "Beloved, now are we children of God, and it is not yet made manifest what we shall be. We know that, if he shall be manifested, we shall be like him; for we shall see him even as he is." (1 John 3: 2.) And the following completes the climax: "For our citizenship is in heaven; whence also we wait for a Saviour, the Lord Jesus Christ; who shall fashion anew the body of our humiliation, that it may be conformed to the body of his glory, according to the working whereby he is able even to subject all things unto himself." (Phil. 3: 20, 21.) When Christ dwells in the heart, we have love perfecting the faith which roots the life in him, a thoughtful knowledge, entering by degrees into the unsearchable riches of his love to us; and the filling the soul, itself weak and empty, up to the perfection of likeness to him, so renewing and deepening through all time and eternity the image of God in our very being.]

3. PAUL MAGNIFIES THE GRACIOUS POWER OF GOD WHICH WORKS ALL FOR US AND WITHIN US
3: 20, 21

20 Now unto him that is able to do exceeding abundantly above all that we ask or think, according to the power that worketh in us, 21 unto him *be*

---

20 Now unto him that is able to do exceeding abundantly above all that we ask or think,—[In thinking of God it is as if we thought of space—however far our conceptions may travel there is still infinity beyond. Paul had asked much in this prayer, and thoughts can always travel beyond words, yet the excess of God's power beyond both was infinite. The excess is denoted by a double term of abundance, as if the apostle wished to fill our minds with the idea of absolute infinity of the gracious power in God.]

according to the power that worketh in us,—This power is none other than the power "which he wrought in Christ, when he raised him from the dead." (1: 20.) The power that is actually at work in us has only to be exerted to confer on us immense spiritual strength; but as infinite as is his capability to help, his power to help us is determined by the nature and manner of those spiritual aspirations and cravings which the power of his grace within us has produced. Unless we desire knowledge he cannot enlighten us. Our spiritual contractedness limits his power to help us.

21 unto him be the glory in the church—The church, being the creation of God's love in Christ and the receptacle of his communicative fullness, is the instrumentality formed for his praise. His worship is a daily tribute to the divine majesty and bounty. The life of her people in the world, her warfare against sin, her ceaseless ministries to human sorrow, and need proclaim the divine

the glory in the church and in Christ Jesus unto ⁹all generations for ever and ever. Amen.

⁹Gr. *all the generations of the age of the ages.*

---

goodness, righteousness, and truth. She reflects the light of God's glory and makes it shine into the midst of the benighted world. [Nor does the church alone render this praise and honor unto God. The display of God's manifold wisdom in dealing with mankind is drawing the admiration and praise from the celestial world. (3: 10.) The story of redemption is the theme of endless songs in heaven. All the celestial hosts join in concert with the redeemed from the earth, and swell the chorus of their triumph.]

and in Christ Jesus—This denotes that this act of adoration is to be done in immediate connection with the work and person of Christ Jesus; for it is he who has brought about the whole scheme of redemption from which the act of adoration and praise springs.

unto all generations for ever and ever.—[This is a cumulative expression of great force. This glory is to be given to God during all the ages of time and eternity. "His name shall be continued as long as the sun: and men shall be blessed in him." (Psalm 72: 17.) "I will make thy name to be remembered in all generations: therefore shall the peoples give thee thanks for ever and ever." (Psalm 45: 17.) The stream of time rolls on world without end, but the glory is to continue throughout all the ages of eternity. "Unto him that sitteth on the throne, and unto the Lamb, be the blessing, and the honor, and the glory, and the dominion, for ever and ever." (Rev. 5: 13.)]

Amen.—This word is used for the purpose of adopting as one's own what has just been said. The word is limited to the religious atmosphere, being on human lips, an expression of faith that God holds the thing true, or will or can make it true.

PART SECOND
PRACTICAL EXHORTATIONS
4: 1 to 6: 24

SECTION ONE

THE PRINCIPLES NECESSARY TO THE DEVELOPMENT AND GROWTH OF THE CHURCH
4: 1-24

1. THE UNITY OF THE CHURCH OF CHRIST
4: 1-6

1 I therefore, the prisoner in the Lord, beseech you to walk worthily of the calling wherewith ye were called, 2 with all lowliness and meekness, with

---

1 I therefore,—Because God had provided for them such an abundant salvation and had given them full liberty to use all the means of grace.

the prisoner in the Lord,—He was a prisoner because he was in the Lord and for his sake. It was as a Christian and the cause of Christ that he suffered bonds. He speaks as a prisoner not to excite sympathy, nor merely to add weight to his exhortation, but rather as exulting that he was counted worthy to suffer for Christ's sake.

beseech you to walk worthily of the calling wherewith ye were called,—They had been called to a higher life, calling or walk, as servants of God. When a man by faith enters into Christ Jesus (Gal. 3: 26), he accepts the call of God to live the life of Jesus Christ, to obey the will of God, and walk according to the precepts he laid down. [The true grace in the heart must show itself by true devotion to the Lord in the life.]

2 with all lowliness—This is a low estimate of one's self, founded on the consciousness of guilt and weakness, and a consequent disposition to be low, unnoticed, and unpraised.

and meekness,—There is a natural connection between humility and meekness, and therefore they are here joined together as in so many other places. Meekness is that unresisting, uncomplaining disposition of mind which enables us to bear without irritation or resentment the faults and injuries of others. It lays hold

longsuffering, forbearing one another in love; 3 giving diligence to keep the unity of the Spirit in the bond of peace. 4 *There is* one body, and one

---

on the sovereign will of God as our supreme good, and delights in absolutely and perfectly conforming itself thereto.

with longsuffering,—[This is an attendant of the Christian walk closely connected with the other two, but introduced by itself. It means not taking swift vengeance, not inflicting speedy punishment. It is meekness towards the sins of others, and the more difficult to exercise because justice seems at times to be against it. It is prompted by recalling that we were called when sinners, that all of our privileges are proofs of God's long-suffering.]

forbearing one another—[This defines the walk still further, but is in reality a vicarious setting forth of how long-suffering is exhibited.]

in love;—[Love is an all-inclusive affection, embracing not only every other affection proper to its object, but all that is proper to be done to its object; for love spontaneously seeks to please its object, so in the case of men to God, it is the native wellspring of a voluntary obedience. It is, besides, the most personal of all affections. One may fear an event, one may hope an event, one may rejoice in an event; but one can love only a person. It is the tenderest, and most unselfish, the most divine of all affections.]

3 giving diligence to keep the unity of the Spirit—Christians are to give diligence to stand *one in the teachings of the Spirit,* to be united in walking according to his instructions. There were Jews and Gentiles in the church, and they were to maintain peace among themselves. Complete and perfect oneness in spirit, in heart, and in one body all springing from the oneness of God in the hearts of all, is the purpose and end of the gospel of Christ among men. The spirit that promotes unity and harmony among men comes from God. Unity and harmony of action are impossible in a way not provided by God. The unity is gained and maintained by doing the will of God. It requires no negotiations or arrangements among men to unite them as one in Christ. If we are in Christ, we cannot help being one with all who are in Christ. All in Christ are one with him and in him. Nothing can keep two persons in Christ separated. They will flow together. Christ came to

Spirit, even as also ye were called in one hope of your calling; 5 one Lord,

remove all division walls and hindering causes and make of the many families and nations of earth one new man in Christ. All human teachings, inventions, and institutions are occasions of discord, stumbling, and division. To divide the spiritual body of Christ is as cruel a crime against God and man as it was to pierce the fleshly body of Jesus with the spear. The hearts of those who add human inventions are not right in the sight of God. The example of perfectness before God that we are to follow is that of Jesus who had no will save to do the will of him that sent him, and to finish his work.

in the bond of peace.—They were to live in accord under the teaching of the Spirit and maintain peace among themselves. The state of mind and heart that inspired the unity of the body is the gentle, long-suffering, forbearing spirit that keeps down strife and divisions in the body, crushes out selfishness, sordid spirit of the flesh, and makes each seek not his own but another's good. The spirit that bears patiently, suffering for well-doing, is the one that is well-pleasing to God, and the one that promotes the unity and harmony of the body of Christ.

4 **There is one body,**—The church of the Lord Jesus Christ, in which his Spirit dwells. It is the one spiritual body of the Lord Jesus Christ. The church at Ephesus was the body of Christ at that place.

and one Spirit,—There is but one Spirit to give life, to guide, and direct that one body. The body animated and guided by the one Spirit cannot be divided. It must be a unit.

even as also ye were called in one hope of your calling;— There is one calling to follow Jesus Christ, and one hope of the home in heaven as a result of that calling.

5 **one Lord,**—This one Lord is Jesus Christ, crucified, buried, risen, exalted, and invested with supreme authority in heaven and on earth. To the Jews out of every nation, Peter declared: "Let all the house of Israel therefore know assuredly, that God hath made him both Lord and Christ, this Jesus whom ye crucified." (Acts 2: 36.) To the Gentiles, also, Peter preached

one faith, one baptism, 6 one God and Father of all, who is over all, and

him as "Lord of all"; and "to him bear all the prophets witness, that through his name every one that believeth on him shall receive remission of sins." (Acts 10: 36, 43.) Thus the door of faith was opened to the Gentiles, as it had been to the Jews, into one and the same kingdom under one and the same Lord. Hence Paul emphasized the fact that "there is no distinction between Jew and Greek: for the same Lord is Lord of all, and is rich unto all that call upon him." (Rom. 10: 12.) As Lord of all, he "is on the right hand of God, having gone into heaven; angels and authorities and powers being made subject unto him." (1 Pet. 3: 22.)

one faith,—One living, life-giving faith that works by love, and is made perfect by these works; that purifies the heart and fits it for a true temple of God, "a habitation of God in the Spirit." Only those whose faith is regulated by the word of God and whose purposes and daily life are conformed to the will of God can be one in Christ. This oneness must be a spiritual and practical oneness, not simply an assent of the mind to the truths of God. Oneness with and in Christ is the only source of spiritual and divine power. The great need of the church today is divine presence and spiritual power. This can be gained only by a closer walk with God; a more perfect conformity of the lives, the feelings, purposes, and life of professed Christians to the will and Spirit of God.

one baptism,—One burial of him whose heart is purified by faith, who has been crucified with Jesus Christ to sin, that he may rise to walk in newness of life with the risen and glorified Savior.

6 one God and Father of all, who is over all, and through all, and in all.—The Creator, Preserver, and Benefactor of all things, who overrules in, through the universe, and dwells and works in every obedient heart "both to will and to work, for his good pleasure." (Phil. 2: 13.) This perfect and complete unity in the creation, preservation, and direction of the universe and of all the loyal and true subjects of God is given as the strong and irresistible appeal for unity among the children of God, in his body, guided by his Spirit. It is not a plea for denominational union. There were no denominations in the days of Paul. It is an earnest plea for unity and oneness in the congregation of believers in Christ in a given locality in doing the work of God on earth. It is a grievous sin against God for men to destroy the unity of the body of Christ by personal ambition and strife and bickering.

2. DIVERSITY OF GIFTS IN THE GLORIFIED CHRIST AND THE PURPOSE OF ALL
4: 7-16.

through all, and in all. 7 But unto each one of us was the grace given according to the measure of the gift of Christ. 8 Wherefore he saith,
    [10]When he ascended on high, he led captivity captive,
    And gave gifts unto men.

[10]Ps. lxviii. 18.

---

7 **But unto each one of us was the grace given according to the measure of the gift of Christ.**—This likely refers to those endowed with spiritual gifts presented in the following verses, and Christ bestowed those gifts or offices as he saw each was gifted to receive and use them. The miraculous gifts did not change the talents, the dispositions, or faculties of those receiving them. They enabled them to work miracles and to know the truth, and the powers bestowed were such as were suited to the talents and dispositions of those to whom they were given.

8 **Wherefore he saith, When he ascended on high,**—The giving of these gifts to men was dependent upon his ascending on high, just as he said to his disciples: "It is expedient for you that I go away; for if I go not away, the Comforter will not come unto you; but if I go, I will send him unto you." (John 16: 7.)

he led captivity captive, and gave gifts unto men.—*Captivity* refers to death, as death had held dominion over every living thing on earth. Jesus Christ went down into death's inner prison, and struggled with the powers of death and hell; bursting asunder the bars of death, and rose a triumphant victor over the power of death and hell. In his triumph he secured man's resurrection, and won his crown as King of kings and Lord of lords. By virtue of his victory over death, his angelic convoy, as it approached the city of God, cried: "Lift up your heads, O ye gates; and be ye lifted up, ye everlasting doors: and the King of glory will come in." (Psalm 24: 7-11.) In this glorious ascension, convoyed by an angelic host, he led death a captive, a conquered captive, in his train. Since that day, death reigns not as an unconquered and independent sovereign, but by the permission and subject to the will of its conqueror and captor—Christ the Lord. But the question arises: "If death has been conquered by the Lord, is held captive by him, is subject to his will, and reigns by his permission, why does he permit death still to reign over all that is on the earth?"

Death is an evil, truly, but not the greatest of evils; sometimes as a result, and must exist as a restrainer, an antidote for greater evils. So death is an evil, but not the greatest evil. Sin is a greater evil than death. Death is the prison house for sinners—the boundary line beyond which no active rebel against God can ever pass. Without, then, the restraining of death, man must have been an eternal sinner. Now, this side of that line he may set God at defiance; he may stiffen his neck and harden his heart. On that side his knee must bow; his stubborn will must flex, and in hell he must pay the fearful penalty of his rebellion against God by submission to its horrors forever.

Then death is the prison house of sin. Let sin cease to abound, and death will be destroyed. Would we then seek to destroy death, we must do it by destroying that greater evil which brought death, and still retains it in and over this world—sin is a rebellion against God. Death came into the world, not as the result of the rule and reign of God. When God ruled over the world, and man, the great head over the under creation, maintained his true allegiance to God, his Spirit was the pervading, controlling power of the world, then death was unknown, and only things which administered to man's well-being and promoted his happiness. When man turned from obedience to God and transferred the allegiance of the world from God to the devil, then God's Spirit no longer dwelt in a kingdom ruled over by the wicked one. But the devil became the ruling, controlling, animating principle in the earth. As a result of this transfer, spiritual death came, and man with his brother engaged in strife, bitterness, wrath, and bloodshed. All

9 (Now this, He ascended, what is it but that he also descended [11]into the lower parts of the earth? 10 He that descended is the same also that as-

[11]Some ancient authorities insert *first*.

---

the institutions of earth, built by man under this evil spirit, partake of this same spirit, and are subject to the same rule of the evil one.

9 **(Now this,**—These words introduce an explanatory statement of the correctness of the application of the preceding verse.

He ascended,—This implies a previous corresponding *descent*, which must be from heaven to earth, as Jesus said: "And no one hath ascended into heaven, but he that descended out of heaven, even the Son of man, who is in heaven" (John 3: 13), and he could not ascend to give gifts to men without previously descending.

what is it but that he also descended into the lower parts of the earth?—The reference here is to the Messiah who came to earth from heaven, his original dwelling place, to destroy the power of the devil; to annihilate his kingdoms, cast out the evil spirit inseparable from them; reassert the authority of God, reestablish his rule and kingdom; make his Spirit again the lifegiving and pervading influence of this world. When this work is accomplished, death will no longer riot on perishing mortals: those in the bondage of death will rise from their imprisoning graves; bitterness, wrath, strife will cease among men, then shall the prophecy of Isaiah (11: 6-9) be fulfilled. This is to be the result of the reign of the kingdom of God on earth. The fullness of that reign and the rule of that Spirit will usher in the glorious millennial morn. Whoever, then, strives to reinstate God's authority, God's Spirit, God's kingdom, and to destroy the authority, spirit, dominion, and institutions that have sprung up under the rule of the wicked one, is a coworker with God—with Jesus Christ, who "also himself in like manner partook of the same; that through death he might bring to nought him that had the power of death, that is, the devil; and might deliver all them who through fear of death were all their lifetime subject to bondage." (Heb. 2: 14, 15.) And in destroying the devil with his institutions, and their fruits, he destroys the necessity and the cause of death—destroys death itself.

cended far above all the heavens, that he might fill all things.) 11 And he gave some *to be* apostles; and some, prophets; and some, evangelists; and

---

10 **He that descended is the same also that ascended far above all the heavens, that he might fill all things.)**—His ascension was necessary to the completing or finishing the work for which he came into the world—the re-establishing the kingdom of God on earth. He must be crowned the conquering Lord, ere his kingdom could be established, or send the Spirit to guide that kingdom, before proper gifts and appointments upon his subjects, to guide them into all truth, and develop them into the full stature of the Lord.

11 **And he gave some to be apostles;**—Here are enumerated the gifts bestowed on the disciples by him when he ascended on high, in the order of the fullness and importance of these gifts. Strictly speaking, the term apostle applies only to the twelve and to Paul. It should be taken here in its strict sense. It is generally agreed that only those are apostles who were commissioned by Christ himself; were witnesses of the resurrection, because they had seen the risen Lord (Acts 1: 21, 22; 22: 14, 15; 26: 16; 1 Cor. 15: 5-8); had a special inspiration (Eph. 2: 20; 3: 5; John 14: 26; 16: 13-16); and that their authority was supreme (Gal. 1: 8, 9). [It must be understood that the apostles completely set in order what things were to be taught and practiced by Christians. They left no successors. Their teaching, therefore, as recorded in the New Testament is the rule of faith and practice, and their institution and example the infallible guide in the order and administration of the church for all time.]

and some, prophets;—The prophets were inspired to make known the will of God after it had been revealed to them through the apostles. [Prophets acted and spoke under the extraordinary divine impulse and inspiration, whether in predicting or in teaching. Naturally their service accompanied and supplemented that of the apostles and so entitled them to be mentioned in this connection. Like that of the apostles, the function of the prophets ceased to be necessary when the foundation had been securely laid.]

and some, evangelists;—Evangelists were those who were supplied with the gifts to go into destitute fields to make known

some, pastors and teachers; 12 for the perfecting of the saints, unto the work of ministering, unto the building up of the body of Christ: 13 till we all

---

the gospel. [They seem to have acted under apostolic direction, and were the missionaries of the time.]

and some, pastors and teachers;—Those endowed to feed and teach those already Christians the duties and obligations resting on them as children of God. All these were miraculously endowed, spiritually gifted to perform the work for which they had talent and turn or disposition. These gifts were to endure until the perfect will of God was made known, and were intended to teach the children of God until the scriptures were completed. Then the gifts were to cease.

12 **for the perfecting of the saints,**—The endowed teachers were given to the church for the purpose of instructing the saints in the full and complete will of God, that they might be perfect in character. The first and highest purpose of God in giving the Spirit to direct and guide man and the object for which the church was established is the perfection of the saints in the spiritual knowledge, that they may make the perfection of their lives the one great leading and absorbing end and aim of their lives.

unto the work of ministering,—Here we see the perversion of the meaning of the Spirit, in the use of the term *ministering*. Preaching is the prominent idea connected with the work of the ministry at the present day. The preacher is *the minister*. Originally the minister was the individual who performed the most menial and laborious work in the congregation—physical labor for the congregation—who waited upon the sick, fed the hungry, and labored for the relief of sorrow, distress, and the physical ills of the offcast of earth. There are two different words used in the Greek to designate the work of serving and the work of preaching the gospel. *Ergon diakonias* indicated the work of serving; *ergon evangelistes* the work of preaching the good news of salvation. The term used here, translated *ministering,* is the one which designates work of serving or ministering to the wants of the afflicted—first of the household of faith; secondly, of all the suffering mortals of the earth.

attain unto the unity of the faith, and of the knowledge of the Son of God,

unto the building up of the body of Christ:—This is the third end for which Jesus gave the gift of the Spirit. This embraces the teaching necessary to bring men into the church, and to perfect, build up their character and to direct their work after having entered it. These gifts were to direct Christians in perfecting themselves in knowledge and obedience, for the work of caring for the needy and suffering, and for their teaching the gospel of the Son of God; and the Christians, the duties and obligations laid on them. The order of these works should be observed. Enumerations in the Scriptures began with the greatest and ended with the least. The list of the apostles began with Peter and ended with Judas Iscariot. Then the first and most important work of the church is to seek to perfect themselves in the divine knowledge and Christian character. Second, to look after the poor, afflicted, and destitute of the children of God, and then after the preaching of the word and building up of the church. This order of God is effective. We reverse the order, neglect the obligation to perfect the character, and the second lesson, too, and devote our energies to the third and last. We fail of the last because we neglect the first and second. If the saints would perfect their own characters in righteousness and true holiness, and care for the needy and helpless, then converting all possible to be converted would be an easy matter. The work done by these gifts is just the work performed by the word of God after it had come in its fullness.

13 till we all attain unto the unity of the faith, and of the knowledge of the Son of God,—This work of the Spirit was to continue until they come to the oneness of faith through the full knowledge of the Son of God that is necessary to make man perfect in faith. This does not mean that any one individual member is perfect in knowledge or in faith; but the knowledge to this end has been given to the church through one member supplementing the weakness of another, for all members have not the same gifts or works to perform in the church. These gifts were partial; each person was instructed by the gift given to him to do the work for which he was naturally qualified. But the gifts differed as the tal-

unto a fullgrown man, unto the measure of the stature of the fulness of Christ: 14 that we may be no longer children, tossed to and fro and carried about with every wind of doctrine, by the sleight of men, in craftiness, after

ents of man differed, so it took all the different gifts to give full instruction.

unto a fullgrown man, unto the measure of the stature of the fulness of Christ:—When the completed instruction was given, it was collected in the New Testament, as the perfected will of God, and the gifts of the Spirit vanished. The same thing is taught by the following exhortation given by Paul to the Corinthian church: "But desire earnestly the greater gifts. And moreover a most excellent way show I unto you." (1 Cor. 12: 31.) The "most excellent way" he describes as follows: "Love never faileth: but whether there be prophecies, they shall be done away; whether there be tongues, they shall cease; whether there be knowledge, it shall be done away. For we know in part, and we prophesy in part: but when that which is perfect is come, that which is in part shall be done away." (1 Cor. 13: 8-10.) This clearly teaches that spiritual gifts were partial and temporary in their office, and would cease when the perfect will of God was completed and revealed to man. When that was come the church of Christ would approximate in its workings the work of a completed man in Christ.

14 that we may be no longer children,—The end of the full knowledge of the will of God being made known would be that the servants of God might be no more children. [The word used here and in 1 Cor. 3: 1; 13: 11; Heb. 5: 13 is a word almost always applied in a bad sense, like our word childish—not to the guilelessness, the trustfulness, or the humility of children, which the Savior emphatically blessed (Matt. 18: 2-4), but to their unforeseeing and unthinking impulsiveness. The distinction is marked in these words: "Brethren, be not children in mind: yet in malice be ye babes, but in mind be men." (1 Cor. 14: 20.) Thus it describes shallowness and crudeness: liability to disturbance and by every external impression from without, so as to be "everything by turns and nothing very long."]

tossed to and fro and carried about with every wind of doc-

the wiles of error; 15 but ¹²speaking truth in love, may grow up in all things into him, who is the head, *even* Christ; 16 from whom all the body fitly

¹²Or, *dealing truly*

trine,—This sets forth the infinite variety of such influences. The varying wind carries about the waves, or the ship deserted is at the mercy of the waves and wind. Those immature and unstable run after every new teacher; having little knowledge or stability, excitable, dependent on their surroundings, they fall a ready prey to the various teachers of error. The readiness of professed Christians now to follow every new idea or visionary dream that some plausible and pretentious adventurer may bring is discouraging. Yet this evil must have been greater in the days of spiritual gifts, when new revelations were being made, than they are now. Wordy and plausible men would come claiming to be spiritually endowed with new revelations, and the ill-taught and unstable converts were ready to run after anything that might be presented.

by the sleight of men, in craftiness, after the wiles of error; —[This emphasizes the dishonesty and trickery of false teaching. Its authors use all the arts of deception to persuade the unstable that their self-made doctrine was the divine truth. It denotes error in practice, a wrong way of life or action. It means a craftiness, furthering the scheming, deceitful art which has for its results the false way of life that strays fatally from the truth.]

15 but speaking truth in love,—Speaking the truth in love is the means of promoting the growth and harmony of the body of Christ. Men are not only brought into the body of Christ through the truth, but their growth and work in the church are promoted through the truth.

may grow up in all things into him, who is the head, even Christ;—The Christian, being grounded and rooted in the faith in Christ, who is the head of all things, should move as he directs, just as all the members of the fleshly body move at the will of the head. Christ practiced perfectly what he taught. The things he taught were the outgrowth of his own life, so that were we to practice fully the truths he taught, our lives would conform to the life of Christ,

framed and knit together ¹⁸through that which every joint supplieth, according to the working in *due* measure of each several part, maketh the increase of the body unto the building up of itself in love.

¹⁸Gr. *through every joint of the supply.*

---

16 from whom all the body fitly framed and knit together—The human body is used to illustrate the church. Jesus is the head, and from him, as the head, the church, as the body, is fitly joined together and compacted by being knit together. The truth is the means that Christ and the Spirit use. Then the body grows up into Christ the head. Just as the human body is connected with the head by joints and ligatures, so the spiritual body is united and grows up into the head by spiritual joints. With that head all the members are united.

through that which every joint supplieth, according to the working in due measure of each several part, maketh the increase of the body unto the building up of itself in love.—By every member working effectually in his place and sphere, they all make increase of the body unto the building up of itself in love. The point is emphasized here that every member has his work to do, his office to fill. By this joint and harmonious working of all the parts, the body grows into the well-proportioned body of Christ, all moved and governed by him as the living head. This union is, of course, a spiritual union, as Christ is Spirit, and the union with him is a spiritual union. The church is a spiritual body. The only manifestation of the church is where the Spirit controls the bodies of men and brings them into obedience to the gospel; so the physical bodies under the control of the Spirit separate themselves from the world as servants of Christ. The apostle says: "But ye are come unto mount Zion, and unto the city of the living God, the heavenly Jerusalem, and to innumerable hosts of angels, to the general assembly and church of the firstborn who are enrolled in heaven, and to God the Judge of all, and to the spirits of just men made perfect, and to Jesus the mediator of a new covenant, and to the blood of sprinkling that speaketh better than that of Abel." (Heb. 12: 22-24.) These are the associations into which the entrance into Christ brings man. These are all spirits; the relation is a spiritual one; and when the spirits of men become subjects of this kingdom or members of this body, these spirits control the bodies they inhabit and separate them from the world and bring them into subjection to Jesus Christ. These bodies of men, controlled by the Spirit of God, are the only manifestations of the church visible to men in the flesh. This shows the close relation that the church and every individual member bears to Christ the head. This relation is a spiritual one and is regulated by the Spirit of the head permeating all the members of the body. But the Spirit does this through the truths he presents. Spiritual influences are directed to the spirit of man that thinks, considers, wills, purposes, and acts in accord with that will.

The evil in the church is that we lay too exclusive stress on certain offices and work, too little in that universal work of each and every member of the body. The welfare and development of the whole body is dependent upon the proper workings of each and every member. In the human body there can be no proxy work. One member cannot do the work of all or any other member without injury to the other members and to the whole body. It is even so in the spiritual body of Christ.

3. AN EXHORTATION TO A HOLY LIFE, FROM THE FACT THAT THEY DIFFERED FROM OTHER GENTILES
4: 17-24

17 This I say therefore, and testify in the Lord, that ye no longer walk as the Gentiles also walk, in the vanity of their mind, 18 being darkened in their

---

17 **This I say therefore, and testify in the Lord,**—[The apostle having in the preceding section taught that Christ had destined his church to perfect conformity to himself, and made provisions for that end, as a natural consequence solemnly enjoins on those in Christ to live in accordance with this high vocation.]

that ye no longer walk as the Gentiles also walk,—[Christ has called into existence and formed a new world. Those who are members of his body are brought into another order of being from that to which they had formerly belonged. They should therefore walk in quite another way—no longer as the Gentiles, for his readers, though Gentiles by birth (2: 11), are now of the household of faith—the church of Christ, the "commonwealth of Israel" (2:

understanding, alienated from the life of God, because of the ignorance that

---

12). Though born Gentiles, Paul distinguishes his readers from *the* Gentiles who were their natural kindred. Where he testified of their walk, he exclaims: "but ye did not so learn Christ" (verse 20), it appears that there were those wearing Christ's name and professing to have learned of him who did not thus walk. This indeed he expressly asserts: "For many walk, of whom I told you often, and now tell you even weeping, that they are the enemies of the cross of Christ: whose end is perdition, whose god is the belly, and whose glory is in their shame, who mind earthly things." (Phil. 3: 18, 19.) This warning we naturally associate with that given in verse 14. The reckless and unscrupulous teachers against whose seductions he guards the churches of Asia Minor tampered with the morals, as well as with the faith of their disciples, and were drawing them back insidiously to their former habit of life.]

in the vanity of their minds,—[After the leading of their own vain and fleshly minds. Christians are to walk after Christ the head, not after the vain efforts of the unconverted heathen to find happiness in the gratification of the depraved lusts. *Vanity* betokens a waste of the whole rational powers on worthless objects. This is the characteristic of heathenism, evil in its most refined forms.]

18 **being darkened in their understanding,**—Having the understanding so warped and perverted, so overruled by debasing lusts, that they could not understand the true good of the person.

alienated from the life of God, because of the ignorance that is in them, because of the hardening of their heart;—They were made averse to the life of God and the complete subjection of their minds to him by the wicked and corrupting lusts. The same causes and effects are presented in the following: "Because that, knowing God, they glorified him not as God, neither gave thanks; but became vain their reasonings, and their senseless heart was darkened. Professing themselves to be wise, they became fools, and changed the glory of the incorruptible God for the likeness of an image of corruptible man and of birds, and four-footed beasts, and creeping things." (Rom. 1: 21-23.) This shows that men es-

[4: 18-20.] EPHESIANS 85

is in them, because of the hardening of their heart; 19 who being past feeling gave themselves up to lasciviousness, ¹to work all uncleanness with ²greediness. 20 But ye did not so learn Christ; 21 if so that that ye heard him, and

¹Or, *to make a trade of*
²Or, *covetousness* Comp. ch. 5. 3; Col. 3. 5.

---

teeming themselves so wise that they can walk without God became fools and gave themselves up to the rule of fleshly lusts.

19 who being past feeling gave themselves up to lasciviousness,—These lusts dominated all their feelings, directed their thoughts, warped and blinded their minds, perverted their judgments, so that they, becoming past feeling and sense of shame or right, gave themselves over to follow the lusts and with greediness run into all lascivious practices. This is the essential result of separation from God. Cut loose from him, man must follow the flesh, and as was said of man before the flood: "And God saw the earth, and, behold, it was corrupt; for all flesh had corrupted their way upon the earth." (Gen. 6: 12.)

[There is nothing more terrible than the loss of shame. When modesty is no longer felt as an affront, when there fails to rise in the blood and burn upon the cheeks the hot resentment of a wholesome nature against things that are foul, when we grow tolerant and familiar with their presence, we are far down the slopes to hell. It needs only the kindling of passion, or the removal of the checks of circumstances, to complete the descent. The pain that the side of evil gives is a divine shield against it.]

to work all uncleanness with greediness.—Insatiable greed, the selfish desire for more, whether in the form of avarice or lust. The business of committing uncleanness moves on in this atmosphere of unsatisfied greed; the two constantly interact. The intimate connection of avarice and lust is suggested, and the history of those times furnishes many fearful illustrations.

20 But ye did not so learn Christ;—This intimates that many had come into the church ill-taught in the truth as Jesus taught it. [To preach Christ is to set him as the object of supreme love and confidence, so to "learn Christ" does not mean merely to learn his doctrines, but to attain the knowledge of Christ as the Son of God, God in our nature, the holy one of God, the Savior from sin, whom to know is holiness and life. Any one who

were taught in him, even as truth is in Jesus: 22 that ye put away, as concerning your former manner of life, the old man, that waxeth corrupt after the lusts of deceit; 23 and that ye be renewed in the spirit of your mind, 24 and

---

has thus learned Christ cannot live in darkness and sin. Such knowledge is in its very nature light. When it enters, the mind is refined and purified.]

21 if so be that ye heard him, and were taught in him, even as truth is in Jesus:—In the early church there were very many that were imperfectly taught in the truth of Christ. With no written standard of truth given, men were ill-taught and moved by personal feeling and ambition, taught many things not compatible with the truth, hence in the earliest days of the church sects and parties were more common in proportion to the number of members claiming to follow Jesus than at any other period.

22 that ye put away, as concerning your former manner of life, the old man,—The new life required that they put off the "old man"—the old manner of life, which was corrupt. [The resistance, the subduing, the absolute overcoming of those sinful propensities and habits, and the abandoning of those sinful acts which are so contrary to the new principles of spiritual life begotten through the gospel is the putting off of the "old man"; represented here under the figure of laying off an old garment, that another and better one may be put on.]

that waxeth corrupt after the lusts of deceit;—The old habit or manner of life which was put off or laid aside was corrupt—sinful through deceitful lusts. The lusts are deceitful because they promise happiness if gratified, when they always bring misery. The man away from God is led by these lusts, and they always work corruption of life and degradation of character and bring misery.

23 and that ye be renewed in the spirit of your mind,—The spirit of the mind is the spirit that directs the mind, which before becoming Christians was under the control of fleshly lusts, seeking happiness only in the gratification of them. Henceforth as Christians the spirit that animates the mind must direct its energies to the elevating of man, doing good, in denying ungodliness and fleshly lusts, and living soberly, righteously, and godly in this present world. (Tit. 2: 12.)

put on the new man, ³that after God hath been created in righteousness and holiness of truth.

³Or, *that is after God, created &c.*

24 and put on the new man, that after God hath been created in righteousness and holiness of truth.—Jesus Christ was God manifest in the flesh. He was the perfect likeness of God, after which the Christian is to model his life. He came as the final and perfect teacher to prepare man to dwell with God. He gave the precepts that would fit man in character to dwell in his presence. He not only gave the precepts, but he also gave the example in his own life of what they would make of man if perfectly practiced. Christ is the only perfect teacher of earth—he perfectly practiced what he taught, and if perfectly obeyed will make man in life just what Christ was. All the instruction as to how to live was illustrated in his own life. If we will carefully examine the record of his life, we will not be at a loss to know how to apply them in our own life. When we determine what he would do, we learn what we should do. Hence, Paul said: "Be ye imitators of me, even as I also am of Christ" (1 Cor. 11: 1); and Peter: "For hereunto were ye called: because Christ also suffered for you, leaving you an example, that ye should follow his steps" (1 Pet. 2: 21); and John: "He that saith he abideth in him ought himself also to walk even as he walked" (1 John 2: 6). The precepts, examples, and provisions he gave were all to help man to form the character that will fit him to dwell with God. Man is fitted for union with God only in so far as he follows the teachings of Jesus.

SECTION TWO

SUNDRY PRECEPTS
4: 25 to 5: 21

1. EXHORTATION AGAINST SPECIAL SINS
4: 25-30

25 Wherefore, putting away falsehood, [4]speak ye truth each one with his neighbor: for we are members one of another. 26 [5]Be ye angry, and sin not:

[4]Zech. viii. 16.
[5]Ps. iv. 4.

---

25 Wherefore, putting away falsehood,—Because we have put on the new man and are to follow the life of Christ, we are to put away all falsehood, misrepresentation, and all deceit. All intentional deceiving is falsehood—lying—whether by speaking falsely, concealing the truth, or by acts misleading others. In our dealings and transactions, we should always seek to maintain a Christian character, a pure, spotless, unsullied integrity. A determination to tell the truth, though it strip us of our property and bring upon us obloquy and shame, is the true characteristic of the Christian. The conduct of Christians should be such as to guarantee unto the world that they will not deceive, conceal, or overreach for the sake of gain, or for some coveted position.

speak ye truth each one with his neighbor:—We have common aims and interests, and should be careful to act with frankness, candor, and spotless integrity in all our dealings with our fellow men. In our actions we are speaking for Christ, not for ourselves. Christ benefits us just to the extent that he causes us to seek to act at all times as he would have us act.

for we are members one of another.—We are members of the same body, have the same interests, and should not deceive one another. While this admonition has special reference to our bearing toward our fellow Christians, it is equally true that we are to be truthful and upright in our dealings with all men. God hates a liar, and he says of all liars, "their part shall be in the lake that burneth with fire and brimstone; which is the second death." (Rev. 21: 8.) It is thought by some that it is strange that Paul should admonish Christians long after their conversion to quit lying and be truthful. The Holy Spirit recognizes things just as

let not the sun go down upon your ⁶wrath: 27 neither give place to the devil.

⁶Gr. *provocation.*

---

they are. But few children of Adam ever attain the divine model of truthfulness, and it requires constant admonition from God and watchfulness on the part of man to be truthful as he should be. I know of no church now to whom, were the Holy Spirit writing, that he would not feel the necessity of warning them to "put away falsehood, speak ye truth each one with his neighbor."

26 **Be ye angry, and sin not:**—This is not an exhortation to be angry, neither is it a prohibition to be angry. Anger is not necessarily sinful. God is angry with the wicked every day. Christ at times had his heart stirred to its very depths with indignation and anger (Mark 3: 5), being grieved and angered at the hardness of heart of the people. Oftentimes the Christian is brought face to face with sin, corruption, and crime so iniquitous that it would be a sin not to manifest deep indignation—a holy indignation. But when he becomes so aroused there is great danger of sinning, of rashly doing a wrong that cannot be corrected, he must be doubly guarded lest he sin. There is oftentimes more true herosim in the Christian, unseen by man, choking back the rising passion and refusing to give expression to the angry feelings when he has so provoked and annoyed by those he loves than in performing deeds of great danger that the world calls great. But a feeling of angry indignation that in its first arousing is harmless, or even praiseworthy, by being harbored and kept alive, soon degenerates into malice and hatred which is always exceedingly sinful. There is possibly no more cause of sin and the difficulty in a church than being ignorant of the Lord's instruction as to how to control wrath after it is aroused.

let not the sun go down upon your wrath:—Let your wrath subside quickly. Wrath cherished soon develops into malice. He who cherishes angry, bitter, or vindictive feelings in his heart toward another will soon come to feel a hatred that will destroy all the pure and holy influences of the soul, and destroy the peace of the bosom in which it dwells, and the happiness of all around.

27 **neither give place to the devil.**—To cherish anger is to give place to the devil. When angry the devil suggests the cher-

28 Let him that stole steal no more: but rather let him labor, working with

ishing of the ill feelings; but we are neither to cherish anger, nor are we to allow him to take advantage of our being angry. The Lord says: "resist the devil, and he will flee from you." (James 4:7.) Refuse to follow the evil passions and they will subside. If we dally with sin, if we trifle with right, if we indulge and cherish passions that lead to sin, we shall be overtaken in crime and must become the helpless slaves of the devil.

28 **Let him that stole steal no more:**—This implies that they had been given to stealing, either before or after their conversion. There is a close relation between lying and stealing. (The world calls only that stealing which is taken under cover of darkness or in secrecy, without a pretext of ownership. God regards and calls the obtaining of what belongs to another by false representation, by concealment of defect, by taking undue advantage, all gaining goods without a fair and just consideration, *stealing*.) Gaining by such unfair means is so common that the world calls it *sharpness, shrewdness,* etc., but all such names when probed to the bottom indicate dishonesty. The man is *shrewd*, is *sharp*, when he studies to take advantage of his fellow men to get more than the just and fair value of his goods, or to get his neighbor's goods at less than their value. Every man is entitled to the market value of his goods. People generally regard those thieves only whom the law has convicted of pilfering, and who are generally among the poor and needy. But in the eyes of the Lord he is a thief who takes from another his rightful due. The tradesman who deals in short weights and measures, and overcharges for his wares, is a thief; the servant who does not occupy faithfully in his master's service the hours and faculties for which he is paid is a thief; the physician who prolongs his visits to his patient beyond what is necessary in order to get gain is a thief. Are Christians cultivating and practicing that spirit of candor, frankness, and honesty that satisfies the man of the world that he will not be unfairly dealt with, that advantage will not be taken of his ignorance, or that he will be overreached in consequence of necessities, or that the goods that he purchases will be just as represented?

his hands the thing that is good, that he may have whereof to give to him

but rather let him labor, working with his hands—Instead of making a living by stealth or dishonesty, let him rather work with his hands is the way approved by God. Nothing has a better tendency to make a man moral, honest, and upright in his deportment and character than manual labor for a living. This is frequently commended: "But we exhort you, brethren, that ye abound more and more; and that ye study to be quiet, and to do your own business, and to work with your hands, even as we charged you." (1 Thess. 4: 10, 11.) "For even when we were with you, this we commanded you, If any will not work, neither let him eat. For we hear of some that walk among you disorderly, that work not at all, but are busybodies. Now them that are such we command and exhort in the Lord Jesus Christ, that with quietness they work, and eat their own bread." (2 Thess. 3: 10-12.) Laboring with the hands seems to have been regarded by the apostles as an important agent in destroying the disposition, and removing the temptation to steal; in other words, of promoting honesty. A hard-working, industrious man is seldom a dishonest man. A community is usually honest in exact proportion to the number of its citizens who engage regularly in honest, productive labor. Its prosperity is also in the same ratio. When parents educate and train their children to live by manual labor, they start them in the path of honesty. Christians, then, should foster and encourage the members of the church to engage in callings of physical industry. No man or woman can live in Christian life faithfully without some regular industrial calling. Idlers, male and female, have no heritage in the kingdom of God.

the thing that is good,—The Christian must confine his labor to the thing that is good. He cannot, without violating the law of the Spirit, engage in any calling whose general results on society are evil. But it must be a calling, the fruits of which are good to humanity. To bring this about, industry and energy, economy and prudence in business are required, and the danger is that, in bringing these to bear on life, we cultivate the love of money and let it become the leading purpose of life and gain the mastery over us. We are to be in the world as strangers and pilgrims, not drinking into the spirit of the world, but into the Spirit of God. Connected with the legitimate calling of life are many things that are hurtful to man. A Christian ought to keep his conscience and his hands clean of all that is connected with or that leads to sin. Any calling or manner of conducting a calling of life, the general effect of which is to prevent our children from being trained to seek first the kingdom of God and his righteousness, itself is sinful and unfit for a child of God. Yet there are many Christians, while not wholly denying the faith themselves, who in their anxiety for wealth and honor place themselves and families in such surroundings that their ruin is almost sure. When parents set a higher value on worldly attainments than on service to God, none see it sooner than their children, and aided as they are by fleshly tendencies of their own natures, and encouraged by the influence of the world, they will more than likely follow the evil course, and, like Lot's daughters who married in Sodom, will prefer the associations that lead to destruction rather than to the pathway that leads to eternal life.

that he may have whereof to give to him that hath need.—The Christian is to work industriously and energetically at that which is good, live economically, and save with prudence, and avoid debt and obligations for the future and use his means liberally for the relief of the poor and needy, the widow and the fatherless, for in this way he promotes the honor of God.

29 Let no corrupt speech proceed out of your mouth,—This is an admonition that demands earnest attention from all professed Christians to make sure that no corrupt or impure communication proceed out of their mouths. All conversations that excite and inflame evil thoughts, feelings, and passions are prohibited. Sometimes preachers compromise their character, destroy their influence, and injure the cause of Christ by foolish jesting, backguardism, and corrupting anecdotes and incidents. The Holy Spirit commands Christians to put away malice, railings, and shameful speaking out of their mouths (Col. 3: 8), and Christ says: "I say unto you, that every idle word that men shall speak, they shall give account thereof in the day of judgment. For by thy words thou

such as is good for [7]edifying as the need may be, that it may give grace to them that hear. 30 And grieve not the Holy Spirit of God, in whom ye

---

[7]Gr. *the building up of the need.*

---

shalt be justified, and by thy words thou shalt be condemned." (Matt. 12: 36, 37.) Thus Christ demands of Christians a pure, elevated, and ennobling conversation calculated to administer grace to the hearers.

but such as is good for edifying as the need may be,—[The effort to build up must be adapted to the place and time and to the persons whose edification is sought. In other words: "Let your speech be always with grace, seasoned with salt, that ye may know how ye ought to answer each one." (Col. 4: 6.)]

that it may give grace to them that hear.—[This is the purpose of that which has just been commanded, and should be made the purpose of those who obey it, because profitable conversation is so rare that our social intercourse seldom has such an exalted aim as this.]

30 **And grieve not the Holy Spirit of God,**—The Holy Spirit is God's medium of communication with man, his representative here on earth. We reach God through the Spirit. Then what pleases God pleases the Spirit; what grieves God grieves the Spirit. The prophet says: "But they rebelled, and grieved his holy Spirit: therefore he was turned to be their enemy, and himself fought against them." (Isa. 63: 10.) The Holy Spirit was in the prophets and through them taught the people the law of God. They refused to hearken to it and rebelled and sinned against him, and God turned and fought against them. Again, referring to the frequent rebellings against Moses, the Holy Spirit, speaking through the Psalmist, said: "How oft did they rebel against him in the wilderness, and grieve him in the desert!" (Psalm 78: 40.) They provoked and grieved the Spirit by their frequent murmurings and rebellions against Moses and his law in the journey through the wilderness from Egypt to the land of Canaan. Distrusting his promises and disobeying his commands grieved him and provoked the Lord to destroy them. He says: "Forty years long was I grieved with that generation, and said, It is a people that do err in their heart, and they have not known my ways: wherefore I sware

in my wrath, that they should not enter into my rest." (Psalm 95: 10, 11.) The Holy Spirit since the ascension of Christ is the representative of God on earth; to grieve God now is to grieve the Holy Spirit. The commands of the Spirit are the commands of God. To violate the commands of the Spirit grieves him. In the passage before us are a number of commands given by the Spirit. Those who violate any of these or any other commands of the Spirit grieve the Spirit as they grieve God by violating a command of God. There is nothing obscure in this work of the Spirit of God. He is a person with the peculiarities of action and being acted upon common to other persons, modified only by his divine characteristics.

in whom ye were sealed—A seal is a sign guaranteeing and confirming a promise, or obligation. To this end the Holy Spirit as an indwelling Comforter to all baptized believers in Christ is given. The influences of the Spirit are exerted through the truth, revealed in the scriptures and confirmed to our faith. All the instructions given by the Spirit to the apostles for the enlightenment, guidance, comfort, and help of the world are recorded in the scriptures for the benefit of the world. Hence the apostle says: "Every scripture inspired of God is also profitable for teaching, for reproof, for correction, for instruction which is in righteousness; that the man of God may be complete, furnished completely unto every good work." (2 Tim. 3: 16, 17.) It is through the Spirit then in his teachings and guiding power that all Christians are sealed or confirmed until the day of redemption, complete and thorough from the thralldom of sin and the grave. They are sealed men, sealed after their conversion by the bestowal of the Holy Spirit.

unto the day of redemption.—The day of redemption refers to the "second coming of Christ," as it is called, when he will redeem his people from the bondage of corruption and give them the eternal inheritance in the presence of God.

2. EXHORTATION TO TAKE THE LOVE OF GOD IN CHRIST AS THE PATTERN FOR IMITATION
4: 31 to 5: 2

were sealed unto the day of redemption. 31 Let all bitterness, and wrath, and anger, and clamor, and railing, be put away from you, with all malice: 32 and be ye kind one to another, tenderhearted, forgiving each other, even as God also in Christ forgave [8]you.

---
[8]Many ancient authorities read *us*.

---

31 Let all bitterness,—Bitterness is that frame of mind which willfully retains angry feelings, ready to take offense and liable to break out in anger at any moment.

and wrath, and anger,—[These are synonymous words, the former being the passionate outburst of resentment in rage, the latter the settled individual. In these the smoldering bitterness kindles into flame.]

and clamor,—Clamor is the loud self-assertion of an angry man, who attempts to make every one hear his grievance. Christians are to be calm and serious. Harsh contentions and strife, brawls, and tumults are to be unknown among them.

and railing,—The railer is the one who carries the war of his tongue into the camp of his enemy, and gives vent to his grievance in abuse and insult.

be put away from you,—These sins were rife among the heathen; and there may have been some among Paul's readers who found it difficult to refrain from their indulgence. Especially was this true when Christians were being subjected to severe persecutions; but they must lay all these aside. Cherished, they ferment and sour in the heart, and destroy one's peace of soul. To remember and dwell upon wrongs received is destructive to Christian character.

with all malice.—All the sins mentioned are various exhibitions of malice—that is, evil-mindedness or malignity. By the law of human nature they rise out of their temper, and react upon it so as to itensify its bitterness, and must be resisted and cast out. This spirit is sensual, and devilish in its influences.

32 and be ye kind one to another, tenderhearted, forgiving each other,—Be kind and helpful to one another, tenderhearted, compassionate, full of mercy, not cherishing vindictive feel-

1 Be ye therefore imitators of God, as beloved children; 2 and walk in

ings, ready to forgive, as God has forgiven you. The kindness and mercy of God to man, his readiness and anxiety to forgive is held up as a model to the Christian. We should be ready and anxious to forgive as God is anxious to forgive us.

even as God also in Christ forgave you.—What lesson does this teach? How does God forgive? To forgive is to hold and treat an offender as though he were not guilty. A man cannot hold one as innocent until he repents of his sin, ceases to sin, and corrects his wrongs so far as possible. God cannot forgive sin in this sense so long as man persists in it. God never forgives sin until it is repented. But while man was a sinner God loved him and was so anxious for him to repent, cease to sin, that he might forgive him, that he gave his own Son to die to lead him to repentance. Man ought to hold himself in a forgiving spirit toward those who sin against him. He ought to be anxious for him to repent that he may forgive him. He should do good to him to bring him to repentance. Man ought at all times to cherish the forgiving spirit and be ready to do good to those who sin against him, that he may bring them to repentance.

5: 1 **Be ye therefore imitators of God,**—He had just given the example of God in forgiving us and urged that in like manner we should forgive one another. [This phrase is unique and striking. The word *therefore* implies that this imitation of God must be chiefly in his essential attribute of love. It is instructive to observe that the Lord's startling command: "Ye therefore shall be perfect, as your heavenly Father is perfect" (Matt. 5: 48), is explained both by the context and the parallel passage, to mean, "be ye merciful, even as your Father is merciful" (Luke 6: 36). God's mercy in forgiving us suggests a rule of conduct for us in the mutual relation of Christian fellowship. The model to be followed is seen in Jesus Christ—a *divine-human personality,* in which God's exceeding kindness is manifested, while every expression seen in Christ, his person, his words, his acts, his sufferings, express really the loving-kindness of God. When, accordingly, Jesus Christ is taken as the model of that which Christians should be in their relations with one another, it is not alone as the model of that which

love, even as Christ also loved you, and gave himself up for ⁰us, an offering and a sacrifice to God for an odor of a sweet smell.

⁰Some ancient authorities read *you*.

Christians should be in their relations with one another, it is not alone as the model of a perfect humanity, but also as a model of such a humanity, expressing what is divine in utmost tenderness, compassion, and love.]

as beloved children;—He exhorts us to be imitators of God in his forgiveness and in his loving spirit, because beloved children should always imitate, and will always strive to imitate, what is good in a beloved father. Forgiving love being one of the great glories of our Father, it has been made peculiarly attractive in our eyes because it has been exercised by him toward us, therefore, it ought to induce us to show the same spirit.

2 and walk in love,—Love prompts to do good, to benefit, to deny self to help. [The imitation must take effect in the practical, unmistakable form of a loving course of life.]

even as Christ also loved you, and gave himself up for us,—He who was the Lord (John 1: 1), in heaven, with God, endowed with honors and glories with the Father that surpassed all other honors and glories of the universe, saw man had brought death and ruin, temporal and eternal, upon himself, that he was helpless and hopeless in that ruin. With man in this condition, heaven lost its charm to him. He gave it all up; he came to earth, clothed himself with human weakness and human infirmities to rescue man. Jesus Christ, imbued with the true spirit of heroism, served and suffered for man. He found more pleasure in the crown of thorns and the cross of Calvary, with the door open for man's return to his Father's house, than he found in heaven, with all its glories, with the door shut against man. This was heroism, this was vicarious service and suffering. Jesus is the truest, the greatest hero of the universe. Let us adore and honor him as such.

an offering and a sacrifice to God for an odor of a sweet smell.—The odor of such a sacrifice was a sweet incense to God. With such he was well pleased. If we sacrifice to do good and to save others from sin, such sacrifices will be a sweet savor to the Lord—he will be pleased with those who make such sacrifices.

3. SPECIAL WARNINGS AGAINST SINS OF UNCLEANNESS
5: 3-14

3 But fornication, and all uncleanness, or covetousness, let it not even be named among you, as becometh saints; 4 nor filthiness, nor foolish talking, or jesting, which are not befitting: but rather giving of thanks. 5 For this

---

3 But fornication,—Not only fornication, but everything of the same nature, or that leads to it, is to be avoided. Fornication embraces all unlawful indulgence of the lusts.

and all uncleanness,—Unnatural and perverted indulgence of the lusts as in Sodom (Gen. 19: 5-8), as pictured in Rom. 1: 27-32.

or covetousness,—This is the unlawful desire of what belongs to another, or such an excessive desire for it as to lead to the use of unlawful means to obtain it. Such a desire is the worship of it. The desire for it is above the desire to obey God. God is disobeyed to obtain it, hence it is idolatry, because wealth becomes the object supremely loved and sought. He who, therefore, sacrifices duty to God, who makes gain the great object of his pursuit, is a covetous man. He cannot be a Christian, and should not, according to the apostle, be recognized as such.

let it not even be named among you, as becometh saints;—The inconsistency of all such sins with the character of saints is such as should forbid the very mention of them among Christians. Instead of indulging in such conversation, their thoughts should turn to joyful words of praise and thanksgiving to God.

4 nor filthiness,—Obscene and degrading practices. [Not simply obscenity, but whatever is vile or disgusting in speech or conduct.]

nor foolish talking,—Such talk as is characteristic of fools. That is, frivolous and senseless.

or jesting,—Supposed to be witty repartee that ridicules modesty and throws contempt on the virtue of good men and women.

which are not befitting:—Foolish talking and jesting are not the ways in which Christian cheerfulness should express itself. [All witty speech uttered for its own sake is not fitting for a Christian whose tongue is to become consecrated to the service of Christ.]

ye know of a surety, that no fornicator, nor unclean person, nor covetous man, who is an idolater, hath any inheritance in the kingdom of Christ and God. 6 Let no man deceive you with empty words: for because of these things cometh the wrath of God upon the sons of disobedience. 7 Be not ye

---

but rather giving of thanks.—[This is the proper tone of Christian speech, and this will drive off the evil habits of which mention has just been made. The blessedness in Christ is the source of joy and gladness, but its joy is expressed in thanksgiving and praise.]

5 For this ye know of a surety, that no fornicator, nor unclean person, nor covetous man, who is an idolater, hath any inheritance in the kingdom of Christ and God.—Cannot become their servants. [What a doom awaits the covetous man! He, like the sensualist, is to be excluded from the kingdom of God. For unto the impenitent and unbelieving there is but one home in eternity. Hell is made up of the profane, the sensual and the vile; and its supremest horrors arise from its being the place where will be gathered all the corrupt and unholy dwellers of a fallen world; all who are so impure that they cannot be admitted into heaven.]

6 Let no man deceive you with empty words:—Some false teachers doubtless taught that such practices did not affect the character of a child of God. That as sin abounded, grace could much more abound. [Here it seems that the apostle had in view, not only worldly condonation of evil or low heathen morality, but to some who held that the things done in the body, being evil only in the body, could not touch the spirit.]

for because of these things cometh the wrath of God upon the sons of disobedience.—Participants in such sins, in whatever age of the world, in heathen or Christian lands, are under the wrath of God on account of them and while they thus remain can therefore have no inheritance in the kingdom of Christ and God.

7 Be not ye therefore partakers with them:—If they partook of their sins, they would necessarily partake of their punishments. They should therefore refuse all partnership with them. Their natural instinct recoiled from partnership in their punishment, so their spiritual instinct should recoil from partnership in their sin.

therefore partakers with them; 8 for ye were once darkness, but are now light in the Lord: walk as children of light 9 (for the fruit of the light is in all goodness and righteousness and truth), 10 proving what is well-pleasing

---

8 for ye were once darkness,—The Gentile Christians were formerly in their heathenish darkness, and practiced such abominations. [They who walk in darkness are said to be themselves *darkness*—new sources, so to speak, of the darkness which hates and quenches the light, both to themselves and to others. The light which was in them becomes darkness.]

but are now light in the Lord:—The light which blesses men is all concentrated in Jesus Christ. As the light, he imparts new possibilities of life to those who otherwise were hopelessly dead in trespasses and sins. The light of Christ enters into the heart through faith, and produces a high and spiritual order in the life that is thus begotten and sustained, as the apostle says, by "the light of the gospel of the glory of Christ. . . . Seeing it is God, that said, Light shall shine out of darkness, who shined in our hearts, to give the light of the knowledge of the glory of God in the face of Jesus Christ." (2 Cor. 4: 4-6.)

walk as children of light—Having been taught the truth as it is in Jesus, and being in the light, they were to walk according to the teachings of this life, as children reared in the light.

9 (for the fruit of the light—The fruit of the light, of knowing and doing this truth of God, is to produce a life in goodness and righteousness and truth. [The metaphor is a striking one, but literally correct, inasmuch as light is the necessary condition of that vegetative life which grows and yields fruit, while darkness is the destruction, if not of life, at any rate of fruit-bearing perfection.]

is in all goodness—[This stands first, as the most visible and obvious form of Christian excellence—that for which every one looks in a religious man, and which all admire when it is seen. Goodness is love embodied; it is the sanctification of the heart and its affections, renewed and governed by the love of God in Christ. Love, as the Christian knows it, is of God, for "herein is love, not that we loved God, but that he loved us, and sent his Son to be the propitiation for our sins." (1 John 4: 10, 11.) This is the faith

unto the Lord; 11 and have no fellowship with the unfruitful works of dark-

that makes good men—the best in the world. So "the fruit of the light is in all goodness."]

and righteousness—[The principle of righteousness includes everything in moral and spiritual worth, and is often used to denote in one word the entire fruit of God's grace in man. Righteousness is loyalty to God's holy and perfect law revealed through Jesus Christ; it is the love of that law in man's innermost spirit, it is the quality of a heart one with "the law of the Spirit of life in Christ Jesus" (Rom. 8: 2), reconciled to it as it is reconciled to God himself in Christ Jesus.]

and truth),—Truth signifies the inward reality of goodness and righteousness. Truth does not mean veracity alone, the mere truth of the lips. Truth of words requires a reality behind itself. The acted falsehood is excluded, the hinted and intended lie no less than that expressly uttered. Beyond all this, it is the truth of the man that God requires—speech, action, thought, all consistent, harmonious and transparent, with the light of God's truth sinning through them. Truth is the harmony of the inward and the outward—correspondence of what the man is in himself with which he appears to be. Now, it is only children of light, only men thoroughly good and upright who can, in this strict sense, be men of truth.

10 **proving what is well-pleasing unto the Lord;**—The exhortation given in verse 8, interrupted by the enforcement introduced in verse 9, is now continued and explained. Believers are required to walk as children of light examining and determining from a prayerful study of the scriptures what is acceptable to the Lord. They are to regulate their conduct by a regard to what is well-pleasing to the Lord. (Rom. 12: 2; 1 Thess. 5: 21.) That is the ultimate standard of judging whether anything is right or wrong, worthy or unworthy of those who have been enlightened by the gospel. This injunction comes fitly, therefore, in connection with the foregoing earnest exhortation, as to the kind of living suitable to those who are "light in the Lord."

11 **and have no fellowship with the unfruitful works of darkness,**—Have no part, be not partakers in these works

ness, but rather even ¹⁰reprove them; 12 for the things which are done by them in secret it is a shame even to speak of. 13 But all things when they are ¹¹reproved are made manifest by the light: for everything that is made

¹⁰Or, *convict*
¹¹Or, *convicted*

---

which grow up in heathen darkness. They are called unfruitful, since they bear no good fruit, no good results to him who practices them or to the world, but only evil and degrading. [Those who have things in common; who are congenial; who have the same views, feelings and interests; and who therefore delight in each other's society are said to be in fellowship. In this sense believers have fellowship with God and with each other. So we are said to have fellowship in anything in which we delight and of which we partake. To have fellowship with the works of darkness, therefore, is to delight in them and to participate in them. All such association is forbidden as inconsistent with the character of the children of light.]

but rather even reprove them;—Condemn them, testify both by precept and example that they are degrading. [When the Spirit is said to reprove men of sin (John 16: 8-11), it means that he sheds such light on their sins as to reveal their true character, and to produce the consequent consciousness of guilt and pollution. Paul says the effect of preaching the gospel produces conviction—which is explained by saying: "The secrets of his heart are made manifest." (1 Cor. 14: 25, 26.) The duty, therefore, here enjoined is to shed light on these works of darkness; to exhibit them in their true nature as vile and destructive. By this method they are corrected. So we see that so far as human agency in the production of sin is concerned, it is limited to the holding forth the word of life; or letting the light of divine truth shine into the darkened minds of men, and upon their evil deeds.]

12 **for the things which are done by them in secret it is a shame even to speak of.**—It is thought that this refers to the impure lascivious practices performed in the worship of the heathen gods. All the worshipers indulged in lewd practices as part of their worship. It was done in the secret recesses of the temple.

13 **But all things when they are reproved are made manifest by the light:**—All those wicked practices performed in secret,

5: 13, 14.] EPHESIANS 103

manifest is light. 14 Wherefore *he* saith, [12]Awake, thou that sleepest, and arise from the dead, and Christ shall shine upon thee.

---

[12](?) Comp. 1 Tim. iii. 16.

---

which he commanded them to reprove, are exposed in their hideousness and corruptness through the light of the gospel.

for everything that is made manifest is light.—Whatever makes manifest the wicked and evil results of these practices is *light*.

14 Wherefore he saith,—It is not known who said this. Probably Christ. It is thought by some to be a portion of a hymn sung in that age of the church, referring to Jesus.

Awake, thou that sleepest,—This is addressed to those persons so sunk in their degrading practices of heathenism, both in their worship and in their social life, and are addressed as asleep. [The sleeper is one not yet a Christian, on whom the light is about to shine.]

and arise from the dead, and Christ shall shine upon thee.—They were dead in trespasses and sins, and in view of this terrible condition, the appeal was made. The call was: Awake from your lethargy, the sleep of death, and Christ shall give you light. Jesus said: "Verily, verily, I say unto you, The hour cometh, and now is, when the dead shall hear the voice of the Son of God; and they that hear shall live." (John 5: 25.) [This does not mean that the dead must be revived before they hear the voice of the Son of God, but that his voice causes them to live. So the passage before us does not mean that those asleep must arise from the dead and come to Christ for the light; but the light which Christ sheds around him through the gospel has power to awaken the sleeping dead. Thus the passage is a confirmation of what is said in verse 13, that everything made manifest by the light is *light*.]

4. EXHORTATION TO CHRISTIANS TO REGULATE THEIR CONDUCT WITH WISDOM, TO MAKE GOOD USE OF OPPORTUNITIES, AND INSTEAD OF INDULGING IN RIOTOUS PLEASURES TO EXPRESS THEIR JOY AND THANKFULNESS IN SPIRITUAL SONGS
5: 15-21

15 Look therefore carefully how ye walk, not as unwise, but as wise; 16 [13]redeeming the time, because the days are evil. 17 Wherefore be ye not

---
[13]Gr. *buying up the opportunity*.

---

15 Look therefore carefully how ye walk,—See that you walk strictly, but consider well the kind of strictness. Do not walk loosely without fixed principles of action; but make sure that your rules are of the true kind. Many are strict who are not wisely strict; they have rules, but not good rules. We are to ascertain the clear line of right as revealed by the word of the Lord, and then keep to it strictly.

not as unwise, but as wise;—Not as fools who close their eyes to the light, but to the wise who take in the full light. [This clause explains first on the negative, and then on the affirmative side of the foregoing: both the strictness of their walk and the way in which that strictness was to be shown were to reflect the spirit of wise men and not of fools. It is not folly that is reproved, but easy-mindedness, want of earnest consideration in a matter so infinitely vital, so as to know what is truly best, and affords a lesson of consistency to those who behold their walk.]

16 redeeming the time,—So use the time left as to rescue as far as possible the time already lost in the days of darkness when you lived in sin.

because the days are evil.—The times were evil tempting them back into sin. [Evil days mean days in which evil abounds. This is parallel to the expressions, "evil and adulterous generation" (Matt. 12: 39), and "this present evil world" (Gal. 1: 4). Because sin abounds is a good reason why Christians should seize upon every opportunity to do good; and also why they should make the most of time. The same exhortation is found in these words: "Walk in wisdom toward them that are without." (Col. 4: 5.) In the passage before us, Paul says to walk in wisdom "redeeming the time." So that this right use of time, or this seizing

foolish, but understand what the will of the Lord is. 18 And be not drunken with wine, wherein is riot, but be filled [14]with the Spirit; 19 speaking [15]one

[14]Or, *in spirit*
[15]Or, *to yourselves*

---

of every opportunity for doing good, is in both places represented as the evidence and the effect of wisdom, that is, of divine truth which is the wisdom of God, which he has revealed. (1 Cor. 2: 6-13.) Paul most likely had in view the special difficulties of the then present time, but his words have a permanent bearing on each following period with its new phases of difficulty, all related as they are to the permanent underlying difficulty, *sin*.]

17 **Wherefore be ye not foolish,**—He who closes his eyes and ears to the truth is unwise. [The wherefore bears on all the preceding argument—because ye are children of light; because the light is so valuable and so indispensable; because your whole circumstances demand so much care and earnestness. Foolish is equivalent to senseless.]

but understand—To understand is both to know and to lay to heart, as in the parable of the sower: "When any one heareth the word of the kingdom, and understandeth it not"—does not consider or ponder it—"then cometh the evil one, and snatcheth away that which hath been sown in his heart." "And he that was sown upon the good ground, this is he that heareth the word, and understandeth it; who verily beareth fruit, and bringeth forth, some a hundredfold, some sixty, some thirty." (Matt. 13: 19, 23.) Then wisely seek to understand what the will of the Lord is, and then endeavor to do it.

what the will of the Lord is.—To know his purpose toward us and toward the world, and the true purpose of our life. Hence, "unto man he said, Behold, the fear of the Lord, that is wisdom; and to depart from evil is understanding." (Job 28: 28.) And: "The fear of Jehovah is the beginning of wisdom; and the knowledge of the Holy One is understanding." (Prov. 9: 10.) [The will of the Lord is the great rule of the Christian life; to know and in the deeper sense understand it is to walk wisely and to walk surely.]

18 **And be not drunken with wine,**—The best protection against any evil is to learn self-control and self-government. [Of

to another in psalms and hymns and spiritual songs, singing and making

all the evils that oppress and outrage and destroy mankind, there is none greater than intemperance. For proof turn to our jails, asylums, police courts, lodginghouses, newspapers, streets, and highways. It is an evil very great, very common, very real, very ruinous. It is an individual, a social, a national evil. It is an evil which produces untold misery, poverty, and wretchedness which no figures can possibly set forth. It injures the body, blunts the finer feelings of the soul, clouds the intellect, ruins the health, and unfits for daily life. It brings poverty, and blights the home. It destroys the peace of mind and destroys the prospect of heaven.]

wherein is riot,—[Recklessness—incapable of denying itself of anything, and naturally passing this want of restraint into profligacy. Drunkenness is at once the cause and effect of utter recklessness. It is the effect of self-abandonment, by which the sensual and passionate elements of the nature are stimulated to frenzy, while self-controlling judgment is drugged to sleep. It is the cause of yet greater recklessness: for as their passions and appetites become jaded, they need stronger and stronger stimulants, till the whole nature, bodily and mental, is lost in delirium or stupor, which sinks lower and lower into helpless ruin.]

but be filled with the Spirit;—To be filled with the Spirit and to have the word of God dwelling in the heart are one and the same thing. The presence of the Spirit in his miraculous demonstrations and in his ordinary influences was received by keeping his commandment.

19 **speaking one to another**—This specifies one of the ways in which the condition of being filled with the Spirit would express itself. They were to seek and promote the purity of heart by songs of praise and thanksgiving. From the beginning praise was an important part of public worship, and is designed to be to the end of the world. It is made clear that it was practiced by the Savior himself and the apostles. (Matt. 26: 30; Acts 16: 25.) It is difficult to draw the distinction between songs described as *psalms,* *hymns,* and *spiritual songs.* The difficult arises from the fact that while each term originally denoted a distinct and separate kind of song, frequently two, or even the three distinct kinds sometimes,

were combined in one song, and the terms came to be used interchangeably.

in psalms—Psalms are songs devoted to the praise of God, extolling his name, power, character, and works. The songs of David are mainly of this character, hence were called *psalms*.

and hymns—Hymns are songs of praise, thanksgiving, and supplication, teaching our dependence on God and his willingness to hear and bless.

and spiritual songs,—Spiritual songs are those intended to inspire and cultivate feelings of spiritual devotion and to bring the spirit of man into harmony with, and under the control of, the Spirit of God.

Some claim that *psallo* carries with it the idea of a mechanical instrumental accompaniment, but if the word in the New Testament means to sing with a mechanical instrument, it is not only allowable but *obligatory to it.* I give a general definition of the word: "(1) To touch, feel, stir, or move by touching, *especially:* to pull, twitch or twang with the fingers; (2) to pull and let go again, to pull, twitch or twang with the fingers; (3) usually of the string of musical instruments, to play a musical instrument with the fingers, instead of the plectrum." Beyond doubt it means the vibration of a string or cord that produces a sound—and refers to the music of stringed instruments. It does not originally mean a hymn sung to the music of a stringed instrument, but to the twanging or vibration of the cord that makes the music. No one who has examined the subjects doubts that this is the original meaning and applies to all sounds and music made by the vibration of the cords of the instrument. As such it embraces the speaking organs of the human voice as much as the harp.

The human voice is the most complicated, delicate, and perfect musical instrument known to man. It is the perfection of the Maker's handiwork as a musical instrument, and is capable of more musical combinations and harmonies far sweeter and more varied than any and all instruments of human make, even than those "invented by David." All the varied sounds and all the multiplicity of intonations of the human voice are made by the tension and vibration of the vocal cords within the throat and mouth. The word *psallo* then would, and did from the beginning, embrace the

melody with your heart to the Lord; 20 giving thanks always for all things

music of the voice as well as that made by stringed instruments of man's invention. The voice is a stringed instrument of God's make. Nor is it singular that as the use of the voice was so much more common and universal than that of any other instrument, the word should come to be applied exclusively to the music made by the voice, unless it was specifically said to be by some other instrument. This is what did come to pass. Especially this was true of the use of the word among the Jews, who in their later period of disaster and sorrow dropped the use of the instrument, but continued to sing the same songs that had been sung in former days to the accompaniment of the harp and other instruments. They were still psalms when sung without the instrumental accompaniment. When David admonished them to praise God with the harp, he did not trust to the word *psallo* to designate and declare it. For *psallo* then referred as well to the singing without the instrument as with it. Hence it was necessary to connect with psallo the instrument used to determine what instrument accompanied the singing or whether any was used save the human voice. So the word unqualified in New Testament times came to mean only to sing.

singing and making melody with your heart to the Lord;— Bring the thoughts and feelings of the heart into harmony with the sentiment of the song. It is the sentiment that is sung that constitutes the worship; there is no acceptable worship in music distinct from the sentiment sung. The music of the song is only a means of impressing the sentiment sung on the hearts of both singer and hearer. What is sung must be the outgrowth of the word of God dwelling richly in the heart. It is done by speaking the word of God in song. The purpose is to praise God. No performance of an instrument can possibly grow out of the word of God in the heart; a mechanical instrument cannot speak that word either to praise God or to teach and admonish one another. The sound of the instrument drowns the words sung and hinders the teaching and admonition. The use of the instrument hinders and destroys the essential purpose of the worship in song. It works an entire change in the song service; it sooner or later changes it from a service of praise to God into a musical and artistic entertainment that pleases and cultivates the fleshly and sensual nature. A more

in the name of our Lord Jesus Christ to ¹God, even the Father; 21 subjecting yourselves one to another in the fear of Christ.

¹Gr. *the God and Father.*

---

hurtful change could not be made in the worship than this change in its spirit and purpose. If it was a sin to change the appointments of God in the patriarchal and Jewish dispensations, which were sealed by the typical blood of animals, much more is it a sin to change the ordinances and appointments of the Christian dispensation, sealed by the Son of God. (Heb. 10: 28, 29.)

20 **giving thanks always for all things**—The giving of thanks seems to be a part of the service performed in singing. Thanksgiving for all blessings, temporal and spiritual, at all times, and in all places is proper from man to his Creator from whom he receives life, health, and all blessings. We need to sing the praises of God, to give thanks unto his name, not only that we may please God and benefit the people, but we need most of all the influence of it upon our own hearts. Speaking his praise, remembering and giving thanks for his mercies, softens and opens our hearts to a fuller appreciation of his blessings, fills them with fuller sense of gratitude to God, and fits us more and more to dwell with and enjoy him in the fullness of his blessings forever. We ought to continually praise the Lord, for his praise is comely to the upright.

in the name of our Lord Jesus Christ to God, even the Father;—All these things must be done in the name of the Lord Jesus Christ. We are servants and can act only in his name. Only those who come in his name can find acceptance with God. So only the servants of Christ who come to the Father in his name can be blessed, [for without Christ we would not have him as our Father to thank, still less to know him as the Father]

21 **subjecting yourselves one to another**—They were to submit to each other in the relationships they stand as defined in the following verses. [There is, however, a certain connection of idea with the preceding section also, and especially with the encouragement of a Christian enthusiasm in the last clause. The strong and frequent emphasis laid in the New Testament on subjection, whether to civil powers (Rom. 13: 1-7; 1 Pet. 2: 13-17); domestic authority (6: 1-9; Col. 3: 18-24; 1 Pet. 2: 18 to 3: 7); or to those whom the Lord has placed over the church (1 Thess.

5: 12, 13; 2 Thess. 3: 14, 15), probably indicate a tendency in the first glimpse of Christian liberty, to disregard the wholesome restraints, laws of daily life. Hence the caution here, preparatory to the more detailed teaching of subjection which follows.]

in the fear of Christ.—But all submission must be in the fear of the Lord. He is to stand first in our fear, then his fear to regulate our submitting to each other in the different relations. The submission of the wife to the husband, the child to the parent, the servant to the master, when other motives fail, because the Lord requires it, is accepted by God as service to him, which he will reward.

SECTION THREE

SPECIAL DUTIES IN HOUSEHOLD RELATIONS
5 : 22 to 6 : 9

1. RELATION OF HUSBANDS AND WIVES CONSECRATED AS A TYPE OF THE UNION OF CHRIST AND HIS CHURCH.
5 : 22-33

22 Wives, *be in subjection* unto your own husbands, as unto the Lord. 23 For the husband is the head of the wife, as Christ also is the head of the

---

22 **Wives, be in subjection unto your own husbands,**—He begins here to specify the different classes that must submit to other classes. God first created man, then from him took woman. Man was first in the order of time, the stronger and more robust in person, God made him the head, and laid it on the wives to submit unto him in the fear of the Lord. This means submit to the husband so far as she can do it, without violating the prior and higher command to obey God. The first and highest duty is to God. [The submission is that of love, respect, and reverence; which is befitting the relation she holds to her husband. In her sphere, she is spiritually on an equality with man, but as a husband he is the natural and scripturally recognized head and leader in the family. Her submission must be in accordance with the principles of righteousness, and nothing is required of her inconsistent with her Christian character. This submission of the wife, when rightly understood and practiced, accords with her inner nature, is in harmony with her relations to God and others, and is productive of the fullest development of her character, her highest happiness and good.]

as unto the Lord.—When all other motives fail to lead the wife to obey the husband, when he is hard and harsh, fails to appreciate her kindness and love, and she is discouraged and disheartened, she is then to remember to submit and bear, because God commands it. She can find solace and comfort and strength to bear, because she is doing it as service to the Lord, knowing that he will reward it as service done to him.

23 **For the husband is the head of the wife, as Christ also is the head of the church,**—Here the headship of the husband is

church, *being* himself the saviour of the body. 24 But as the church is subject to Christ, ²so *let* the wives also *be* to their husbands in everything. 25 Husbands, love your wives, even as Christ also loved the church, and gave

---

²Or, *so* are *the wives also*

---

carried out, and illustrated by the headship of Christ over the church. The church is represented as the bride, the wife of Jesus Christ; as Christ is its head, guide, and supporter, so the husband is to the wife. The point of conflict between the authority of the husband and the authority of God cannot rise in the case of Christ and the church, as Christ cannot require things contrary to the will of God.

being himself the saviour of the body.—As Christ is the Savior of the church so the husband is the preserver and supporter of his wife.

24 But as the church is subject to Christ, so let the wives also be to their husbands in everything.—The wife is to be submissive to her husband in everything, as the church is to Christ, as the Son of God. He requires nothing save what God requires. This in everything is necessarily modified as above by everything compatible with obedience to God.

25 Husbands, love your wives, even as Christ also loved the church, and gave himself up for it;—Having illustrated the duty of the wife to the husband by the church's subjection to Christ, he refers to the love of Christ for the church to illustrate and enforce the duty of the husband to love and cherish his wife. [The love here required of the husband is not of passion, but of the soul in its spiritual purity and from its innermost depths. It should be Christlike, patterned after God's love, self-forgetful, self-sacrificing, and self-devoting, even unto death.]

26 that he might sanctify it,—Christ died, gave himself up that he might sanctify the church and perfect it. [The sanctification of the church is the purpose of the grace of God. It was God's purpose "before the foundation of the world, that we should be holy and without blemish before him in love" (1: 4), and the mission of Jesus Christ in the world was to that end; this was the object of his death on the cross. In his prayer for his disciples, on the night in which he was betrayed, Jesus said: "Sanctify them in the truth: thy word is truth. . . . And for their sakes I sanctify

[5: 26.] EPHESIANS 113

himself up for it; 26 that he might sanctify it, having cleansed it by the ³washing of water with the word, 27 that he might present the church to

---

³Gr. *laver.*

---

myself, that they themselves also may be sanctified in truth." (John 17: 17, 19.)

having cleansed it by the washing of water—This refers to the forgiveness of sins, according to the word of God. Commentators almost without exception understand "by the washing of water" to refer to baptism. This unity of sentiment is very decisive. It was the washing with water with which the Ephesian Christians were familiar, and which could not fail to occur to them as the washing intended. Besides, nothing more is here attributed to baptism than is attributed to it in many other places in the word of God. Jesus in the commission said: "He that believeth and is baptized shall be saved" (Mark 16: 16); to the convicted multitude on the day of Pentecost, Peter said: "repent, ye, and be baptized every one of you in the name of Jesus Christ unto the remission of your sins" (Acts 2: 38); and Ananias said to Saul: "Arise, and be baptized, and wash away thy sins" (Acts 22: 16); and many other passages testify the same thing.

with the word,—Peter says: "Having been begotten again, not of corruptible seed, but of incorruptible, through the word of God, which liveth and abideth." (1 Pet. 1: 23.) And James says: "Of his own will he brought us forth by the word of truth, that we should be a kind of firstfruits of his creatures." (James 1: 18.) In these passages the "word of God," or "the word of truth," is the instrument of regeneration. God's will is the origin of it. Paul said to the Corinthians: "For though ye have ten thousand tutors in Christ, yet have ye not many fathers; for in Christ Jesus I begat you through the gospel." (1 Cor. 4: 15.) He regards the gospel in the same attitude that James and Peter represent it. The gospel is here the seed, the instrument of conversion of the Corinthians. Of the Gentiles Peter said that God "made no distinction between us and them, cleansing their hearts by faith." (Acts 15: 9.) To the Thessalonians Paul said: "God chose you from the beginning unto salvation in sanctification of the Spirit and belief of the truth: whereunto he called you through our gos-

himself a glorious *church,* not having spot or wrinkle or any such thing; but that it should be holy and without blemish. 28 Even so ought husbands also to love their own wives as their own bodies. He that loveth his own wife

---

pel, to the obtaining of the glory of our Lord Jesus Christ." (2 Thess. 2: 13, 14.) Here again the belief of the truth is the instrument of sanctification and salvation. Whether, then, we call it the *truth,* the *word,* the *word of God,* the *gospel,* it is called the seed, the incorruptible seed of the new birth by which the sinner is begotten, sanctified, purified, and saved.

27 that he might present the church to himself a glorious church,—The church having been washed in the members being baptized into Christ, the work of Christ is to perfect it, that he might present it to himself a glorious church.

not having spot or wrinkle or any such thing;—Her glory consisted in her purity—without spot or stain upon her garments or character, as a pure and chaste woman, true to her husband. Spots indicated the indiscretions of youth, and wrinkles in the garments indicated carelessness or the decay of age, as wrinkles in the face. He was so perfecting the church that it would have neither the indiscretions of youth nor the feebleness and decay of age.

but that it should be holy and without blemish.—Christ died not only to redeem the church out of the world, but also to perfect it after it was separated from the world. [The design of Christ's death as here expressed is to render the church perfectly holy, but there can be no doubt as to when this end is to be attained, for in this life neither scripture nor experience affords an example; still if one should attain this blessed state, it cannot be affirmed of the whole body of believers. It is then when the righteous dead shall be raised in the likeness of the Son of God, and those who shall be alive shall be changed. (1 Thess. 4: 15-18.) When this corruptible shall have put on incorruption and this mortal shall have on immorality—it is then that the church shall be made ready as a bride adorned for her husband. (Rev. 21: 2; 19: 6-8.)]

28 Even so ought husbands also to love their own wives as their own bodies.—As Christ redeemed the church and loves it, so ought husbands to love their own wives. Christ loved the church better than he did his own fleshly body. He sacrificed

loveth himself: 29 for no man ever hated his own flesh; but nourisheth and cherisheth it, even as Christ also the church; 30 because we are members of

it that he might establish the church. The church became the spiritual body which was dearer to him than the fleshly body.

He that loveth his own wife loveth himself:—So the wife becomes part of the body of the husband. The twain are one. [This is so because she is one with him, and their interests are identified; because by this, he really promotes his own welfare as much as he does when he takes care of his own body. A husband's kindness to his wife will be more than repaid by the happiness which she imparts, and all the real solicitude which he shows to make her happy will come to far more than it costs. If a man wishes to promote his own happiness in the most effective way, he should follow the Lord's instruction to show love and kindness to his wife.]

29 **for no man ever hated his own flesh;**—As no man ever hated his own flesh, he ought not to hate or be bitter against his wife.

but nourisheth and cherisheth it, even as Christ also the church;—[The husband's love for his wife should be that of the highest character, a love that shrinks at no sacrifice in order to bless and ennoble the wife of his bosom. It must be of the same kind as that which prompted Christ to give himself for the salvation of the world. The aim of the true husband should be to make the character of his wife a glorious character, without spot or blemish.]

30 **because we are members of his body.**—We, as members of the church, which is the body of Christ, are members or partakers of his body. Our union with him is close and strong. He is head in the sense that from him all the strength and power comes, all the wisdom descends. He is the center to which all the members are bound, from him all the impulses and guidance flow. The members of the church should be as subject to the mind of Christ as the members of the body are subject to the will of its head. The head through the nervous organization conveys its mandates to the members of the body, and they move at its slightest wish and obey faithfully its mandates. Christ the head of the church

his body. 31 ⁴For this cause shall a man leave his father and mother, and shall cleave to his wife; and the two shall become one flesh. 32 This mys-

⁴Gen. ii. 24.

---

bears his mandates to the body through the mind. The will of Christ is contained in the New Testament. That the will may be conveyed to the body, we must take that will into the mind, learn it, study it, and have it so in the heart that it molds the mind and guides the very emotions. In this way only can we have the mind of Christ. When we learn the mind that was in Christ, we must perform it willingly, as the members of our body obey our own mind. This is the only way of receiving the mind of Christ; the only way of receiving his Spirit that we may be guided thereby. Unless we have, and are guided by the mind of Christ, we are none of his. Let it sink deep into every mind that our lack of obedience is a lack of faith or trust in God.

31 **For this cause shall a man leave his father and mother, and shall cleave to his wife;**—Because of this intimate relation and oneness between husband and wife, as between Christ and the church, as ordained in the beginning: "Therefore shall a man leave his father and his mother, and shall cleave unto his wife: and they shall be one flesh." (Gen. 2: 24.) The wife is the other part of himself. [The relation of parentage is one of common flesh and blood, and stands at the head of those natural relations which we do not make, but into which we are born. The relation of marriage is the most sacred of all the ties into which we are not born, and which we do make for ourselves, in accordance with a true or supposed harmony of nature. It becomes, says the Lord, a relation not of common flesh and blood but of *one flesh*. Itself originally voluntary, it supersedes all natural ties. The Lord therefore says, "They are no more two, but *one flesh*. What therefore God hath joined together, let no man put asunder." (Matt. 19: 6.) Hence marriage is strikingly that unity with Christ—voluntarily initiated by the Lord, voluntarily accepted by us—which yet so supersedes all natural ties that it is said: "If any man cometh unto me, and hateth not his own father, and mother, and wife, and children, and brethren, and sisters, yea and his own life also, he cannot be my disciple." (Luke 14: 26.)]

tery is great: but I speak in regard of Christ and of the church. 33 Nevertheless do ye also severally love each one his own wife even as himself; and *let* the wife *see* that she fear her husband.

---

and the two shall become one flesh.—When a man selects a woman to be his wife, she becomes the complement of himself—that which is needed to make the complete man, so the two are one. It takes both to make one being as originally created. This union must be indissoluble in the sight of God.

32 This mystery is great: but I speak in regard of Christ and of the church.—This union of the two is a great mystery, he illustrates it by Christ and the church.

33 Nevertheless do ye also severally love each one his own wife even as himself;—Notwithstanding he speaks of Christ and the church, let every man so love his wife as he loves himself—make her a part of himself, in his thoughts, feelings, purposes, and regard her comfort and happiness as he does his own, and do for her as he does for himself.

and let the wife see that she fear her husband.—Let the wife see that she respects and honors her husband. [Reverence consists of love and esteem which produce a care to please, and a fear which awakens caution lest just offense be given. There should be such a mutual love and confidence that the known wish of the husband should be a law to the wife; and that the known desires of the wife should be the rule which the husband would approve.]

2. THE RELATION OF PARENTS AND CHILDREN
6: 1-4

1 Children, obey your parents in the Lord: for this is right. 2 [5]Honor

[5]Ex. xx. 12; Dt. v. 16.

---

1 Children, obey your parents—After speaking of the relations of husband and wife, next comes that of parents and children. The child is begotten, conceived, and brought into existence by the parents. It is a part of themselves, each imparting of their own life and being to the child. They take care of it, sustain it, and the child looks to the parent as the parent looks to God. In gratitude to the parent and as a means of training, it is to trust and obey God as it grows older. God has always required the child to obey the parent; under the Mosaic law, he said: "If a man have a stubborn and rebellious son, that will not obey the voice of his father, or the voice of his mother, and, though they chasten him, will not hearken unto them; then shall his father and his mother lay hold on him, and bring him out unto the elders of his city, and unto the gate of his place; and they shall say unto the elders of his city, This our son is stubborn and rebellious, he will not obey our voice; he is a glutton, and a drunkard. And all the men of his city shall stone him to death with stones: so shalt thou put away the evil from the midst of thee; and all Israel shall hear, and fear." (Deut. 21: 18-21.) This was a son in his minority, but when the parents grow old and infirm in body and mind, and the child has reached the strength and wisdom of manhood, honor then demands support and help, but always with deference, kindness, and respect.

in the Lord:—This limits the submission. That is, whatever can be done in obedience to the parents without violating the law of God, that do; but beyond this no child dare go without deep condemnation upon itself. The fearful doom of those who fail to obey God in order to please parents or propitiate the world is given in the following: "He that hath my commandments, and keepeth them, he it is that loveth me: and he that loveth me shall be loved of my Father, and I will love him, and will manifest myself unto him. . . . If a man love me, he will keep my word: and my Father will love him, and we will come unto him, and make our abode with him. He that loveth me not keepeth not my words: and the word which ye hear is not mine, but the Father's who sent me." (John 14: 21-24.) When one does the will of parents rather than obey the commandments of God, or when he fails to do the commandments of God to please any earthly being, he shows that he loves that being more than he loves God. Whenever one fails to bear whatever cross stands in his way, he fails to obey God in order to save his life even, he cannot be a disciple of the Lord. (Luke 14: 26, 27; 17: 33.)

for this is right.—The same obligation and restriction in obeying parents, not only for gratitude and love of the parent, but because God requires it. In obeying the parent the child obeys God. This is the added obligation. But the child old enough to be

thy father and mother (which is the first commandment with promise), 3 that it may be well with thee, and thou ⁶mayest live long on the ⁷earth. 4 And, ye fathers, provoke not your children to wrath: but nurture them in the chastening and admonition of the Lord.

⁶Or, *shalt*
⁷Or, *land*

---

accountable to God is under higher obligation to obey God than it is to obey the parent. It must disobey the parent in order to obey God when their requirements conflict. The first duty is to God.

2 Honor thy father and mother (which is the first commandment with promise),—This is one of the ten commandments written on tables of stone at Sinai. To honor father and mother is to discharge faithfully the duties the child owes them—obedience in childhood, respect, reverence through life, tender care, and support in old age, and kindness and love at all times. This is the first commandment that has a specific promise connected with it.

3 that it may be well with thee, and thou mayest live long on the earth.—The blessings come as the result of the character that loves and honors the parent, and then God, and preserves from the fatal ruin of the stubborn and rebellious son. [This blessing is the heritage of dutiful children in every land. The obedience of childhood and youth rendered to a wise Christian rule forms in the young the habit of self-control, self-respect, diligence, promptitude, faithfulness, and kindness of heart, which are the best guarantees for happiness and success in life.]

4 And, ye fathers, provoke not your children to wrath:— Fathers are cautioned against an excessive severity that provokes bitter, wrathful rebellion. Children should be corrected and retained from self-will and should be trained to be obedient to their parents from earliest childhood; but this should be done in love for the child. The child will come to appreciate this and to love and honor the parent for the restraint and correction given.

but nurture them in the chastening and admonition of the Lord.—Kindly and earnestly train them in the discipline of the Lord. It may be severe, but it is for the good of the child, and is prompted by love. In no point do Christians fail more than in the training of their children in the Lord. They allow them to grow up ambitious of worldly preferement, lovers of pleasure, greedy of gain, and frequently scoffers of God. This is due to lack of faithful training. The obedience of childhood and youth rendered to a wise Christian rule forms the habit of self-control, self-respect, diligence, faithfulness, and kindliness of heart, which are the best guarantees for happiness and success in life. Parents cannot be faithful servants of God without studying his word; treasuring it in their hearts, letting its teachings mold their feelings, direct their lives, and form their character. They must do this to fit them for heaven. In doing so they will teach the word to their children as the chief matter of life. They have brought them into existence, and are under every obligation to bring them up in the chastening and admonition of the Lord.

So great and important were the issues involved concerning the teaching of the law given at Sinai that God said unto Israel: "And these words, which I command thee this day, shall be upon thy heart; and thou shalt teach them diligently unto thy children, and shalt talk of them when thou sittest in thy house, and when thou walkest by the way, and when thou liest down, and when thou risest up. And thou shalt bind them for a sign upon thy hand, and they shall be for frontlets between thine eyes. And thou shalt write them upon the door-posts of thy house, and upon thy gates." (Deut. 6: 6-9.) Again, he says: "See, I have set before thee this day life and good, and death and evil; in that I command thee this day to love Jehovah thy God, to walk in his ways, and to keep his commandments and his statutes and his ordinances, that thou mayest live and multiply, and that Jehovah thy God may bless thee in the land whither thou goest in to possess it." (30: 15, 16.) And still further, he says: "Set your heart unto all the words which I testify unto you this day, what ye shall command your children to observe to do, even all the words of this law. For it is no vain thing for you; because it is your life, and through this thing ye shall prolong your days in the land, whither ye go over the Jordan to possess it." (32: 46, 47.) This was said concerning the law of Moses, sealed with the typical blood of animals; we have the spiritual and eternal law of God, sealed with the blood of his beloved Son, the Savior of the world, concerning which it is said: "Therefore we ought to give the more earnest heed to the things that were heard, lest haply we drift away from them. For if the word spoken through angels proved stedfast, and every transgression and disobedience received a just recompense of reward; how shall we escape, if we neglect so great a salvation? which having at the first been spoken through the Lord, was confirmed unto us by them that heard; God also bearing witness with them, both by signs and wonders, and by manifold powers, and by gifts of the Holy Spirit, according to his own will." (Heb. 2: 1-4.) Parents who fail to teach their children sin against God, themselves, their children, and how shall they escape the wrath of God on account of their neglecting this solemn warning?

3. THE RELATION OF MASTERS AND SERVANTS MADE A BROTHERHOOD OF SERVICE TO ONE MASTER
6: 5-9

5 [8]Servants, be obedient unto them that according to the flesh are your [9]masters, with fear and trembling, in singleness of your heart, as unto

[8]Gr. *Bondservants.*
[9]Gr. *lords.*

---

5 Servants, be obedient unto them that according to the flesh are your masters,—The apostle recognized the slavery of human beings in both master and slave. Slavery is a political relation, established by political governments. The Lord did not violently interfere with political relations. It was not an indisoluble relationship like husband and wife, parent and child. Slavery was in force in all the countries to which letters were addressed. Indeed, it was in force in all countries at that time. Christ did not propose to break up such relations by violence. He recognized the relationship, regulated it, and put in operation principles that in their workings would so mold public sentiment as to break down all evil relations and sinful institutions. Slavery was so treated.

with fear and trembling,—With earnest, conscientious care and reverence. [The fear enjoined is no dread of human displeasure, or the master's whip or tongue. It is the same "fear and trembling" with which the child of God is to work out his "own salvation." (Phil. 2: 12.) The inward work of the soul's salvation and the outward work of the busy hands on the farm, in the

Christ; 6 not in the way of eyeservice, as men-pleasers; but as ⁸servants of Christ, doing the will of God from the ¹⁰heart; 7 with good will doing ser-

¹⁰Gr. *soul*.

---

mine, at the factory, or in the lowest domestic duties—all alike are to be performed under a solemn responsibility to God and in the presence of Christ who understands every kind of work, and will render to each of his servants just and exact reward.]

in singleness of your heart,—The honest desire to do right for its own sake, with inward sincerity, knowing it was their duty; and even if it was irksome, doing it pleasantly, with no feeling of reluctance, but genuine good will.

as unto Christ;—The Christian servant was required to obey his master not only from fear, but for conscience' sake. It was not only to please the master, but to please Christ. It was an added obligation to fidelity in the service rendered.

6 not in the way of eyeservice, as men-pleasers;—Eyeservice is either work done only to please the eye, which cannot bear to be tested; or it may be good work done only when the master's eye is upon the worker. This was a vice not peculiar to slavery, but it enters into all forms of service. Dishonest work is to be avoided quite as much as dishonest words. An acted lie is as dishonorable as a spoken one.

but as servants of Christ,—The servants of Christ must apply the principles of Christ to their work.

doing the will of God from the heart;—The service was to be a faithful service, rendered from the heart, with a singleness of heart for the benefit of the master. [To do the will of God in this way may sometimes require Christian courage. In these days there are labor unions and combinations among workmen, with a view of protecting their rights. They may sometimes be dominated by selfishness, and act tyranically; and a Christian workman may be in the position of choosing between the Lord and incurring the ill will of his fellow workers. If he is worthy of the Lord, he will not, to please his fellow workers, render unfaithful work, but will brave the consequences of rendering faithful service because he must be faithful to Christ rather than to men.]

vice, as unto the Lord, and not unto men: 8 knowing that whatsoever good thing each one doeth, the same shall he receive again from the Lord, whether *he be* bond or free. 9 And, ye ⁹masters, do the same things unto them, and forbear threatening: knowing that he who is both their Master and yours is in heaven, and there is no respect of persons with him.

---

7 with good will doing service,—Much of the service required of slaves was done from fear and grudging; but the Christian slave must do the will of God in the service of men, as Jesus Christ did it—with meekness and fortitude and unvaried love. The work will thus be rendered from inner principles, with thought and affection and resolution spent upon it.

as unto the Lord, and not unto men:—As a Christian he must do it willingly, and cheerfully as unto the Lord, for he accepts only cheerful service.

8 knowing that whatsoever good thing each one doeth,—The Lord requires fidelity in any relation his servants occupy as service to him. They must be faithful in all relations of life.

the same shall he receive again from the Lord, whether he be bond or free.—When the servants are so because they trust the Lord, he will reward them whether bond or free. So if the master be harsh and unreasonable, and the slave be discouraged from service, he will still do it from the fear of the Lord, and look forward for God to reward him.

9 And, ye masters, do the same things unto them, and forbear threatening:—He commands the masters to act towards their slaves from the fear of God. The spirit that threatens is a bitter, dictatorial one, lacks kindness and consideration, and greatly exasperates and embitters the servant.

knowing that he who is both their Master and yours is in heaven,—God will reward the master with good or evil as he treats his servants. God rewards the master for his course toward his servant as well as the servant's course toward his master.

and there is no respect of persons with him.—God no more respects the person of the master than that of the servant. Indeed, he makes no allowance for him because of his superior station.

[The general principles underlying this section are applicable to all the relations of employer and employee. The employee is warned against eyeservice, exhorted to faithful labor as in the sight of God, bidden to look unto a higher recompense than the temporal wages, because he serves a higher Master. The master is reminded of the equality of all before God, and warned that position does not avail in his sight, and exhorted respecting the duties to him involved in the duties of an employer. Here, and here only, is the true social science. Duties to one another are duties to Christ.]

SECTION FOUR

FINAL EXHORTATION AND CONCLUSION
6: 10-24

1. THE ARMOR OF GOD AND THE FIGHT AGAINST THE POWERS OF EVIL
6: 10-20

10 [11]Finally, [12]be strong in the Lord, and in the strength of his might. 11 Put on the whole armor of God, that ye may be able to stand against the

---
[11]Or, *Henceforth*
[12]Gr. *be made powerful.*

---

10 **Finally,**—In this section Paul draws his epistle to a conclusion, and by this word quickens the attention of his readers, and prepares them for a counsel eminently mighty in itself of what had already been said.

be strong in the Lord,—He now gives admonition as to their general deportment. We become strong in the Lord by drawing near to God in a more faithful and trusting obedience to him, a closer walk in the footsteps of Jesus Christ.

and in the strength of his might.—[Though the redemption in Christ is complete and free, yet between the beginning and the final consummation there is a continual conflict—it is something real and arduous. It is not only real, but is difficult. It is one in which true believers are often grievously tried; and multitudes of weak believers utterly fail. He knew that to meet these mighty foes they needed to be fully armed for the conflict. To be strong in the Lord indicates the relation to Christ in which alone the strength can be experienced. (2 Cor. 12: 9.) The might is Christ's, but by faith it becomes our strength. Strong trust, courage, endurance, hope, love may all be had from him, if our fellowship be maintained in uninterrupted vigor.]

11 **Put on the whole armor of God,**—God does not clothe Christians with this strength and power without earnest effort on their part, and without their making just such efforts and doing just what he commands. The spiritual or inner man becomes strong only by experience. God has prepared and furnished armor to be used by the Christian soldier. It is composed of weapons both defensive and offensive, those which ward off the blows of the

wiles of the devil. 12 For our wrestling is not against [18]flesh and blood, but

[13]Gr. *blood and flesh.*

enemy and with which they are to strike offensive blows to conquer others. [We are thus taught from the outset that as the strength which we need is not from ourselves, so neither are the means of offense and defense. Nor are they means of man's devising. This is a truth which has been overlooked by many professed Christians in all ages of the church, to the injury of those who profess to be children of God. Instead of relying on the arms which God has provided, men have always been disposed to trust to that which they have provided for themselves or which have been prescribed by others.]

that ye may be able to stand—The Christian soldier ought to be prepared on all sides, so as to want nothing. The Lord has provided arms for repelling every attack. It remains for him to apply them to use. [To quicken our vigilance, he reminds us that we must not only engage in open warfare, but that we have a crafty and insidious foe to encounter, who frequently lies in ambush.]

against the wiles of the devil.—[These are the devil's treacherous methods of warfare and his subtle plans of battle. *Wiles* are acts or means of cunning deception; something as a ruse or stratagem, by which he is enabled to trick or deceive. The idea here is that the devil does no carry on an open warfare. He does not meet the Christian soldier face to face. Hence the necessity of being constantly armed to meet him whenever the attack is made. He presents the world in an alluring aspect; invites to pleasures that seem to be harmless, and leads in indulgence until we have gone so far that we cannot retreat.]

12 **For our wrestling**—Wrestling is a technical word of the Greek athletic contests. It was probably suggested by the word *stand*. For the wrestler's work is to maintain his position and to throw his adversary. And it is a most graphic picture of the Christian life. For, unlike military conflict, each one contends alone against a personal contestant, and can gain the victory only by intense personal effort and watchfulness. This suitability of the word led Paul to drop for a moment the military metaphor in-

against the principalities, against the powers, against the world-rulers of this darkness, against the spiritual *hosts* of wickedness in the heavenly *places*. 13

volved in the word armor, to which he returns in the next verse, and to borrow another metaphor from the athletic festivals.

is not against flesh and blood,—This denotes mankind as limited by the constitution of the human body. The Christian struggle is not against persons so limited. This is true even when we have resolute human opponents. For these are but instruments of unseen and more tremendous foes.

but against the principalities, against the powers,—The signification of this and the following terms, and the analogy of scripture, renders it certain that the reference is to evil spirits. For the angels that sinned and were cast out of heaven, it is said: "God spared not angels when they sinned, but cast them down to hell, and committed them to pits of darkness, to be reserved unto judgment." (2 Pet. 2: 4.) And again: "Angels that kept not their own principality, but left their proper habitation, he hath kept in everlasting bonds under darkness under the judgment of the great day." (Jude 6.) They are now subject to Satan their prince. They are now called those who are first in high rank; and *powers*, those invested with high authority. These terms have probably reference to the relation of the spirits among themselves.

against the world-rulers—This expresses the extent of the dominion of these invisible foes—the term is extended only to the rulers of the most widely extended realms; there is no part of the earth to which their influence does not extend, and where this dark rule does not show itself. (Luke 4: 6.)

of this darkness, against the spiritual hosts of wickedness—These evil spirits reign over the existing state of ignorance and alienation from God. That is, the world in its apostasy is subject to their control; or "this darkness" is equivalent to kingdom of darkness. Rulers of the kingdom of darkness, which includes in it the world as distinguished from the true people of God. Our conflict, therefore, is with the potentates who are rulers of the kingdom of darkness as it now is.

in the heavenly places.—Undoubtedly the places here meant are those in which are found the hosts of wicked spirits against whom believers are in perpetual struggle, and in which they need the panoply of God described in the following verses. These places cannot be called "heavenly" because of heavenly enjoyment experienced by these occupants, but for some other reason. The allusion is the same as in the following: "And you did he make alive, when ye were dead through your trespasses and sins, wherein ye once walked according to the course of this world, according to the prince of the powers of the air, of the spirit that now worketh in the sons of disobedience." (2: 1, 2.) If our "adversary the devil, as a roaring lion" (1 Pet. 5: 8), if he is "going to and fro in the earth, and from walking up and down in it" (Job 1: 7), his activity is in the same place precisely in which the angels are employed. He is often at church, and sometimes in the pulpit. He is at work in places that are heavenly, to angels, though they are far from being heavenly to him. Paul often speaks of the Christian life as a conflict, but only here does he name the opponent. In 1 John 5: 4, 5, the enemy to be conquered is *the world*. This calls attention to the outward and visible form, and the multiplicity, of the foes arrayed against us. In 1 John 4: 4-6, the power of this multiform antagonist is traced to one animating and personal principle. In 2 Cor. 4: 4, Paul says "the god of this world" proves his hostility by blinding "the minds of the unbelieving, that the light of the gospel of the glory of Christ, . . . should not dawn upon them." And the passage before us speaks of various superhuman powers acting under the directions of one supreme foe, the devil.

[At the head of the ranks of wicked spirits is the devil. The subject is a forbidding one, but the levity with which it is treated in many circles, the number of those who scorn the idea of personal evil spirits whose sole aim is to antagonize the Lord's work, grace among men, justifies some reflections on it. Probably there is no criminal known to men that has so many *aliases* as the devil. I subjoin a partial list of names given him by the Lord Jesus Christ and the Holy Spirit: Evil One (Matt. 13: 19); Enemy (Matt. 13: 39); Beelzebub (Mark 3: 22); Prince of Devils (3: 22); Strong One (Luke 11: 21); Murderer (John 8: 44); Liar (8: 44); Father of Lies (8: 44); Prince of This World (12: 31); Satan (Acts 5: 3); God of This World (2 Cor. 4: 4); Belial (6:

Wherefore take up the whole armor of God, that ye may be able to withstand in the evil day, and, having done all, to stand. 14 Stand therefore,

---

15); Serpent (11: 3); Spirit of Evil (Eph. 2: 2); Tempter (1 Thess. 3: 5); Adversary (1 Pet. 5: 8); Angel of the Abyss (Rev. 9: 11); Apollyon (9: 11); Abaddon (9: 11); Great Red Dragon (12: 3); The Dragon (12: 7); Great Dragon (12: 9); The Old Serpent (12: 9); Devil and Satan (12: 9); Deceiver of the Whole World (12: 9); Accuser (12: 10). Here are twenty-seven names given the devil, each of which is descriptive of his energy, and his power. The Lord Jesus himself calls him "the prince of this world," a title which invests him with marvelous authority. Paul calls him "the god of this world." Both describe the sphere of the devil's influence, and both have to do with that strange, lawless, and godless thing called "the spirit of the twentieth century." How profoundly this spirit of the age is dominated by the devil and interpenetrated vicious influence which every observant Christian perceives. There is scarcely a beneficial invention of this age that is not perverted into an instrumentality for evil. With such a foe confronting him, the Christian needs "the whole armor of God," which is fully provided and freely given.]

13 Wherefore take up the whole armor of God,—Having all these wicked spirits to fight, he admonishes them to take unto themselves the whole armor of God. [The repetition of the counsel given emphasizes its importance. The language used distinguishes it from all manner of merely human precautions, defenses, or disciplines. It is a special provision for the believer in response to his prayerful trust in God.]

that ye may be able to withstand in the evil day,—The commandment to be strong in the Lord is fully associated with our having done all, because leaning on almighty strength implies the effort to put forth strength by our own instrumentality; when God's strength comes to us it contrains us to do all that can be done by us or through us, as Paul exhorted: "So then, my beloved, even as ye have always obeyed, not as in my presence only, but now much more in my absence, work out your own salvation with fear and trembling; for it is God who worketh in you both to will

having girded your loins with truth, and having put on the breastplate of righteousness, 15 and having shod your feet with the preparation of the

---

and to work, for his good pleasure." (Phil. 2: 12, 13.) [We are to leave nothing undone that can contribute to the success of the battle; then we shall be able to stand, or stand firm.]

and, having done all, to stand.—It is important to bear in mind through the whole context that the central idea is *preparedness*, not progress or conquest; ideas of which the gospel is full, but which are not present here. [The scene is filled with the marshalled hosts of the evil one, bent upon dislodging the Christian from the one possible vantage ground of life and power—union and communion with the Lord.]

14 **Stand therefore, having girded your loins with truth,**— The girding the loins gives strength to labor. The truth of God taken into the heart is as a girdle to give strength to the loins. [The belt was an essential part of the soldier's equipment. Passing around his loins, it was of special use in keeping other parts of the armor in place and in securing the proper soldierly attitude and freedom of movement. The girding is the soldier's own act by the help of God's grace. It is subjective truth. In that of harmony of knowledge with the objective truth given in the gospel, of the inward practical acknowledgement of the truth as it is in Christ. The subjective application means obviously the personal grace of candor, sincerity, and truthfulness, as it is used also of the veracity of God. (Rom. 15: 8.) It seems simplest, therefore, and most accordant with usage to take it so here. And this plain grace of openness, truthfulness, reality, the mind will practice no deceits and attempt no disguises in our intercourse with God, is indeed vital to Christian safety and essential to the due operation of all other qualities of character. This is a wonderful source of strength, and requires much attention, careful thought, prayerful reading and meditation, to arm ourselves with the truth.]

and having put on the breastplate of righteousness,—The breastplate was to protect the breast and chest, and the vital organs within. Righteousness is the breastplate God has furnished man to protect himself from the darts the enemy may hurl at him.

¹⁴gospel of peace; 16 withal taking up the shield of faith, wherewith ye shall

₁₄Gr. *good tidings.* See Mt. 4. 23 marg.

Righteousness is gained by doing the will of God. The righteousness of God is that plan of obedience to him, that he has ordained through which to save man. (Rom. 8: 1-11.) Man clothes himself with that righteousness of God by walking in the way God has marked out for him to walk. "My little children, let no man lead you astray: he that doeth righteousness is righteous, even as he is righteous." (1 John 3: 7.) Jesus did the will of God and for that reason was righteous. All who do God's will are righteous, for "if ye know that he is righteous, ye know that every one also that doeth righteousness is begotten of him." (1 John 2: 29.) Then to put on the breastplate of righteousness is to obey God.

15 and having shod your feet with the preparation of the gospel of peace;—Since the Christian warrior is to stand, he must have no unprotected and uncertain foothold. Preparedness is the thought here. As his fighting was so much of a hand-to-hand conflict, a firm footing was exceedingly important. His sandals were accordingly not only bound firmly to his feet and ankles, but were thickly studded with hobnails, to give a sure footing to those who would stand firm. The Christian soldier's preparedness in this regard, he is to find in the gospel of peace. [It is that principle of steadfastness which has its origin in a sense of oneness with God, and so of divine aid in any emergency. The paradox here, of *peace* as part of the panoply of the holy *war*, is as significant as it is beautiful. The Christian soldier's foothold needs to be settled, sure, and restful, just in proportion to the stress around him. The peace of justification (Rom. 5: 1), and its accompaniment, "the peace of God, which passeth all understanding," guarding the heart and thoughts in Christ Jesus (Phil. 4: 7), are just then most necessary to the Christian's spirit and most real to his consciousness, when put to the test in the evil day. Jesus Christ, in himself, is ground of vantage; a clear view and personal hold of him is the secret of a true foothold upon him. Paul himself, when facing death, stood in this strength when he wrote the following: "For which cause I suffer also these things: yet I am not

be able to quench all the fiery darts of the evil *one*. 17 And take the helmet

---

ashamed; for I know him whom I have believed, and I am persuaded that he is able to guard that which I have committed unto him against that day." (2 Tim. 1: 12.)]

16 withal taking up the shield of faith,—The shield to which reference is made was four feet long and two and one-half feet wide. It was held on the left arm and could be used to protect the entire body, and was very essential to the safety of the combatant. Joined together, these large shields formed a wall, behind which a whole body of troops could hide themselves from the rain of the enemies' missiles. [Such is the office of faith in the conflicts of life; it is the Christian soldier's main defense. To increase our faith it is necessary to study regularly the word of God, since belief cometh of hearing "the word of Christ." (Rom. 10: 17.) But in order that our faith may be strengthened and fixed as a part of our being, it is necessary that we give expression to our convictions in our daily life. No thought or feeling enters into the formation of our characters or becomes permanent until it controls the actions of our bodies and becomes a part of our being. Faith itself is accepted by God only when it has molded the actions of the body and made the body subject to its control. The conviction of the heart becomes a part of our being and enters into our character only when it prompts the body to action.]

wherewith ye shall be able to quench all the fiery darts of the evil one.—Faith in God furnishes the shield that will ward off all the darts of the wicked one. [On the shield of faith the darts of Satan are caught, their points broken, and their fire extinguished. The shields were made of wood, covered on the outside with thick leather, which not only deadened the shock of the missile, but protected the frame of the shield from the fire-tipped darts. These flaming arrows, armed with some quickly burning and light combustible material, if they failed to pierce the warrior's shield, fell in a moment extinguished at his feet. It is not likely that Paul means by the *fiery darts* incitement to passions in ourselves, inflammatory temptations that seek to rouse the inward fires of anger and lust. The fire belongs to the enemy who shoots the dart. It

of salvation, and the sword of the Spirit, which is the word of God: 18 with

signifies malignant hate with which Satan hurls his slander and threats against the people of God through his human instruments. An unwavering faith wards off and quenches this fire, so that the soul never succumbs to its heat.]

17 And take the helmet—The Roman soldier's helmet was a cap made of thick leather or brass, fitted to the head. It was used to guard the head from a blow by a sword, a war club, or a battle-axe.

of salvation,—According to the analogy of the preceding expressions, "the breastplate of righteousness," and "the shield of faith," salvation is itself the helmet. That which adorns and protects the Christian, which enables him to hold up his head with confidence and joy, is the fact that he is one of the redeemed, made meet to be a partaker of the inheritance of saints in light, who has been delivered out of the power of darkness into the kingdom of the Son of his love, in whom there is redemption, the forgiveness of sins. (Col. 1: 12, 14.) [To the Christian soldier, the assurance of salvation is very important for the following reasons: To be firm and steadfast in the faith, he must have scriptural assurance of pardon or salvation from past sins, and he must have a well-grounded hope of the future and final salvation. This can be attained only by "them that by patience in well-doing seek for glory and honor and incorruption." (Rom. 2: 7.)]

and the sword of the Spirit,—This is the sword which the Spirit puts into the hands of the Christian, which he must accept and use.

which is the word of God:—The Spirit gave the word of God to the Christian, that he might use it both as a defensive and offensive weapon. It is that which God has spoken, his word, the Bible. This is "sharper than any two-edged sword." (Heb. 4: 12.) It is the wisdom of God and the power of God. It commends itself to reason and conscience. It has the power not only of truth, but of divine truth. [The Lord promised to give a word and wisdom which all their adversaries should not be able to gainsay or resist. (Luke 21: 15.) In opposition to all error, to all false philosophy, to all false principles of morals, to all sophistries

all prayer and supplication praying at all seasons in the Spirit, and watching

---

of vice, to all suggestions of the devil, the sole, simple and sufficient weapon is the word of God. It puts to flight all the powers of darkness. The Christian finds this to be true in his individual experience. It dissipates his doubts; it drives away his fears; it delivers him from the power of Satan. It is also the experience of the church collectively. All her triumphs over sin and error have been accomplished through the word of God. So long as she uses this and relies on this alone, she goes forward conquering; but when she turns aside to reason, science, tradition, or the doctrines and commandments of men, then she is at the mercy of the adversary—the devil.]

18 **with all prayer and supplication**—In this verse there still lingers some reference to soldiers on guard. Prayer is the general word for worship appropriated to God alone; supplication, used also towards man, is one element of such worship—asking what we need from God. [Paul says: "In nothing be anxious; but in everything by prayer and supplication with thanksgiving let your requests be made known unto God." (Phil. 4: 6.) In this we have first the general word *prayer* and then the two chief elements of worship, *supplication with thanksgiving*. It is not armor or weapons that makes the soldier. There must be courage and strength; even then he needs help. As the Christian has no resources of strength in himself, and can succeed only as aided from above, the apostle urges the duty of prayer.]

praying at all seasons in the Spirit,—[Believers should pray on all occasions, as Jesus said: "They ought always to pray, and not to faint" (Luke 18: 1), and Paul exhorted Christians to "pray without ceasing" (1 Thess. 5: 17). It is obvious, therefore, that prayer includes all converse with God, and is the expression of our feelings and desires which terminate in him. True prayer is spiritual and comes from a heart filled with heavenward longings and aspirations, changing our prayer from a cold form to heartfelt realities. The ordinary habit of the soul should be prayerful, realizing the presence of God and looking for his grace and guidance.]

and watching thereunto in all perseverance and supplication for all the saints,—The conflict of which Paul has been speak-

thereunto in all perseverance and supplication for all the saints, 19 and on my behalf, that utterance may be given unto me ¹⁵in opening my mouth, to make known with boldness the mystery of the ¹⁴gospel, 20 for which I am an

¹⁵Or, *in opening my mouth with boldness, to make known*

---

ing is not merely a single combat between the individual Christian and Satan, but also a war between the people of God and the powers of darkness. [No soldier entering into a battle fights for himself alone, but for all his fellow soldiers also. They form one army, and the success of one is the success of all. In like manner Christians are united in one army and therefore have a common cause; and each must pray and fight for all. Such is the communion of saints as set forth by the Holy Spirit that they can no more fail to take this interest in each other's welfare than the eye can fail to sympathize with the foot.]

19 and on my behalf, that utterance may be given unto me in opening my mouth,—Paul was a man of like passions and infirmities with us. His inspiration revealed unto him the will of God concerning man, and what was needed to carry forward God's work among men. Seeing clearly his duty and responsibility, and seeing what he most lacked to enable him to do the work, he prayed to be strengthened and guarded against the weaknesses and dangers that beset him. A lack of courage to speak at all times the full truth of God was one of the besetting sins of the early preachers. No more courageous man ever lived than Paul; yet he felt there was danger that he might fail to speak the whole truth of God to the world, and prayed, and asked others to pray for him that he might have the courage to preach it faithfully. If one of such natural courage as he felt such danger and the necessity for praying for courage, how much more should we poor mortals feel the need of following his example. Our courage is not now tested exactly in the same way his was; but it is none the less fully tested, and we need the courage to do our full duty to God and man His courage was tested by the danger of persecution, imprisonment, and death.

to make known with boldness—This includes frankness and boldness of spirit, of which this unrestrained declaration of truth is the expression. Men now as often fail to preach the whole truth of God with boldness and fullness, because it is unpopular and excites

ambassador in ¹chains; that in it I may speak boldly, as I ought to speak.

¹Gr. *a chain*.

opposition of the public, as it did in apostolic days from fear of imprisonment and death. Courage to preach boldly and fully the whole truth of God is the crying need of preachers and teachers of God's word. The word of God is corrupted, its teachings are perverted, and his truth is compromised, because they lack courage to speak boldly the whole truth. This weakens the church, and deprives men of the blessings of God's help. He blesses only those who speak the whole will of God. Not to do so is to stain our souls with the blood of our fellow men.

the mystery of the gospel,—The mystery of the gospel is that the Gentiles are fellow partakers of the promise in Christ Jesus, through the gospel. (3: 1-7.)

20 **for which I am an ambassador in chains;**—Paul was then in Rome, a prisoner, wearing chains for preaching the truth. He was an ambassador of God to the world to proclaim terms of pardon, as he says: "We are ambassadors therefore on behalf of Christ, as though God were entreating by us: we beseech you on behalf of Christ, be ye reconciled to God." (2 Cor. 5: 20.) Ambassadors are representatives of governments which send them. Paul, as sent by Christ with authority to preach in his name, and to negotiate with men, proclaiming the terms of reconciliation and urging their acceptance, was in an eminent sense an ambassador. He was an ambassador in chains, yet he did not lose his courage, but preached with as much boldness as ever.

that in it I may speak boldly, as I ought to speak.—Every one who speaks in the name of the Lord ought to speak his word boldly, fearlessly, and fully as it is, no matter how unpopular it may be.

2. COMMENDATION OF TYCHICUS
6: 21, 22

21 But that ye also may know my affairs, how I do, Tychicus, the beloved brother and faithful minister in the Lord, shall make known to you all

---

21 But that ye also may know my affairs, how I do,—Having referred to his captivity, he knew it would be natural for the Ephesians to desire more information about how he fared and his state of mind in captivity. The information regarding Paul and his friends would not be confined to the letter, but would be given no doubt also by Tychicus by word of mouth.

Tychicus,—He was of the province of Asia, in Asia Minor, of which Ephesus was the capital. (Acts 20: 4.) He accompanied Paul on his last journey from Corinth to Asia, although he is not, like Trophimus, actually named with Paul in Jerusalem. It is highly probable that he was one of the "messengers of the churches" spoken of in Second Corinthians (8: 18-23), as sent to bear the alms to Jerusalem We now find him again with Paul, and made by him the bearer of this epistle and the one to the Colossians. He is alluded to as still his companion in the interval between the first and second captivity (Tit. 3: 2), and in the second captivity is dispatched once more to Ephesus (2 Tim. 4: 12).

the beloved brother and faithful minister in the Lord,—[The character and career of Tychicus are such as show him altogether worthy of the confidence reposed in him by Paul, who sent him again and again on important work, which could be performed only by a man of ability and of high Christian character and experience. Thus all that is known of Tychicus bears out the description given by Paul himself, that he was a beloved brother, a faithful minister and fellow servant of the Lord. The two qualities by which he is noted—lovableness and fidelity—have not only served to embalm his name, but to show that he had a character much like that of Paul.]

shall make known to you all things:—It is supposed that this has reference to his commission as bearer of this epistle. As so sent, Tychicus would be a messenger direct from Paul, and could make known to these brethren, whose solicitude in his behalf was certainly great, all the particulars of his life in the Roman prison.

things: 22 whom I have sent unto you for this very purpose, that ye may know our state, and that he may comfort your hearts.

22 whom I have sent unto you for this very purpose, that you may know our state, and that he may comfort your hearts. —[This serves to explain the absence of personal remembrances, allusions, and messages in this epistle. Tychicus, in whom Paul had full confidence, would deliver them all by word of mouth. The concluding words show that it was not to gratify any personal feeling that Paul directed Tychicus to make this communication; but knowing how much they felt for him, he believed it would be a comfort to hear how he fared. To pagans, imprisonment was always dreadful; it was well for them to know how Christians could glory in tribulations. (Rom. 5: 3.) Tychicus, the beloved brother, was well fitted to apply this comforting view of his state.]

3. BENEDICTION AND BLESSING
6: 23, 24

23 Peace be to the brethren, and love with faith, from God the Father

23 Peace be to the brethren,—The peace for which Paul prayed to be among those in Christ is the fruit of peace with Christ and God. [Such peace guarding the thoughts and heart of each Christian, nothing contrary thereto will arise among them. There can be no clashing of interests, no selfish competitions, no strife as to who shall be the greatest. The awe of God's presence with his people, the remembrance of the dear price at which the church was purchased with his own blood (Acts 20: 28), the sense of Christ's lordship (1 Cor. 15: 25), and the sacredness of the brotherhood (1 Cor. 3: 16, 17), should check all turbulence and rivalry and teach us to seek the things that make for peace (1 Pet. 3: 11).]

and love with faith,—Love includes peace, and more; for it labors not to prevent contention only, but to help enrich in all ways the body of Christ. [By such toil of love, faith is made perfect. As faith grows and deepens, it makes new channels in which love may flow. To the Thessalonians Paul wrote: "We are bound to give thanks to God always for you, brethren, even as it is meet, for that your faith groweth exceedingly, and the love of each one of you all toward one another aboundeth." (2 Thess. 1: 3.) This is the sound and true growth of faith.]

and the Lord Jesus Christ. 24 Grace be with all them that love our Lord Jesus Christ ²with a *love* incorruptible.

²Or, *in incorruption*. See Rom. 2. 7.

---

from God the Father and the Lord Jesus Christ.—Peace among Christians is the fruit of peace with God through Christ. With such peace guarding the thoughts and heart of each Christian, nothing contrary thereto will arise among them. Calm and quiet hearts make a peaceful church. There are no clashing interests, no selfish competitions, no strife as to who shall be greatest.

24 Grace be with all them that love our Lord Jesus Christ— God's grace is to those who love Christ, and for those who continue to love him is this grace continued. If our love to Christ fails, grace ceases to rest upon us. God does not look with favor upon those who turn from faith in his Son. [Of such persons, Paul said: "If any man loveth not the Lord, let him be anathema. Maranatha." (1 Cor. 16: 22.) God's love is not a love of indifference; but a love of choice, Jesus said: "If a man love me, he will keep my word: and my Father will love him." (John 14: 23.) God cannot grant his grace to those who have seen and hated him in his Son and image. By that hatred they refuse his grace, and cast it from them. On the other hand, sincere love to the Lord Jesus Christ opens the heart to all the rich and purifying influences of divine grace. If we love Christ, we shall love his people.]

with a love incorruptible.—[This love is the life of the body of Christ. In it lies the church's immortality. The gates of death prevail not against her, rooted and grounded as she is in love to the risen and immortal Christ. May that love be maintained in deathless power!]

COMMENTARY ON THE EPISTLE
TO THE PHILIPPIANS

CONTENTS

	Page
INTRODUCTION	145
I. Philippi	145
II. Origin of the Philippian church	146
III. The Philippian church	151
IV. Time and place of writing	152

SECTION ONE
ADDRESS AND SALUTATION (1: 1, 2) 155

SECTION TWO
SITUATION AND LABORS OF THE APOSTLE AT ROME (1: 3-30) 157

1. Thanksgiving and prayer for the church at Philippi (1: 3-11) 157
2. Paul's condition at Rome and state of his mind (1: 12-30) 161

SECTION THREE
THE LORD'S EXAMPLE AND PATTERN FOR THE OBSERVANCE OF HIS CHURCH (2: 1-18) 176

1. Christ's example on the way through humiliation to exaltation (2: 1-11) 176
2. God strengthens believers to walk in obedience to Christ to a glorious end (2: 12-18) 185

SECTION FOUR
PAUL'S ASSISTANTS AND COLABORERS (2: 19-30) 191

1. Timothy and his speedy mission to Philippi (2: 19-24) 191
2. Information concerning Epaphroditus (2: 25-30) 194

SECTION FIVE
WARNINGS AGAINST JUDAISTIC FALSE TEACHERS AND WICKED DECEIVERS IN CONTRAST WITH THE APOSTLE (3: 1 to 4: 1) 199

CONTENTS

Page

1. The spirit of false teachers as distinguished from that of Paul (3: 1-16) 199

2. Opposite destiny of false and true believers (3: 17 to 4: 1) 211

SECTION SIX

FINAL EXHORTATION TO COOPERATION BETWEEN HIMSELF AND THE PHILIPPIAN CHURCH (4: 2-20) 218

1. Individuals exhorted to harmony (4: 2, 3) 218

2. General exhortation to joyfulness (4: 4-7) 221

3. General and final summons to Christian progress (4: 8, 9) 224

4. Thanksgiving for the gifts of love from them (4: 10-20) 228

SECTION SEVEN

SALUTATIONS AND BENEDICTION (4: 21-23) 236

INTRODUCTION TO PHILIPPIANS

I. PHILIPPI

Philippi, one of the principal cities of Macedonia, was historically famous in the annals of both Greece and Rome, while to the cause of Christ it is still more of notice as being the first place in Europe which heard the message of salvation from an apostle of Jesus Christ. It stood on the banks of the river Gangites, about ten miles from Neapolis, the seaport town, on a plain to the north of a ridge of hills which connect Mount Pangaeius with the mountainous parts of the interior of Thrace. It was founded by Philip of Macedon, father of Alexander the Great, and called after his own name. In Roman history, Philippi is best known as the scene of the victory (B.C. 42) gained by Augustus and Antony over Brutus and Cassius. It was by Augustus that the city was raised to the dignity among the independencies of the Roman Empire which it enjoyed when it was first visited by Paul.

The Roman colonies were primarily intended as military safeguards of the frontiers, and as a check upon insurgent provincials. They were part of the great system of fortification by which the empire was made safe. They served also as convenient possessions for rewarding veterans who had served in the wars, and for establishing freemen and other Italians whom it was desirable to remove to a distance. The colonists went out with all the pride of Roman citizens, to represent the city in the midst of an alien population. They proceeded to their destination like an army with banners; and the limits of the new city were distinctly marked. Their names were still enrolled in one of the Roman tribes. Every traveler who passed through a colony saw there the insignia of Rome, heard the Latin language, and was amenable, in the strictest sense, to the Roman law. Though the colonists, in addition to the poll tax, which they paid as citizens, were compelled to pay a ground tax, yet they were entirely free from any intrusion by the governor of the province. Their affairs were regulated by their own magistrates. These officers took pride in calling themselves *Praetors*. The primary settlers in the colony were, as we have seen, real Italians; but a state of things seems to have taken place, in many instances, very similar to what happened in the early history of Rome itself. A number of the native provincials grew up in the same city with the governing body; and thus two or three coordinate communities were formed, which ultimately coalesced into one, and we have no reason to suppose that Philippi was different from the rest.

Whatever the relative proportion of Greeks and Romans at Philippi may have been, the number of Jews was small. This is sufficiently accounted for when we remember it was a military, and not a mercantile, city. There was no synagogue at Philippi, but only "the place of prayer" by the riverside. Those who met there on the Sabbath consisted chiefly, if not entirely, of women.

II. ORIGIN OF THE PHILIPPIAN CHURCH

In the course of his second missionary journey, Paul sailed from Troas, accompanied by Silas, Timothy, and Luke, and on the following day reached Neapolis. (Acts 16: 11.) Thence they journeyed to Philippi, about ten miles distant. Of his experiences there we have a singularly full account. (Acts 16: 12-34.) On the following Sabbath Paul, accompanied by his fellow workers, went out to the riverside, and there spoke to the women who had come together to pray, "and a certain woman named Lydia" accepted the apostolic message, "and when she was baptized, and her household, she besought us, saying, If ye have judged me to be faithful to the Lord, come into my house, and abide there. The Lord had said to his apostles: "And into whatsoever city or village ye shall enter, search out who in it is worthy; and there abide till ye go forth." (Matt. 10: 11.) The search on this occasion was not difficult. Lydia voluntarily presented herself to Paul and his fellow workers, and said to them, earnestly and humbly, that since they regarded her "to be faithful to the Lord," her house should be their home. She admitted no refusal to her request, and their peace was on that house.

Thus far all was peaceful and hopeful in the work of preaching the gospel to Macedonia. Those who became obedient to the faith met by the riverside; men and women were converted. It was difficult to foresee the storm that was rising over such a promising outlook. A bitter persecution however was unexpectedly provoked. Paul and Silas were brought into collision with heathen superstition in one of its worst forms, and with the rough violence of colonial authorities. As if to show that the Lord's work is advanced by difficulties and discouragements, rather than by ease and prosperity. Paul who had been supernaturally summoned to labor in a new field, and was cultivating it with good success, was suddenly called away from it, silenced, and imprisoned. In tracing the life of Paul up to this time we have not seen Christianity directly brought into conflict with heathenism. The sorcerer who had obtained influence over Sergius Paulus in Cyprus was a Jew like Paul himself. (Acts 13: 6-12.) The first impulse of the idolaters of Lystra was to worship Paul and Barnabas; and it was only after the Jews had perverted their minds that they began to persecute them. (Acts 14: 8-28.) But as Paul traveled farther from the East, and especially through countries where the Israelites were thinly scattered, he found pagan creeds in immediate antagonism with the gospel; and not merely pagan creeds, but the evil powers themselves which gave paganism its supremacy over the minds of men.

In the case at Philippi we have "a certain maid having a spirit of divination"—the property of masters who kept her for the purpose of gain. This case undoubtedly of demon possession was such as frequently occurred in the gospel narratives. The impression that the ravings of a maniac makes on the mind of the ignorant is well known; and we can easily understand the notoriety which the gestures and words of this demoniac would obtain in Philippi; and it was far from a matter of indifference when she began following after Paul and those associated with him, crying out and saying: "These men are servants of the Most High God, who proclaim unto you the way of salvation. And this she did for many days." The whole city must have become familiar with her words. Paul was well aware of this; and could not bear the thought that the credit even of the gospel should be proclaimed by such unholy means. At length he could bear this Satanic interruption no longer and "being sore troubled, turned and said to the spirit, I charge thee in the name of Jesus Christ to come out of her. And it came out that very hour." Her natural powers resumed their course; and the gains of her masters were gone.

Violent rage on the part of these men was the immediate result. They proceeded therefore to take summary revenge. Laying violent hands on "Paul and Silas, and dragged them into the marketplace before the rulers"; but the complainants must have experienced some difficult in stating their grievance. The slave that had been so lucrative a possession had suddenly become valueless; but the law had no remedy for property depreciated by exorcism. The true state of the case was therefore concealed, and an accusation was laid before the magistrates in the following form: "These men, being Jews, do exceedingly trouble our city, and set forth customs which it is not lawful for us to receive, or to observe, being Romans." The accusation was false. Paul and Silas were not disturbing the colony; for nothing could have been more calm and orderly than their worship and teaching at the house of Lydia, or at the place of prayer by the riverside. The force of the accusation which was adroitly introduced, that they were Jews to begin with, will be fully understood, if we remember, not only that the Jews were generally hated and suspected, but that they had lately been driven out of Rome in consequence of an uproar (Acts 18: 2), and that it was incumbent on Philippi, as a colony, to copy the indignation of the mother city.

Thus we come to appreciate the feelings which caused the mob to rise against Paul and Silas, and tempted the magistrates to dispense with legal formalities and consign the offenders to immediate punishment. The mere loss of the maid's supposed prophetic powers, so far as it was generally known, was enough to cause a violent agitation—for mobs are always more fond of excitement than of truth and holiness. And when they learned, moreover, that these strangers were Jews, and were breaking the laws of Rome, their fury became fanatical. It seems that the magistrates had no time to hesitate if they would retain their popularity. So "the magistrates rent their garments off them, and commanded to beat them with rods." The order was promptly obeyed; for the magistrates gave the prisoners no opportunity to defend themselves, so that even the forms of justice were disregarded. The rods with which they were beaten were those habitually borne in bundles by the lictors, who always attended the Roman praetors; and in order that the beating might be effectually applied, the victims were doubtless strapped, as usual, to the whipping post. After the beating they were consigned to the prison, bleeding and faint from the rods, the jailer received strict instruction to "keep them safely." The jailer entered fully into the spirit of the mob, and carried out the orders with utmost rigor. Locking them up in the inner prison would have kept them safely; but to safekeeping he added torture by means of stocks. With their legs locked in these clamps, they could neither sit nor stand without pain, nor could they find relief by a change of position. The pain grew more intense continually.

A few hours had made a serious change from the quiet scene of the riverside to the interior of a stifling dungeon. But they had learned in whatever state they were therewith to be content. (Phil. 4: 11.) They were even able to rejoice that they were counted worthy to suffer for the name of Christ. Racked as they were with pain, sleepless and weary, they were heard about midnight praying and singing hymns unto God. Such sounds as these were new in a Roman dungeon. When suddenly, as if in direct answer to the prayer of his servants, an earthquake shook the very foundations of the prison, the doors were thrown open, the bars smitten asunder, and the bands of the prisoners loosed. The jailer was awakened in a moment by the earthquake, his first thought was of his prisoners —and in the shock of surprise seeing the doors of the prison open, and supposing that the prisoners were fled—aware that inevitable death awaited him, with the stern and desperate resignation of a Roman official, he resolved that suicide was better than disgrace, and had it not been for the loud exclamation of Paul: "Do thyself no harm: for we are all here," the rash act would have been committed. With this assurance, he dropped his sword, "called for lights and sprang in, and, trembling for fear, fell down before Paul and Silas, and brought them out and said, Sirs, what must I do to be saved? And they said, Believe on the Lord Jesus, and thou shalt be saved, thou and thy house." No time was lost in making known to them "the word of the Lord." All bodily comfort and repose was postponed to the work of saving the soul. "And they spake the word of the Lord unto him, with all that were in his house. And he took them the same hour of the night, and washed their stripes; and was baptized, he and all his, immediately." The prisoners had now become the jailer's guests. His cruelty was changed into hospitality and love. "And he brought them up into his house, and set food before them, and rejoiced greatly, with all his house, having believed in God."

At last the morning broke on the eventful night. In the course of the night the greatest of all changes had been wrought in the jailer's relation to this world and the world to come. From being a slave of a heathen magistracy he had become the servant of the living God, and the head of a Christian family. A change also had come over the minds of the magistrates themselves. Either from reflecting that they had acted more harshly than the case warranted, or from having a more accurate statement of the facts, they sent new orders in the morning to the jailer. The message conveyed by the lictors was expressed in a somewhat contemptuous form: "Let those men go." But the jailer no doubt received it with utmost joy. He felt his infinite debt of gratitude to Paul and Silas, not only for the preservation from a violent death, but for the tidings they had given him of eternal life. When, therefore, the lictors brought the order, he went with them to announce the intelligence to the prisoners, and joyfully told them to leave their dungeon "and go in peace." But Paul, calmly looking to the end of justice and the honor of the cause of Christ, refused to accept his liberty without public acknowledgment of the shameful wrong he had suffered. He now proclaims the fact that he and Silas were Roman citizens. Two Roman laws had been violated by the magistrates in the scourging inflicted on the day before. And this, too, with signal aggravation. They were *uncondemned*. They had no form of a trial, without which, in the case of the citizen, any punishment would have been illegal. And it had been done *publicly*. In the face of the colonial population, an outrage had been committed on the majesty of the name in which they boasted, and Rome had been insulted in her citizens. *"No,"* said Paul, "they have oppressed the innocent and violated the law. Do they seek to satisfy justice by conniving at a secret escape? Let them come themselves and take us out of prison. They have publicly treated us as guilty; let them publicly declare that we are innocent."

The lictors returned to the praetors, and informed them of Paul's demand, and they were alarmed. They felt that they had committed an act which, if divulged at Rome, would place them in utmost jeopardy. They had good reasons for fear even for their authority in the colony; for the people, being "Romans," might be expected to resent such violation of the law. They hastened, therefore, immediately to the prison, and became suppliants of those whom they had persecuted. They brought them at once out of the dungeon, and "asked them to go away from the city."

They complied with the request of the magistrates; but even in their departure they were not unmindful of the dignity and self-possession which ought always to be maintained by innocent men in a righteous cause. They did not retire in any hasty or precipitate flight, but "went out of the prison, and entered into the house of Lydia: and when they had seen the brethren, they comforted them, and departed." (Acts 16: 40.) It was not deemed wise to leave the infant church at Philippi with the mere remembrance of their farewell words of exhortation. Two of their number remained behind: Timothy, of whom the Philippians learned the proof that he honestly cared for their state, that he was truly likeminded with Paul, served with him in the furtherance of the gospel; and Luke, whose praise is in the gospel, remained with the church now planted in Philippi.

III. THE PHILIPPIAN CHURCH

No other church ever gave Paul more joy and satisfaction. In no other part of the empire were there Christians in whom he found such comfort in visiting, or to whom he had more delight in writing. The Philippians had evidently noble qualities before they became Christians. The Macedonians and the Roman colonists were alike fine types of manhood. They preserved the simpler manner of an earlier time. They were truthful and honest, sane and serious. They understood the sacredness of a promise. They brought their instinct of loyalty into the church. The relation was a new alliance and devotion. It did more than enlighten their understanding, it laid hold of their hearts. They were not very easily impressed, but when they were once moved and won they were absolutely faithful—they stood like a Roman phalanx. From first to last they seem never to have given Paul an anxious thought. No wonder he called them "my joy and crown." (4: 1.)

He showed his confidence in them by accepting at their hands favors which he received from no other congregation. His rule was to refuse gifts of money for himself, though he spent not a little time in raising gifts for others, especially for the poor saints in Jerusalem. He knew how likely the acceptance of gifts was to be misunderstood. He could not run the risk of appearing to be mercenary. But he made an exception in the case of the Philippians. He felt that they were too noble to think evil. For them it was blessed to give, and he would not deny them the pleasure. Once and again he gratefully received their ungrudged gifts. They made for themselves a name for liberality. (2 Cor. 8: 1-5.)

They proved how well poverty and generosity may go hand in hand. To Thessalonica and Corinth they had already come with their bounty. (Phil. 4: 16; 2 Cor. 11: 9.) But their latest offering was especially grateful to Paul, it came when his need was the sorest. He was a prisoner, he had grown old and his hands once cunning could now do nothing to support him. Epaphroditus made a journey of seven hundred miles over land and sea, exposing himself to great dangers, to bring the gift of the Philippians. In his lonely prison he was deeply moved, and ere long he poured all his feelings of gratitude into the most affectionate letter he ever wrote.

IV. TIME AND PLACE OF WRITING

This epistle was written by Paul while in "bonds" in the Praetorium (1: 7-13). He sends greetings from Caesar's household (4: 21); he expresses expectation of some crisis in his imprisonment (1: 20-26); and confident hope of visiting Philippi (1: 26; 2: 24). All these indications place it in the first imprisonment of Paul in Rome which we know to have lasted "two whole years" (Acts 28: 30), which certainly began in the year A.D. 61. Therefore its date must be somewhere towards the end of the imprisonment, in the year A.D. 63. Epaproditus had brought the contribution of the Philippians to Paul. He entered into the work there, risking his life and contracting a serious illness; but his life had been spared of Paul and his brethren. Now Paul sends him back to Philippi, though he knows he will be very lonely without him; and he sends with him this letter of acknowledgement of their gifts, filled with commendation and encouragement, gratitude and love.

COMMENTARY ON THE EPISTLE TO THE PHILIPPIANS

SECTION ONE

ADDRESS AND SALUTATION
1: 1, 2

1 Paul and Timothy, ¹servants of Christ Jesus, to all the saints in Christ

---
¹Gr. *bondservants.*

---

1 Paul and Timothy,—Paul associates Timothy with him in this epistle because he was with him at this time in Rome, had labored at Philippi, was known to the church there, and was much beloved and esteemed by Paul as a brother and fellow laborer in Christ. It was customary with Paul to associate those teachers with him, especially those known to those to whom he was writing. He did this not because they were apostles, but simply as brethren, faithful and beloved. Here he does not call himself an apostle as he does in many of his epistles. It is thought that this was because his right to be an apostle had not been called in question in the church at Philippi as at some other places. The question of circumcising the Gentiles had been settled before the gospel had been preached at Philippi. It was the partisanship aroused by this question that called in question his apostolic character and position. When not necessary to vindicate his teaching as from God, he was modest and unassuming and placed himself on an equality with the humblest servant of the Lord Jesus. He assumed no titles or dignities. He felt himself "less than the least of all saints" (Eph. 3: 8), because he had persecuted the church of God. The spirit of Christ and his religion are contrary to the assumption of titles and dignities that lift one Christian above another. Paul never did, save when the truth of God and the faith of Christians were imperiled by his not doing so.

servants of Christ Jesus,—Here he calls himself and Timothy servants, which applies equally to the poorest slave that obeyed God. [When Christ is the Master, the service, though there is no promise that it shall be easy at all times, is transfigured always into the perfect freedom of the loving and devoted heart.]

Jesus that are at Philippi, with the ªbishops and deacons: 2 Grace to you and peace from God our Father and the Lord Jesus Christ.

ªOr, *overseers*

---

to all—[The word *all*, which occurs again and again (1: 2, 7, 8, 25; 2: 17; 4: 21), springs from the deep affection of Paul for the Philippian church, whose beautiful spirit of unity, promptness in obedience, and liberality made it possible to include *all* its members without exception in his greeting.]

the saints in Christ Jesus that are at Philippi,—Sanctified, set apart from, separated to, or set apart in Christ as his servants. All such disciples are saints, entitled to the claim of trying to serve God, no matter how weak or liable to err they might be. [At the same time the word suggests holiness of character, as the ultimate goal toward which those who are separated are confidently aiming.]

with the bishops and deacons:—Why these are separately addressed does not appear, as no special instruction is given to them in the epistle. Bishops or overseers among the Gentiles corresponded to elders among the Jews. It shows that there was more than one of both classes in the church at Philippi, as in others. The deacons were the servants of the church, to look after the necessities of the poor.

2 Grace to you and peace from God our Father and the Lord Jesus Christ.—He extends the usual salutation to them in the prayer that God and Jesus Christ would bestow grace and peace upon them. [In grace kindness is always present, with the special thought of entire and marked absence of obligation in the extension of it. It is essentially unmerited and free.]

SECTION TWO

SITUATION AND LABORS OF THE APOSTLE AT ROME
1: 3-30

1. THANKSGIVING AND PRAYER FOR THE CHURCH AT PHILIPPI
1: 3-11

3 I thank my God upon all my remembrance of you, 4 always in every supplication of mine on behalf of you all making my supplication with joy, 5 for your fellowship in furtherance of the ³gospel from the first day until

---

³Gr. *good tidings:* and so elsewhere; see marginal note on Mt. 4. 23.

---

3 I thank my God upon all my remembrance of you,—Paul's treatment by the unbelievers in the city of Philippi was very bitter. He and Silas had been beaten with many stripes, their backs had been lacerated and made bloody by the stripes laid upon them, they had been harshly cast into the inner prison and their feet made fast in stocks; but out of it all a most faithful church had grown that has shown an earnest love for Paul, that followed him in his labors and sufferings with their prayers and their contributions for his help, so that every time he called them to remembrance his heart overflowed with thanksgiving to God for them. He always cultivated a cheerful and thankful heart. [As he reviews his whole relation to them from the very beginning of his work there, the total impression left upon his mind to the very time he was writing was nothing but the most hearty thanksgiving.]

4 always in every supplication of mine on behalf of you all making my supplication with joy,—Paul's remembrance of them took the direction of joyful supplication to God to bless them. [His whole remembrance of them caused gratitude, and this finds expression in every prayer. His prayer for them was the outflowing of an entirely joyful heart. Often he prayed for his brethren with deep grief and tears, but not so for this devoted church. For them he had made supplication with joy, for there was nothing in their condition to hinder emotions of gratitude and praise. This gives them a unique place among the churches of the New Testament.]

5 for your fellowship—This means more than the contribution of their means for his support. This help was the fruit of the

now; 6 being confident of this very thing, that he who began a good work in you will perfect it until the day of Jesus Christ: 7 even as it is right for me

---

fellowship. Fellowship means to share with, to participate in the same things. To fellowship Jesus is to partake of or take part in his poverty and want, to share in his sorrows, his sufferings, and self-denial in this world, as well as to partake of the joys and hopes, the consolations and blessedness of this world, and the hopes and glories of the world to come. We must suffer with him if we would reign with him. Here it certainly refers to their sympathy, common faith with Paul in the truths he had taught them, common sufferings they had endured for the truth, and the watchful interest with which they followed him and the prayers in his behalf, and the contributions sent to him. Paul desired both the prayers in his behalf and the contributions sent him. The contributions for their good (4: 16), that would abound to their account, but the prayers for his good and help. He was more desirous of the spiritual help that came through their prayers than for the material help bestowed in their gifts.

in furtherance of the gospel—From the first day of their conversion they had been moved to sympathetic cooperation towards its furtherance. For this end the Philippian church worked together, either one with another, or the whole body with Paul and others.

from the first day until now;—This fellowship had been continuous, from the first act of Christian love, when Lydia constrained Paul and his companions to come into her house and abide there, to the sending of relief to his necessities in Rome. [Constancy is the great test of personal worth. A fellow worker always ready to cooperate is beyond price.]

6 **being confident of this very thing,**—[The constancy of their fellowship and labor gave to the apostle a personal certainty that the work would be continued.]

that he who began a good work in you will perfect it—Paul gave God the credit really as well as in form for having begun the work. It was done through Paul and his fellow laborers, but God directed them to go, had been with them, had sustained and upheld them, and in every trial and trouble had been with them to deliver

[1: 6-8.] PHILIPPIANS 159

to be thus minded on behalf of you all, because ⁴I have you in my **heart,** inasmuch as, both in my bonds and in the defence and confirmation of **the** ³gospel, ye all are partakers with me of grace. 8 For **God is my witness, how I long** after you all in the tender mercies of Christ Jesus. 9 And this I

⁴Or, *ye have me in your heart*

---

them, and to turn their sufferings to the glory of God. [His admonition is: "Work out your own salvation with fear and trembling; for it is God who worketh in you both to will and to work, for his good pleasure." (2: 12, 13.) Paul with fear and trembling did the will of God, and God worked through him to will and to work the things that pleased God.]

until the day of Jesus Christ:—God had begun the work among them and Paul had confidence that he would perfect it, still through his chosen agents until the day of Jesus Christ—the coming of Christ, or until death when they would go to him.

7 even as it is right for me to be thus minded on behalf of you all,—[This confidence is accorded as their just due; not in mere charity, but in the love that springs from his experience of them. This implies strong proof of their sincerity and excellence.]

because I have you in my heart,—The ground for this was because he loved them dearly as the first fruits of his labor in Europe, now the most promising field, [and the depth of his love warrants the fullness of his confidence.]

inasmuch as, both in my bonds and in the defence and confirmation of the gospel, ye all are partakers with me of grace.— This love had been intensified by their love to him, both while he was a prisoner and while he was standing for the defense and confirmation of the gospel among strangers and amid bitter persecutions, they had shared his grace. They remembered him, prayed for him, sent to his help time and again, sent messengers to know his condition in prison, ministered to his wants (2: 25), and they themselves were bearing persecution for Christ's sake. In doing and suffering these things they were partakers of his grace.

8 For God is my witness, how I long after you all—God knew how he yearned for them and their good.

pray, that your love may abound yet more and more in knowledge and all discernment; 10 so that ye may ⁵approve the things that are excellent; that ye may be sincere and void of offence unto the day of Christ; 11 being filled

⁵Or, *distinguish the things that differ*

---

in the tender mercies of Christ Jesus.—Paul was willing to suffer for them as Jesus had suffered for them. [That divine tenderness is the element in which Paul's love lives and breathes.]

9 **And this I pray, that your love may abound yet more and more in knowledge and all discernment;**—He prays for an increase, a growth in their love, by knowing more and more of the will of God. Their growth in the knowledge of God's will, and discerning his work, increased his love to God and man, and fitted them more and more to cherish the same love for man that God cherishes. Through knowing God's will we come to more fully understand him, we more faithfully obey him, walk in closer union with him, partake more fully of the presence and blessings of his Spirit, and come to take more fully of his character.

10 **so that ye may approve the things that are excellent;**— This increase in the knowledge of God enables man to understand and approve the things that are excellent, to discern between the good and the evil. [If we distinguish between the things that differ, it is for the sake of approving what is excellent. In this process we are not merely to distinguish the good from the bad, but the best among the good. This is a true description of Christian wisdom, love growing continually richer in knowledge and spiritual discernment.]

that ye may be sincere—[Sincerity denotes truth and uprightness; and agreement of heart and tongue. Sincerity is opposed to double-mindedness; or deceit, when the sentiments of the heart are contrary to the language of the lips.]

and void of offence unto the day of Christ;—Offence is the cause of stumbling. It may mean without giving or receiving offense, that by the increase of the knowledge of God's will, one may neither find occasion or cause of stumbling himself nor be the cause of others stumbling in the Christian race. [Having nothing against which either themselves or others may strike their foot and fall.]

with the ⁶fruits of righteousness, which are through Jesus Christ, unto the glory and praise of God.

⁶Gr. *fruit.*

---

11 **being filled with the fruits of righteousness,**—Righteousness comes through the plan God has ordained to make men righteous. When a man does this God makes him righteous, clothes him with his own righteousness and the blessings that come to a man as a result of being clothed with the righteousness of God. He becomes a partaker of the divine nature, conforms his character to the character of God, and God bestows on him the privileges and blessings of a child.

which are through Jesus Christ,—These fruits are the same as the fruits of the Spirit. (Gal. 5: 22.) They all come through Jesus Christ. Without him, without the help he bestows, and out of him, these fruits could never be borne in the life of a Christian. [This conformity to what is right however is defined as that which is by Jesus Christ, and thus is that which begins in the soul at its entrance into the new life through faith. Faith works by love, and the result is right living. The fruits of righteousness grow more abundantly as the love abounds more and more in knowledge and all perception, until the Christian appears at the tribunal full of its fruits.]

unto the glory and praise of God.—That they are borne in the life of the child of God is to the glory and praise of God who provided to redeem and rescue man.

2. PAUL'S CONDITION AT ROME AND STATE OF HIS MIND
1: 12-30

12 Now I would have you know, brethren, that the things *which hap-*

---

12 **Now I would have you know, brethren,**—Paul was and had been for some time, when this letter was written, a prisoner in Rome. He had appealed from the trials and decisions at Cæsarea and Jerusalem to the emperor at Rome. For a long time, it seems, the trial before Cæsar was delayed. He was allowed to live in his own hired house, guarded by a soldier for two years. From this epistle it would seem that the trial had taken place, and he was awaiting the verdict, expecting to be released, yet uncertain.

pened unto me have fallen out rather unto the progress of the ⁸gospel; 13 so that my bonds became manifest in Christ ⁷throughout the whole prætorian guard, and to all the rest; 14 and that most of the brethren in the Lord, ⁸being confident through my bonds, are more abundantly bold to speak the

⁷Gr. *in the whole Praetorium.*
⁸Gr. *trusting in my bonds.*

[Inasmuch as they might have looked upon his imprisonment in Rome as a hindrance to the spread of the gospel, his first thought was to dispel such an anxiety. God had so wrought that what seemed a loss had proved a great gain.]

that the things which happened unto me have fallen out rather unto the progress of the gospel;—This seems to show that his recent trial had brought his condition before the people and afforded an opportunity to present the gospel to all those in the palace and in other places. It had given the gospel a publicity among all classes and in all places as could not otherwise have been gained. So he tells the Philippians who watched his course with such an affectionate interest that these things which had occurred in connection with his trial had turned out to the advancement of the gospel.

13 **so that my bonds became manifest in Christ throughout the whole praetorian guard,**—[By his trial in Rome it became manifest throughout the whole Praetorian guard that his imprisonment was no political matter, neither was it on account of any crime he had committeed; but was wholly due to his union of life and action with Christ.] The household of Cæsar was composed of his attendants, courtiers, officers, and guards. Some of Cæsar's household, probably his servants and humbler class of his retainers, became obedient to the faith. It is probable that the employees in the lower orders connected with the household would pass unnoticed in such things as readily as in any other position in the empire.

and to all the rest;—[To all the Roman public, as distinguished from this special class. This phrase points to an extended development of Paul's personal influence.]

14 **and that most of the brethren in the Lord, being confident through my bonds, are more abundantly bold to speak the word of God without fear.**—Courage as well as fear is contagious. Seeing Paul preach Christ and him crucified openly

word of God without fear. 15 Some indeed preach Christ even of envy and

before the highest officers and dignitaries of the empire inspired others to do likewise. Paul's defenses of himself consisted in preaching Christ to the rulers and judges, as may be seen from his defense before Festus and Agrippa. His defense made a good impression on the public and "most of the brethren" were encouraged "to speak the word of God without fear," and his inspiring example, his hopefulness, and cheerfulness, even in bonds, encouraged these brethren to lay hold with firmer faith upon the promises of God. [On his coming to Rome, Paul had thanked God and taken courage at the sight of them. (Acts 28: 15.) Now they thank God and take courage at the sight of him and his patient confidence.]

15 **Some indeed preach Christ even of envy and strife;**— Under these circumstances it is difficult to see how any one could be led to preach Christ of envy and strife to add opposition to Paul. While his preaching made a favorable impression, it was not sufficiently popular to lead those not faithful to the Lord to engage in it. It is strange that true believers would do it out of envy. [Were they persons without the love of the gospel, and without personal convictions of its truth? This is impossible. Paul would have regarded such as enemies of the Lord; and such would more likely oppose Christ as well as Paul. Were they then Judaizers? Most assuredly not the mere legalists, such as Paul exposed in the epistle to the Galatians. He certainly could not have rejoiced in the gospel and the Christ they preached. (3: 2; Gal. 6: 7; 5: 3, 10-12; 2 Cor. 11: 4.) It seems more probable, therefore, that they were those who opposed Paul on various grounds and questioned his authority. It is very likely also that the Christians at Rome were without a strong leadership before Paul's coming, and that some of their leaders, jealous of his influence, became personal enemies.] The preaching of these factious adversaries is so insincere that the very contrast between their state of mind and their action carried their condemnation with it. They thought to take advantage of the fact of his bonds, and of whatever these occasioned in the unlimited freedom of his preaching to promote the interest and increase of their own party to make his bonds

strife; and some also of good will: 16 ⁹the one *do it* of love, knowing that I am set for the defence of the ⁸gospel; 17 ¹⁰but the other proclaim Christ of faction, not sincerely, thinking to raise up affliction for me in my bonds. 18

---

⁹Or, *they that are moved by love* do it, *knowing &c.*
¹⁰Or, *but they that are factious proclaim Christ, not &c.*

---

more grievous. Paul says nothing here that many faithful gospel preachers may have not experienced.

and some also of good will:—[These are the same as those mentioned in the preceding verse, but introduced here again under a different point of view, and in contrast with those just described. These preach from good will. Their motive was a personal one also, but how noble and pure. Good will toward Paul who was the appointed proclaimer of the gospel, whose work they regarded as holy, which it was their duty and privilege to help forward, especially now that by his imprisonment he himself was hindered to a great extent from carrying out his mission.]

16 **the one do it of love,**—The preaching prompted by "good will" springs out of love.

knowing that I am set for the defence of the gospel;—[This is the ground of this special manifestation of Christian love, which inspired sympathy with him in his great work, and moved them to preach the gospel committed to his charge.]

17 **but the other proclaim Christ of faction,**—[This is an explanation of the envy and strife. Faction properly implies self-seeking, hence it came to be employed not only of the method of gaining followers, but also of the act. It is the ambition of rival leaders who create parties for egotistic purposes and the serve their own ends, and it is, therefore, of the leaders of the party that was hostile to Paul rather than the followers who are condemned here. From the earliest times the churches were troubled by those who sought adherents only that they might glory in their ability as leaders. Paul found much trouble from the Judaizers among the Galatian churches (Gal. 1: 6-10), and it was the same spirit that was at work in Rome.]

not sincerely,—Their motive was not a pure one, though they might call themselves ministers of Christ.

thinking to raise up affliction for me in my bonds.—[They could do this by preventing the access of inquirers to him, unable

What then? only that in every way, whether in pretence or in truth, Christ is proclaimed; and therein I rejoice, yea, and will rejoice. 19 For I know

as he was to go to them. Loyal fellow workers would have made it a point to bring their hearers under the personal influence of Paul, and also into a personal connection of order with him. Every instance in which the opposite was done was fitted to try severely the spirit of Paul, to afflict him in and through his position of restraint.]

18 **What then?**—What was he to say concerning their preaching, what judgment was he to pass on their motives and conduct?

only that in every way, whether in pretence or in truth, Christ is proclaimed;—The thing that mattered was not his personal feeling or comfort, nor whether Christ was being proclaimed exactly in accordance with his sense of fitness, or the motive which prompted it, he was willing to suffer all things that Christ might be proclaimed.

and therein I rejoice, yea, and will rejoice.—Paul's own sufferings, strifes, imprisonment, and death itself, never for a moment weighed in the matter of preaching the gospel to the world. [These words are a noble testimony of Paul's breadth of mind and toleration, and a notable instance of his power to forget himself when the cause of Christ was at stake. His opponents' method of preaching did not commend itself to him; and their attitude towards him was mean, ungenerous, and painful, yet it was Christ that was being proclaimed, and he, therefore, rejoiced.]

Paul rejoiced because the people heard the gospel, and could thereby be saved from their sins, notwithstanding it was proclaimed to them by envious partisans. But had these converts themselves become envious partisans keeping up strife and division, they would have forfeited their claims to be Christians. They should, therefore, be taught that sects and parties are sinful, and if they imbibe their spirit, and work to build them up, they sin against God. In this teaching we are at a disadvantage with Paul. He was inspired, God was with him, the Spirit taught him. The disciples knew his infallibility, and a word from him carried at once the authority of God. We cannot speak with the personal authority that Paul did. Our judgment will be called in question.

that this shall turn out to my salvation, through your supplication and the

Our appeal must be to the scriptures. It takes time and patience and forbearance and perseverance in that they, not we, are partisans. So we must deal with them in love and with patience and in much prayer, that we may deliver them from their evil ways. When a man believes in Jesus Christ with all the heart, and is led by faith to repent of his sins, be baptized into Christ, that man is a Christian, no matter where he did it. If he goes into parties and sects, he sins just as though he fell into other sins, such as drunkenness and revelry. He is a sinning Christian—an erring brother. Christians should seek to deliver him from his wrong in a spirit of meekness and love, knowing that we are liable to be led into sin.

19 **For I know that this shall turn out to my salvation,**—The salvation referred to must be his deliverance from bondage. This refers back to his imprisonment and defense before the rulers and the good results following.

through your supplication—This, in connection with the prayers of the Christians, together with the guidance of the Spirit, he felt sure would bring about his being set free from imprisonment. He relied much on the efficacy of prayer in his behalf. It is in securing this harmonious working of the elements of grace and nature for good that prayer comes in to effectually aid and bless the work. He writes to the brethren concerning his deliverance: "Who delivered us out of so great a death, and will deliver: on whom we have set our hope that he will also still deliver us; ye also helping together on our behalf by your supplication." (2 Cor. 1: 10, 11.) This shows that the prayers of God's children enter into the working of God's laws and bring good to the persons for whom they are offered. God's providences are the results of the working of God's laws. The spiritual and natural laws work in harmony for the good of those who love and honor God—for the destruction and ruin of those who refuse to honor him. To honor God is to obey his laws; to dishonor him is to refuse that obedience. In the spiritual world as in the material, man has it in his power to thwart and hinder the workings of God's laws, because God has made man with freedom to obey or disobey him. The law of harmony runs through all of God's dealings with man. When Christ

1: 19, 20.]   PHILIPPIANS   167

supply of the Spirit of Jesus Christ, 20 according to my earnest expectation and hope, that in nothing shall I be put to shame, but *that* with all boldness,

---

said, "According to your faith be it done unto you" (Matt. 9: 29), he recognized this law. Hence if a man's faith is strong, he confidently and faithfully complies with the law of God, and the blessings will be abundant. If his faith is weak, his compliance will be imperfect and careless, and the blessings will be few.

and the supply of the Spirit of Jesus Christ,—The spirit of Christ is one that excludes all turning from or neglect of the commands of God, or substitution of other service for that ordained by God, and insists on rigid obedience to the divine will as the only means of union with God. The law of the Spirit requires obedience to the will of God that springs from the heart. It insists upon an obedience to the whole law of God from a heartfelt trust in God. The more trusting the heart is, the more faithful and rigid will be the adherence to the will of God.

20 **according to my earnest expectation and hope,**—[Paul has two things in mind—the preaching of the gospel and his own salvation. In reference to the former, he is earnestly expectant that he shall never be put to shame by the opposition of his adversaries. This feeling enabled him to rejoice in the midst of all their envy and strife. His hope looks on to his own salvation. But he enjoys both these. He awaits the future both of his work on earth and of his call to heaven without fear. Whatever the crisis might be, he looked eagerly for it.]

that in nothing shall I be put to shame,—[He used the phrase elsewhere with special reference to the shame which comes from hopes disappointed and professions unfulfilled. (2 Cor. 7: 14; 9: 14; 10: 8; Rom. 9: 33; 1 Pet. 2: 6.) He says: "Hope putteth not to shame." (Rom. 5: 5.) So probably here; he trusts that in the hour of trial the confidence which he had felt and of which he said: "I can do all things in him that strengtheneth me" (4: 13), may not come to shameful failure, but magnify Christ in all boldness of speech.]

but that with all boldness,—[The peculiar boldness was the freedom of speech. It was a favorite word for the free preaching of the apostles (Acts 4: 13, 29; 14: 3; 18: 26), such boldness

as always, *so* now also Christ shall be magnified in my body, whether by life, or by death. 21 For to me to live is Christ, and to die is gain. 22 ¹But if to

---
¹Or, *But if to live in the flesh* be my lot, *this is the fruit of my work: and what I shall choose I know not*

---

could only be the quality of one whose work had not been frustrated, but to whom the Lord had constantly witnessed to Paul.]

as always, so now also Christ shall be magnified—Here Paul changes the form of his speech, and puts forward that for which he constantly labored—that Christ may be magnified.

in my body,—The body is the spirit's vehicle and implement in action on others. The impression made upon others, "whether by life, or by death," would have to be effected bodily by doing or suffering. [The phrase is no doubt suggested by the idea of death—the death of a martyr in bodily torture or shame. The same idea is suggested in the following: "Always bearing about in the body the dying of Jesus, that the life also of Jesus may be manifested in our body." (2 Cor. 4: 10.) But while the word "flesh" is sometimes used in the New Testament in a bad sense, the body is always regarded as that in which we may "glorify God" (1 Cor. 6: 20) in word and deed. In the passage before us, the whole idea is of Christ in him; hence the body is spoken of simply as the tabernacle of the dwelling presence of Christ and devoted only to *magnify* him.]

whether by life, or by death.—He was ready to live or die as would best magnify and honor Jesus Christ. He had drunk into the spirit of Christ so deeply that he was ready to die to honor him and save his fellow men. [We gather from this, and from 2: 23, that the epistle was written at a time of special suspense and uncertainty, regarding what might be the decision of the court in his case.]

21 **For to me to live is Christ,**—To exalt and glorify Christ was his only incentive in life. [Christ lived in Paul, animated and permeated his entire activity, so that all his words and acts were really said and done by Christ and were therefore an outflow of Christ living in him. Consequently, the personality of Christ was the center and circumference of his entire life. So, in his body the character and greatness of Christ ever appeared. And the varying events of his life, pleasant and unpleasant, showed the greatness of Christ.]

live in the flesh,—*if* ²this shall bring fruit from my work, then ³what I shall choose I know not. 23 But I am in a strait betwixt the two, having the

²Gr. *this is for me fruit of work.*
³Or, *what shall I choose?*

---

and to die is gain.—[Death is a new stage of union with Christ, so he said: "Being therefore always of good courage, and knowing that, whilst we are at home in the body, we are absent from the Lord (for we walk by faith, not by sight); we are of good courage, I say, and are willing rather to be absent from the body, and to be home at with the Lord." (2 Cor. 5: 6-8.) It was not impatience with life that glorified death in his eyes, but his unwavering faith in Christ that caused him to look on death as but the door to a new and more glorious life. Then his union with Christ would be completely realized.]

22 But—[This checked the flow of raptured thought of being with Christ to suggest a consideration that made him hesitate in his choice between life and death.]

if to live in the flesh,—This does not put forward an hypothetical case but a real one. If he continued to live in the flesh, his effort would be to magnify Christ.

—if this shall bring fruit from my work,—Fruit that comes from work bringing souls into the kingdom of the Lord, bringing life to them.

then—If all this was true, if life, and life only, subserved his work, then came the difficulty of choice.

what I shall choose I know not.—Since the earthly life and that alone is the sphere of work, with its fruitage of converted souls, he was so uncertain what to choose that he refrained from any decision.

23 But I am in a strait—This expresses forcibly the intensity of the struggle in his mind.

betwixt the two,—This refers to the alternative between life and death. He was so hedged by the two alternatives that he did not know which way to move. Most of us would have no trouble in making a choice between them; but not so with Paul; and if he were to choose for his own pleasure, it would be to leave this world.

desire to depart and be with Christ; for it is very far better: 24 yet to abide in the flesh is more needful for your sake. 25 And having this confidence, I know that I shall abide, yea, and abide with you all, for your progress and

having the desire to depart and be with Christ;—He had already expressed the desire by saying, "to die is gain." He had grown old; the fleshly ties and hopes had been swallowed up in the higher spiritual life, and the desire of his soul was to depart and be with Christ. He expected to be with him in some very important sense when he departed this life. I do not know of anyone that knows better about this than he.

for it is very far better:—He cannot forget the gain, though his love for the salvation of men may reconcile him to forego it. So, in this further allusion to life with Christ, he intensifies his language by the double comparative—*very far better*.

24 yet to abide in the flesh is more needful for your sake.—He was a helper and instructor of the Philippians and other Christians. The reverence and respect with which they regarded him enabled him to hold them back from many evils. He foresaw that on his death many evils and grievous departures from the faith would follow. (Acts 20: 18-35.) To the Thessalonians he said: "The mystery of lawlessness doth already work: only there is one that restraineth now, until he be taken out of the way. And then shall be revealed the lawless one." (2 Thess. 2: 7, 8.) He who restrained the development of the man of sin was Paul. He would hinder until he was taken out of the way, then would he be developed and revealed. [In this he approaches the reason which confirms him as to what his lot will be. He sees that there is much which lies before him, which God is showing him that he would have him do, and the sense that the churches will be the better for his life, and need of his continued care, brings with it the certainty that God will not call him home.]

25 And having this confidence, I know that I shall abide, yea, and abide with you all,—This knowledge was based on his confidence that, if it was best for him to remain, God would so overrule that the decision of the court would be for his acquittal. [No doubt his mind passed to the whole care of the churches, which came upon him daily, and he sees not without some consolation

1: 25-27.] PHILIPPIANS 171

joy [4]in the faith; 26 that your glorying may abound in Christ Jesus in me through my presence with you again. 27 Only [5]let your manner of life be worthy of the [6]gospel of Christ: that, whether I come and see you or be

[4]Or, *of faith*
[5]Gr. *behave as citizens worthily.* Comp. ch. 3. 20.
[6]Gr. *good tidings.* See marginal note on ch. 1. 5.

---

the further prospect of spending and being spent for Christ's service.]

for your progress and joy in the faith;—He would teach and instruct them, and as they improved in righteousness, the joy and blessedness that came to them through their faith would be increased. [He employs the same word here to denote the advance of the Philippians in the faith as he used to describe the effect of his imprisonment and trial upon the Roman Christians. (1: 12.) His presence at Philippi would have an influence similar to that which it had in Rome and would become an influence to greater activity. This would, in itself, fill their hearts with joy, joy proceeding out of loyal and ever-increasing dependence upon Christ, which is the true prerogative of the mature Christian.]

26 that your glorying may abound—Should he be released, he looked forward to another visit to them. [The idea is that they may obtain a larger and richer increase of that which is their true glory, the possession of the gospel and of the privileges of the Christian life.]

in Christ Jesus in me through my presence with you again. —The immediate occasion of the glorying would be Paul. The ground of glorying would attach especially to him as the representative of the cause which was the great matter of glorying. The ground of glorying was first and comprehensively in Christ; then in Paul as representing Christ; then in Paul's personal presence with them, with his teaching and example and prayers would be the means for attaining the grace of Christ, and so he was able to add, "in me." The rejoicing would be of what the Lord had done, and the help thereto would be Paul's continuance in the flesh.

27 Only—Whatever happens they were to deport themselves as faithful citizens of the kingdom of heaven.

let your manner of life be worthy of the gospel of Christ:— The gospel was to elevate the manner of life into the likeness of

absent, I may hear of your state, that ye stand fast in one spirit, with one

---

that which Jesus lived. He died as a man, that men might live like God; he lived in the flesh, that they might walk in the Spirit. [The Christian must remember that he does not live for himself alone, that he is under "the law of the Spirit of life in Christ Jesus" (Rom. 8: 2), enjoys great privileges, which in turn, lay upon him great responsibilities. One so minded will know that in his actions the interests of others are involved as well as his own, and will make it his aim to live worthy of the gospel.]

that, whether I come and see you or be absent,—[Whether he lives or dies, whether he comes to them again or sees them in the flesh no more, whatever happens to him or them, they were to deport themselves in a worthy manner.]

I may hear of your state,—[He had a deep interest in the life of the whole congregation. All their surroundings as well as their doings and condition were of deep interest to him, for they were his children in the faith.]

that ye stand fast—[He was fully aware of the fact that they were in the midst of many adversities, and that they had to fight for the faith, and he urges them to stand their ground against all foes.]

in one spirit,—The spirit is the highest part of our immaterial nature, which, when enlightened by the Holp Spirit through the word of truth, can arise into communion with God and discern the truth of the spiritual life.

with one soul—[The soul is that element of man's material nature which is nearest his body and directly influenced by it, and through the body by the outer world; and is thus distinguished from the spirit, which is that in man nearest to God and directly influenced by the Spirit of God. The soul, therefore, is the emotional side of man, that which is roused by its surroundings.]

striving for the faith of the gospel;—[Christians are comrades in one struggle, each helping others. All are exhorted to act together, as though the many were impelled by the soul of one man, this harmony being a condition of steadfastness of which he hopes to hear. On this subject of unity too much stress cannot be laid. Unity conditions efficiency and growth and comfort. It is so

soul striving ⁷for the faith of the ⁶gospel; 28 and in nothing affrighted by the adversaries: which is for them an evident token of perdition, but of your

⁷Gr. *with*.

---

in the home and institutions of learning; but pre-eminently so in a body of believers in Jesus Christ. A badly divided, discordant, wrangling church is about the most offensive, as well as the most inefficient thing the eye can look upon. A church in which the sentiment of unity has been displaced by the bitterness of mutual ill will has reached the day when its prosperity is at an end—at an end at any rate until its membership changes its front and comes into a better mood. How much harm has been done to individuals, how the advance of the Lord's kingdom has been hindered, by the unseemly spectacle of disciples of the Lord arrayed in bitterness against each other. Resentments, whims, whisperings, grudges, alienations are all out of place in a company of true believers in the Lord Jesus Christ. They can make no headway in commending the gospel to others, or in magnifying it as the saving power of God, if they themselves were split into factions, and were biting and devouring each other instead of exemplifying a temper of love and unity. Unity would assure them power; they could move forward to conquest.]

28 and in nothing affrighted—The Philippian church was then suffering of their enemies. [The original of this word "affrighted" has in it the suggestions of the action of a horse in a race, which becomes scared and springs aside and runs off wildly. It is getting alarmed and disheartened in the face of some opposing demonstration, or under some fierce assault. It is the timidity and misgiving which says at the outset of the struggle: "It is no use; the enemy is too strong or too cunning; and the surrender might just as well be made now as later on."]

by the adversaries:—[Who were their adversaries? In verse thirty he speaks of them as having the same conflict as he had when at Philippi and then had at Rome. In both instances, most probably, his opponents were heathen. Further, when warning his readers against Jewish malice, what he usually feared was not that they would be frightened into compliance, but that they would be seduced from the right way of the Lord. The pagans at Philippi would struggle hard against a faith which condemned idol

salvation, and that from God; 29 because to you it hath been granted in the behalf of Christ, not only to believe on him, but also to suffer in his behalf: 30 having the same conflict which ye saw in me, and now hear to be in me.

---

worship, for the extant remains at Philippi and in its neighborhood show that they were a very devout heathen community.]

which is for them an evident token of perdition,—The undaunted bearing of the Philippian Christians in the face of opposition and persecution was a token of destruction to their adversaries. It showed that their persecutors were powerless to thwart God's work; that their resistance was working their own spiritual ruin; they they were fighting against God, which could mean only their destruction.

but of your salvation, and that from God;—Their fidelity in maintaining their faith was a token and sign of their deliverance, and that deliverance would come from God. [These words apply to the word "token," and so derivatively both to "perdition" and "salvation." The sign is of God, but it may be read by both sides. Like the pillar of God's presence, it was "the cloud and the darkness" to the one, but "light by night" to the other. (Ex. 14: 20.)]

29 because to you it hath been granted in the behalf of Christ, not only to believe on him, but also to suffer in his behalf:—Paul presents it as a privilege that God granted them not only to believe in Christ, but to suffer with and for him. To Timothy he said: "If we endure, we shall also reign with him." (2 Tim. 2: 12.) After the apostles had been condemned by the council and beaten, it is said: "They therefore departed from the presence of the council, rejoicing that they were counted worthy to suffer dishonor for the Name." (Acts 5: 41.) And Peter says: "But even if ye should suffer for righteousness' sake, blessed are ye: and fear not their fear, neither be troubled." (1 Pet. 3: 14.) Christians ought to esteem it an honor that they are permitted to suffer for the name of Christ.

30 having the same conflict which ye saw in me,—What they had seen of his sufferings must have been when he and Silas were beaten, imprisoned, and their feet made fast in stocks at Philippi. (Acts 16: 22-24.) How deeply this outrage impressed itself on his mind, we see both by his conduct toward the magistrates, and also by his allusion to it: "But having suffered before and been shamefully treated, as ye know, at Philippi, we waxed bold in our God to speak unto you the gospel of God in much conflict." (1 Thess. 2: 2.) Here he uses the remembrance to suggest to the Philippians that their struggle was only the same which he had borne, and borne successfully. The conflict, though called the same, need not be taken to imply that they were exposed to the danger of arrest, imprisonment, and scourging, but that they had to endure sufferings and that their cause was the same. They were soldiers under the same Master, and each had a share in the conflict. The word implies a struggle for a prize and is here used to denote the Christian's position in the world. He is fighting for the mastery, and there are many adversaries.

and now hear to be in me.—They had been informed of his imprisonment, and for that reason had sent Epaphroditus to Rome with their gifts, and they would hear still more from Epaphroditus when he returned to them and delivered the apostle's epistle.

SECTION THREE

THE LORD'S EXAMPLE AND PATTERN FOR THE OBSERVANCE OF HIS CHURCH
2: 1-18

1. CHRIST'S EXAMPLE ON THE WAY THROUGH HUMILIATION TO EXALTATION
2: 1-11

1 If there is therefore any exhortation in Christ, if any [8]consolation of

---
[8]Or, *persuasion*

Paul, having shown them that they should account it a gracious favor of God to be permitted to suffer for the sake of Jesus, proceeds in this section to urge upon them unity among themselves and harmony with the Spirit of Christ.

1 **If there is**—[This implies no doubt of the existence of the following motives, but is simply a tender form of appeal to what is well known to exist.]

therefore—[This is generally connected with: "Only let your manner of life be worthy of the gospel of Christ" (1: 27), so that the notes of steadfastness and unity there are here expanded and based more definitely upon humility and abnegation of self.]

any exhortation in Christ,—[Paul opens this weighty section with an impassioned appeal to the deepest Christian experiences of his readers, and it was calculated to prompt to action and endurance.]

if any consolation of love,—Comfort springs from love and its source. The followers of Christ by giving proofs of their ardent love to each other in cases of distress alleviated the sufferings of the persecuted. Of this the apostle says: "Blessed be the God and Father of our Lord Jesus Christ, the Father of mercies and God of all comfort; who comforteth us in all our affliction, that we may be able to comfort them that are in any affliction, through the comfort wherewith we ourselves are comforted of God. For as the sufferings of Christ abound unto us, even so our comfort also aboundeth through Christ. But whether we are afflicted, it is for your comfort and salvation; or whether we are comforted, it is for your comfort, which worketh in the patient enduring of the same

love, if any fellowship of the Spirit, if any tender mercies and compassions, 2 make full my joy, that ye be of the same mind, having the same love, being

---

sufferings which we also suffer: and our hope for you is stedfast; knowing that, as ye are partakers of the sufferings, so also are ye of the comfort." (2 Cor. 1: 3-7.)

if any fellowship of the Spirit,—People are said to be in fellowship when they are so united that what belongs to one belongs to the other, or what is true of the one is true of the other. Incongruous elements cannot be united. The human heart is said to be full of the Spirit when its inward state, its affections, and its acts are directed and controlled by him so as to be a constant manifestation of his presence. Christians are partakers in common of the same mind as God, Christ, and the Holy Spirit and of the blessings arising therefrom. If they have any partnership in the life and blessings, then they are ready to listen to Paul's plea for unity, for he "spake from God, being moved by the Holy Spirit." (2 Pet. 1: 21.) [The Holy Spirit is the unifying personality in the church. (1 Cor. 12: 4-11.) He alone can bring order out of chaos and preserve harmony in the body of Christ. Unless the Holy Spirit rules, there is excitement and confusion.]

if any tender mercies and compassions,—This is an appeal to their knowledge that God had tender sympathy for them and abounds in service toward them, and that the same tender spirit of affection and mercy for one another should be excited in them. ["Mercies and compassions" serve to emphasize the thought. The appeal is to their hearts. He sought their sympathy in his condition and in his aims. Very naturally he felt that he had a right to their sympathy. To withhold it under the circumstances would have been unkind and cruel. If they had such feelings as are wont to spring up in the soul through the love of Christ, then they would move forward in the way pointed out.]

2 make full my joy, that ye be of the same mind,—It was Paul's highest joy to see them like-minded with Jesus and the Holy Spirit. He beseeches them by the consideration given in verse 1, that as persecuted Christians they should make his joy complete by being moved by the same love, being in perfect agreement one with another. He had suffered so much for them, and

of one accord, ⁹of one mind; 3 *doing* nothing through faction or through

---
⁹Some ancient authorities read *of the same mind.*

---

they had shown such unremitting regard for him by following with their prayers and contributions that he felt impelled to make this appeal unto them.

having the same love,—It is a unity resting on the love of Christ which engenders the love of Christ.

being of one accord, of one mind;—In every letter that Paul wrote to the churches, he pled with them for the unity of the faith, oneness of mind and purpose, perfect accord in the work they should do. For division and strife are themselves sinful, and bring ruin and destruction as their fruits. To the Corinthians he said: "Now I beseech you,. brethren, through the name of our Lord Jesus Christ, that ye all speak the same thing, and that there be no divisions among you; but that ye be perfected together in the same mind and in the same judgment." (1 Cor. 1: 10.) Such was the plea for harmony and unity among the children of God at all places. It is just as essential today that unity be preserved as it was then. Christians do not often divide over what God, Jesus Christ, and the Holy Spirit have said. Divisions come almost always in reference to things not taught in the word of God. Theories, practices, and methods unknown to his word are introduced, and over these men divide and strive. The way to prevent this is given by Paul: "If ye died with Christ from the rudiments of the world, why, as though living in the world, do ye subject yourselves to ordinances, Handle not, nor taste, nor touch (all which things are to perish with the using), after the precepts and doctrines of men?" (Col. 2: 20-22.) The divisions into parties among Christians have arisen chiefly over questions not taught in the scriptures, over the doctrines and commandments of men, introduced into the church. Paul says these are all to perish with the using, or as some translate, "for the destruction of those using them," and asks, "why be subject to them, why use them, when they bring evil and no good?" The principle everywhere taught is, union among the people of God and with God is to be maintained by walking in the ordinances and appointments of God, rejecting all inventions of men. "Thou shalt add nothing to, dimin-

vainglory, but in lowliness of mind each counting other better than himself;

---

ish nothing from the appointments of God" has been the watchword of acceptable service to him from the beginning. Paul in saying, "if any fellowship," did not imply a doubt as to its existence, but it expresses a strong assurance that it did exist, to which the Philippians' own experience would attest. It was an appeal to their knowledge.

3 doing nothing through faction—[A factious man is one who seeks by unscrupulous and subversive methods to gain his own ends. He is active in promoting factions and dissensions. There is no greater foe to unity than this spirit. It causes men to take sides on any question and mars their oneness of aim. The moment a man falls into a factious temper and thinks so much of promoting his own selfish ends, and makes it his chief business to object and find fault, he becomes an element of discord to every one with whom he may be identified. If there is to be any real unity of mind and heart, the factious spirit must be crucified.]

or through vainglory,—This is the desire to triumph one over another. Men sometimes become excited one against another, so that one opposes a thing because the other favors it. They form parties, and act from party feeling. Such a state of mind is condemned here, and in every letter written by the Spirit of God to the churches.

but in lowliness of mind each counting other better than himself;—So far from pursuing this course, let each cultivate a meek and lowly mind as to himself and learn to esteem the virtues and good qualities of others. [The Greek word here translated *lowliness of mind* is also translated *humility* (Col. 3: 12), and *lowliness* (Eph. 4: 2). In the two cases, just mentioned, where the word occurs it comes before meekness and long-suffering, showing that it is only by a wise and lowly estimate of ourselves that we come to know what is due to others. Humility, then, describes the spirit of one who has come to the knowledge of himself in relation to God, and it is, therefore, primarily a Christian grace and not a social virtue. There is no trace in it of the weakness associated with the term in pagan literature. On the contrary, it is the badge of the strong, the first test of a truly great

4 not looking each of you to his own things, but each of you also to the things of others. 5 Have this mind in you, which was also in Christ Jesus:

---

man. For it was the one specific virtue and quality which above all others explains the work and character of Christ, our Savior, who "humbled himself, becoming obedient even unto death." It was the special creation of Christ himself; it was he who brought the new spirit into the world and illustrated it in his own person because he was "meek and lowly in heart." (Matt. 11:29.)]

4 **not looking each of you to his own things, but each of you also to the things of others.**—This means more than to look to the material good of others as well as yourselves. Look to their conditions, surroundings, and the influences brought to bear upon them, and endeavor to see things as they see them, and it will enable you to sympathize more with them in their trials and troubles, and you will come to esteem them the more highly. This is what Paul meant by saying: "I am become all things to all men, that I may by all means save some." (1 Cor. 9:22.) Seek to promote the well-being of others in all things. In doing this one gains his own truest good.

5 **Have this mind in you, which was also in Christ Jesus:**— The exhortation to them is to cherish the spirit of Christian fellowship among themselves which corresponds to the fellowship they enjoyed in Christ Jesus. [It was not an appeal to Christ as the outstanding example of humility that was in question here, although that is implied all through the passage that follows. It is not the Jesus that walked on earth but the Christ incarnate and exalted that is in Paul's mind, and the unity that he pressed upon the Philippian church was to be achieved by the growth of that spirit of fellowship which it had already experienced in its relation to Christ himself. The foundation truth of the exhortation is that Christians must become like Christ in character; apply the same rule to themselves that they see and approve in Jesus. It is not always that Christians put Christ into their business and social relations, or feel the same call for consecration that they love to note in him. The keenest zeal may be displayed in religious work, accompanied by singular laxity in common concerns of daily business and social intercourse. Some people are piously humble on the

6 who, existing in the form of God, counted not the being on an equality with God a thing to be grasped, 7 but emptied himself, taking the form of a

---

Lord's day, but follow the ways of the world during the week.]

6 who, existing—This relates to the existence of Christ before his manifestation in the flesh as he appeared to those in heaven who saw him. [The word *existing* calls attention to the essential being of Christ, corresponding to the idea embodied in the name of Jehovah, and thus implying what is more fully expressed in the following words: "In the beginning was the Word, and the Word was with God." (John 1: 1.)]

in the form of God,—Christ was "the effulgence of his glory, and the very image of his substance." (Heb. 1: 3.) [The word *form* is to be carefully distinguished from *fashion* (which denotes the mere outward appearance which we frequently designate as form); in this there is no notion of a body or form for God, but simply the character of God in his real essence. Christ is described as "the image of the invisible God, the firstborn of all creation." (Col. 1: 15.) John (1: 1) applies *Word* as the expression of God. Christ had the essential attributes of God's nature, actual deity.]

counted not the being on an equality with God—This refers only to relations which describe our Lord's essential and therefore eternal being in the true nature of God. Jesus could not give up his essential character of Sonship. He was the Son of God in the preincarnate state. He was the Son of God after he became the Son of man. Of him it is said: "And the Word became flesh, and dwelt among us (and we beheld his glory, glory as of the only begotten from the Father), full of grace and truth." (John 1: 14.)

a thing to be grasped,—[He did not consider this state of equality with God, his glory at the right hand of his Father, a thing to be held on to at any cost when, by giving up the glory and holding on to the nature of God, he could enter upon his redemptive work for mankind.]

7 but emptied himself,—He emptied himself of all glories, laid aside the honors of his Father's throne, took upon himself the form of man—the nature of the seed of Abraham, took part of flesh

¹⁰servant, ¹¹being made in the likeness of men; 8 and being found in fashion as a man, he humbled himself, becoming obedient *even* unto death, yea, the

---
¹⁰Gr. *bondservant*.
¹¹Gr. *becoming in*.

---

and blood, lived among the lowliest of men, and served in the humble walks of life.

taking the form of a servant,—He was not only made in the likeness of men, but partook of their nature, bore their infirmities, took on himself the form and filled the office of a servant. He was servant of all.

being made in the likeness of men;—He was made in the likeness of men in general, men as they actually are. [Hence the key to the meaning is to be found in the following passages: "For what the law could not do, in that it was weak through the flesh, God, sending his own Son in the likeness of sinful flesh and for sin, condemned sin in the flesh" (Rom. 8: 3); "Wherefore it behooved him in all things to be made like unto his brethren, that he might become a merciful and faithful high priest in things pertaining to God, to make propitiation for the sins of the people" (Heb. 2: 17), and "For we have not a high priest that cannot be touched with the feeling of our infirmities; but one that hath been in all points tempted like as we are, yet without sin" (Heb. 4: 15). It would have been an infinite humiliation to have assumed humanity, even in unique and visible glory; but Christ went beyond this, by deigning to seem like other men in all things, one only of the multitude, and that too in the station which confused him with the commoner type of mankind. The truth of his humanity is expressed in the phrase "form of a servant"; its unique and ideal character is glanced at when it is said, "in fashion as a man."]

8 and being found in fashion as a man,—He still further humbled himself and became subject to death, even the most shameful of all deaths, the death of the cross. [*Fashion* here refers to the outward appearance of Christ, the appeal that he made to the senses, to human observation—his outward appearance was altogether human.]

he humbled himself,—[This expresses plainly and simply the fact of the humiliation of Christ. In outward fashion he be-

death of the cross. 9 Wherefore also God highly exalted him, and gave unto

came as one of us, though he ceased not to be on an equality with God. His whole humiliation from the incarnation to the cross was his own voluntary act: "I lay down my life, that I may take it again. No one taketh it away from me, but I lay it down of myself. I have power to lay it down, and I have power to take it again." (John 10: 17, 18.) That stupendous act of self-sacrifice wholly transcends the reach of human thought. The difference between the greatest king and the meanest slave is absolutely nothing compared with the abyss that separates humanity from deity. That abyss beyond measure is the measure of the love of Christ which passeth knowledge. He despised not the carpenter's shop of Nazareth; he shed a new dignity on labor by his own example; he gave a new glory to humility which had no glory hitherto; he was content to obey. His obedience extended through every detail of his most holy life.]

becoming obedient even unto death,—He still further humbled himself and became subject to death, even the most shameful death of all deaths, the death of the cross. He tasted the depth of human weakness, shame, ignominy, and woe, that he might "be touched with the feeling of our infirmities." (Heb. 4: 15.) He "can bear gently with the ignorant and erring, for that he himself also is compassed with infirmity." (Heb. 5: 2.) Jesus partook of our nature, clothed himself with flesh and blood, became subject to death, "that through death he might bring to nought him that had the power of death, that is, the devil; and might deliver all them who thought fear of death were all their lifetime subject to bondage." (Heb. 2: 14, 15.) All the humiliation and suffering were endured to rescue man from the consequences of sin, death, and destruction from the presence of God forever.

yea, the death of the cross.—Jesus humbled himself to the end and met death as a condemned criminal with all the shame of the cross. He went down to the bottom of darkness, the very depth of humiliation and shame. The body of one that hung on a tree was accursed according to the Mosaic law (Deut. 21: 23), and Paul knew this well (Gal. 3: 13). The Jews stumbled at the cross of Christ, the Greeks thought it foolishness, but Paul came to

him the name which is above every name; 10 that in the name of Jesus every knee should bow, of *things* in heaven and *things* on earth and ¹²*things* under the earth, 11 and that every tongue should confess that Jesus Christ is Lord, to the glory of God the Father.

¹²Or, things *of the world below*

---

see in it the wisdom of God. (1 Cor. 1: 23-25.) Jesus saw the shame of the cross and felt it keenly, but he endured it for the sake of "the joy that was set before him" when he reached the goal and finished his atoning death. (Heb. 12: 2.) Therefore Jesus despised the shame. The cross has come to be his crown of glory.

9 **Wherefore also God highly exalted him,**—Because he thus humbled himself to lift man up, God was highly pleased with him and exalted him beyond the state of glory which he enjoyed before the incarnation.

and gave unto him the name which is above every name;—Gave unto him the name of more honor and glory than any other name of heaven or of earth. He had descended into the grave to lift man up. God exalted him much more highly than he had ever been. Jesus as he approached the sufferings that awaited him prayed: "And now, Father, glorify thou me with thine own self with the glory which I had with thee before the world was." (John 17: 5.) But God exalted him higher than he had been before. To give him a name was to give him authority and honor and glory above every name in heaven or on earth.

10 **that in the name of Jesus every knee should bow,**—God so highly exalted Jesus above every other being that all things in heaven and on earth and under the earth bow the knee to him. To bow the knee is to worship and implore a divine being.

of things in heaven and things on earth and things under the earth,—Beings in heaven or angels and spirits of just men made perfect, all the human beings on earth, and the fallen spirits of the universe will do homage to him as Lord of all.

11 **and that every tongue should confess that Jesus Christ is Lord,**—For the tongue to confess is to acknowledge that Jesus is Lord, is to acknowledge his supremacy. I do not understand that all who thus own him do it for their own salvation. [The Lordship of Jesus came to be the test of loyalty. The password in

the dark days of persecution came to be "Jesus is Lord." This was the *Shiboleth* of the faith. It is even so yet. Vain is the praise of those who refuse to bow the knee to Jesus and to confess him as Lord. "No man can say, Jesus is Lord, but in the Holy Spirit." (1 Cor. 12: 3.) To confess Jesus as Lord was the mark of a true believer.]

to the glory of God the Father.—The spirits from the lower regions who confess that Jesus Christ is Lord do it to the glory of God and to their own shame and ruin—they pay the penalty of their sin in everlasting ruin. And in that ruin they confess Christ as Lord, and themselves as sinners lost and undone by their rebellion. Those who willingly confess him on earth will receive the reward. They and the spirits of the heavenly world confess him to the glory of God, and are blessed in the confession and service they render. After the humiliation of Christ, he was exalted to the throne of God and crowned with glory and honor in heaven and on earth forever.

2. GOD STRENGTHENS BELIEVERS TO WALK IN OBEDIENCE TO CHRIST TO A GLORIOUS END
2: 12-18

12 So then, my beloved, even as ye have always obeyed, not [18]as in my presence only, but now much more in my absence, work out your own salva-

[18]Some ancient authorities omit *as*.

---

12 So then, my beloved, even as ye have always obeyed,—[This is the secret of all the joy in this epistle. In the church there, his words as spoken in Christ's name had aroused them to a diligent effort to put them into practice. He had no cause for grief of any kind over them.]

not as in my presence only,—[Of their early zeal he had been a witness, he now pleads that he may not learn that his presence among them was necessary to sustain their zeal, but that they will prove it to have been of a true nature, a zeal for Christ by their steadfastness while he was away from them.]

but now much more in my absence,—He exhorts them to be more faithful and earnest in their obedience, because they are now deprived of his presence and help and there is need of greater

tion with fear and trembling; 13 for it is God who worketh in you both to will and to work, for his good pleasure. 14 Do all things without murmur-

diligence on their part. This certainly was a wonderful church which so lived as to enable Paul to say: "Even as ye have always obeyed," "from the first day until now." (1 : 5.)

work out your own salvation—To work out one's salvation is to comply with the conditions on which God has promised to save. To so live in accordance with God's word that he will be fitted to be saved. The thing for man to do is to fit himself for salvation, then God will save him. He can be fitted for salvation only by complying with the law God has given to discipline and fit him.

with fear and trembling;—To work out salvation with fear and trembling is to fear God with such reverence and awe that they seek to do his will and tremble lest they should fail to understand that they may do it. Jehovah says: "To this man will I look, even to him that is poor and of a contrite spirit, and that trembleth at my word." (Isa. 66: 2.) [These words occur only three times more in Paul's epistles, and always in reference to obedience. (1 Cor. 2: 3; 2 Cor. 7: 15; Eph. 6: 5.) The fear is not exactly the fear of God, but of the greatness of the task and of the possibility of failure. We are to exhibit the utmost solicitude lest we fail to heed the instruction: "Wherefore let him that thinketh he standeth take heed lest he fall" (1 Cor. 10: 12), and "Therefore we ought to give the more earnest heed to the things that were heard, lest haply we drift away from them. For if the word spoken through angels proved stedfast, and every transgression and disobedience received a just recompense of reward; how shall we escape, if we neglect so great a salvation?" (Heb. 2: 1-3.)]

13 for it is God who worketh in you both to will and to work, for his good pleasure.—When a man with reverence and awe does the will of God, it is God in and through him working to will and to do after his good pleasure. Just as when the son follows implicitly the directions of the father in doing the work the father commits to him, it is really the father through the son doing his own work according to his own will; the father is working through the son. When man gives himself up to God to walk as

ings and questionings: 15 that ye may become blameless and harmless, chil-

God directs, God works through him to do his own good pleasure. If man refuses the obedience, God may overrule his rebellion to accomplish his purposes; but he does not work in or through him or bless him.

Baptism as an act of faith is a declaration of distrust of self and of trust in God. It is an act in which the believer declares distrust in self and commits himself—heart, soul, and body—to God. It is not a work of man. So far from it, it is a solemn declaration that he is dead and not able to work or do anything of himself; he henceforth commits himself to God. He will let God work through him. To follow the law of faith is for man to do nothing of his own, but to submit through faith, with fear and trembling, to the will of God—to walk in the works of God. To do God's work allows no room for boasting. It is to seek blessing in walking in the word of God; it is to receive blessing and strength from God in God's appointed way.

14 Do all things without murmurings and questionings:— Men are inclined to murmur and complain at duties which God has laid on them. But God requires them to put away murmurings and questionings; he does not accept grudging or unwilling service. Even if the service is to suffer like Christ, while the flesh may draw back from the service, the spirit should be willing to do the will of God, should be willing to suffer for his sake. What God requires should be done as he requires it, without questioning upon the part of any. [Both words are used generally and they need not be limited to opposition to God's will alone. They equally applied to the early lives of the Philippians, and to their intercourse with one another (1 Pet. 4: 9; Acts 6: 1), they were to live blamelessly and irreproachably before the world. Such murmurings and questionings would mar their love toward Christ and their brethren. They must avoid these sins if they would have the mind of Christ. (2: 5.)]

15 that ye may become blameless—To do these things cheerfully, gladly, without questioning the requirements, dispensations of God alone enable us to be blameless before him. [To be blameless is to be without fault or stain. To be correct in the ex-

dren of God without blemish in the midst of a crooked and perverse generation, among whom ye are seen as [14]lights in the world, 16 holding forth the

[14]Gr. *luminaries.* Wisd. 13. 2; comp. Rev. 21. 11.

---

ternals of life. It is said of Elisabeth and Zacharias that "they were both righteous before God, walking in all the commandments and ordinances of the Lord blameless." (Luke 1: 6.) And so it was the desire that these brethren should meet all their duties and discharge all their obligations and in all their intercourse with their fellow men be irreproachable.]

and harmless,—[This refers to the internal purity, simplicity, and sincerity which ought to characterize all followers of Christ. To be harmless is to have the innocence of character which has no admixture of evil thought or desire in it. Thus these Philippian Christians were to be outwardly and inwardly correct that they might be no hindrance nor scandal to the name of Jesus Christ; and inwardly correct because no mere outward correctness can long be maintained without inward correctness. These traits are distinguishing marks of the children of God, and they should be cultivated and honored. If the followers of Christ would only see to it that their lives are all blameless and harmless, the cause of Christ would make greater progress.]

children of God without blemish in the midst of a crooked and perverse generation,—The children of God can be without blemish while they are living in the midst of the people who are perverse in their disposition, rebellious in their spirit, and who walk not according to the straight rule laid down by the Master. [It is of very great importance always and everywhere to be without blemish; but when surrounded by people whose views of truth, whose ideas of life, and whose general course of conduct are always wrong, it is of importance beyond estimate to be rightminded and straightforward and clean.]

among whom ye are seen as lights in the world,—They were to shine as lights in the world by holding forth in their lives and in their teaching the word of God. The law of God is a lamp to our feet. [Jesus said to his disciples: "Ye are the light of the world." (Matt. 5: 14.) So Paul says here. In both instances, of course, the idea is of a reflected light. In the highest sense of the words light belongs only to Christ. (John 1: 4; 8: 12.) The two fig-

word of life; that I may have whereof to glory in the day of Christ, that I

ures are blended here. Christians are the lesser lights of the spiritual world—always dim in comparison with the shining of the Sun of Righteousness, but they are still lights. Though they can give only borrowed radiance; they are yet the clearest luminaries which not a few behold. More people have no other conception of Christianity than that they actually see in the lives and doings of professed Christians. They do not go to Jesus Christ, and look at the truth as he speaks it out and lives it out; they do not yield up their minds and hearts to his teaching and come under his guidance, and let him take them forward into the knowledge and fellowship of "the law of the Spirit of life," as revealed in the scriptures, but they watch Christians, and draw their inferences and reach their conclusions from the type of character which they illustrate—"they are the Bible the world reads and studies." If Christians exemplify a new life, if they bring forth the fruits of the life in Christ, they are the luminaries in whose light the multitude will sometimes come to rejoice.]

16 holding forth the word of life;—The word of life is the message of salvation set forth in Christ, and goodness and blessedness by him. It is that teaching given by those who spoke as the Holy Spirit moved them. It was for Christians to hold by it, or to hold it out—the expression may have either meaning; and both senses are here. In order to give light there must be life. And the Christian life depends on having in it the word, quick and powerful, which is to dwell in us richly in all wisdom and spiritual understanding. [This is the secret of the blameless life; and so those who have this character will give light, as holding forth the word of life. For while the word and message of life is to be owned, professed, and proclaimed, yet the embodiment of it in the Christian is the main point here, the character being formed and the practice determined by the word believed.]

that I may have whereof to glory in the day of Christ,—The day when they shall meet Christ when he comes again and gives account for the deeds done in the body. [The frequent use of the words—"the day of Christ"—shows how definite and important in the mind of the early Christians was the coming of the Lord. For

did not run in vain neither labor in vain. 17 Yea, and if I am [15]offered upon the sacrifice and service of your faith, I joy, and rejoice with you all: 18 and in the same manner do ye also joy, and rejoice with me.

[15]Gr. *poured out as a drink-offering.*

---

in that day and not till then will the good work which God is now doing in his people's heart be completed and manifested. For the day of the Lord's return his servants wait when he will present to himself the spotless church. And towards that consummation tends our present growth in the spiritual life.]

that I did not run in vain neither labor in vain.—[Paul desired proof in the light given by his readers to the wicked and sinful world that his own strenuous efforts and frequent weariness for them had not been in vain. Such proof would be to him a ground of triumphant confidence in God. And this exultation would reach forward to that day, ever present to Paul's thought, when the inward spiritual life began on earth and manifested imperfectly here will receive its full and visible consummation in the light of eternity, and earthly toil receive its abundant recompense.]

17 **Yea, and if I am offered upon the sacrifice and service of your faith,**—He adds this to show the spirit he had imbibed from Christ. If the sacrifice of his life was needed to make their faith and service acceptable to God, he would rejoice.

I joy, and rejoice with you all:—[He was glad to make the offering of his life, if this supreme sacrifice was demanded. He would not shrink back, but would meet it gladly, if this, and all the more readily since he could have his joy with them. He was glad on his own account that he had been the instrument in their conversion.]

18 **and in the same manner do ye also joy, and rejoice with me.**—[There were two offerings in Paul's contemplation—his own, as he was poured out on the sacrifice; the offering of the faithful lives of the Philippian Christians which they themselves would make. He did not intimate whether the power of Rome or his own continued toils should be the agency employed to pour his life forth. Both offerings were subjects for joy. He could not restrain his triumph at the one, and in like manner he bade his brethren feel equal joy at the offering which he was making and being strengthened to make unto his Master.]

SECTION FOUR

PAUL'S ASSISTANTS AND COLABORERS
2: 19-30

1. TIMOTHY AND HIS SPEEDY MISSION TO PHILIPPI
2: 19-24

19 But I hope in the Lord Jesus to send Timothy shortly unto you, that I also may be of good comfort, when I know your state. 20 For I have no

19 But I hope—[He had just spoken of the possibility of his own death, which his language suggests as possible; but that conviction now, as elsewhere in this epistle, seems to yield at once to the opposite expectation of a speedy release, or at least of such an improvement in his affairs that he could dispense with the presence and service of Timothy for a season.]

in the Lord Jesus—[This is equivalent to through the Lord *Jesus*. It was to the Lord Jesus he looked in all his need. He realized that he could not even hope for anything except in complete subjection to the Lord's will. It was in him he hoped, as in the Lord his whole life moved. The Christian is a part of Christ, a member of his body—the church. His every thought and word and deed proceeded from him, as the center of volition. Thus he loved the Lord and hoped in him. He had one guiding principle in acting and forbearing to act, "only in the Lord." (1 Cor. 7: 39.)]

to send Timothy shortly unto you, that I also may be of good comfort, when I know your state.—The proposed visit of Timothy to Philippi had a double motive. First of all the thought of the encouragement that the coming of Timothy would produce among the Philippians, an encouragement that was all the more needed perhaps because he had just touched upon the possibility of his own death. But he himself was also to be cheered and comforted by the news that Timothy would be able to send him on his arrival at Philippi. His beloved son in the gospel was to be his representative among them and was to give them that guidance and help which his own enforced absence prevented him from giving. [Also and if the worst happened and death came to himself Timothy was to comfort them in their sorrow concerning his fate.

man likeminded, who will care ¹truly for your state. 21 For they all seek their own, not the things of Jesus Christ. 22 But ye know the proof of him,

¹Gr. *genuinely*.

It was not the first time that he had undertaken on Paul's behalf a mission of this character. He had been sent from Athens to encourage the church at Thessalonica in the face of persecution (1 Thess. 3: 2, 6), and later on from Ephesus to Macedonia and thence to Corinth when Paul himself was unable to pay these churches a promised visit (1 Cor. 16: 10).]

20 **For I have no man likeminded, who will care truly for your state.**—He meant, of course, like-minded with Timothy. This is a high tribute to the fidelity of Timothy, but he richly deserved it. He was such a friend that he was generally anxious about the Philippian church. He was with Paul when the church was established there, and would naturally have a great interest in its prosperity.

21 **For they all seek their own, not the things of Jesus Christ.**—The most of the teachers near Paul at the time of writing this epistle looked after their own interests, not feeling the interest of the disciples at heart. He contrasts them with Timothy. It is a sad state of affairs that at the present time the majority of the preachers are more anxious for their personal aggrandizement than for honoring Christ and saving men. [It seems that when this epistle was written Paul was separated from most of his intimate friends and fellow workers, and that only two of these are mentioned—Timothy and Epaphroditus. But we learn from other epistles written from Rome that there were several other brethren with him during this portion of his imprisonment. It is almost certain that Luke and Aristarchus were in his company, and that they remained with him until after the epistles to the Colossians and Philemon had been written, and they show that Mark, Aristarchus, Justus, Epaphras, Demas, and Tychicus had been added to their number. (Col. 4: 10-14; Phile. 23, 24.) It is probable that before this epistle was written most, if not all, of these had left Rome on different missions assigned to them by Paul. Tychicus had been sent to Colossæ (Col. 4: 7, 8), and it is likely that he was accompanied by Epaphras and Mark who was at that time contemplating a visit to that district (Col. 4: 10). So if

that, as a child *serveth* a father, so he served with me in furtherance of the ²gospel. 23 Him therefore I hope to send forthwith, so soon as I shall see how it will go with me: 24 but I trust in the Lord that I myself also shall

²Gr. *good tidings.* See marginal note on ch. 1. 5.

---

these were away from Rome, engaged in the Lord's work they were not included in the number who "seek their own, not the things of Jesus Christ."]

22 But ye know the proof of him, that, as a child serveth a father, so he served with me in furtherance of the gospel.—Timothy in their midst had proven his worthiness as a minister of Christ, by laboring with Paul as a child would labor with his father. He partook of the same spirit of self-denial and fidelity in Christ and for the salvation of men that Paul showed. His loyalty was impeachable. He stood ready to serve Christ anywhere.

23 Him therefore I hope to send forthwith, so soon as I shall see how it will go with me:—At the time this epistle was written, Paul was awaiting the outcome of his trial, which he hoped would result in his acquittal. Just as soon as the verdict was rendered he would send Timothy with that information. If he should be condemned to death, he would of course have no further occasion for Timothy's services, and if he should be acquitted, he could then spare Timothy's services for a season to visit them and give them full information and encouragement.

24 but I trust in the Lord—[With Paul this expression was far more than a mere form. It was a recognition both of the providential and spiritual government of the Lord. He recognized that the accomplishment of any purpose depended on his will and felt that his life was in his hands. Still he was in danger and the issue of the trial was doubtful, but he was confident it would end in his release. Yet that confidence was conditional and was centered "in the Lord" as was all else in his life. He believed that the Lord's will and his purposes were to be fulfilled in his life, and with that thought in mind he rested his case.]

that I myself also shall come shortly.—[We do not know certainly what he meant by the term *shortly*. The uncertainty as to what whim might strike Nero was an uncertain thing to count upon. It is not likely that he now contemplates going on to Spain as he had once planned. (Rom. 15: 28.) His heart now turns to his old field of labor. (Phile. 22.) His long imprisonment in Cæsarea and Rome had made it very necessary for him to set things in order there. Those *grievous wolves* of which Paul warned the Ephesian elders (Acts 20: 29, 30) had taken advantage of his absence and were causing much trouble and confusion among the churches in Asia. Philippi also makes a strong appeal for his presence and assistance. It is now admitted by nearly all those who are competent to decide on such questions that Paul's appeal to Cæsar terminated successfully; that he was acquitted of the charge laid against him; and that he spent some years in freedom before he was again imprisoned and condemned to death. But farther, we must admit not only that he was liberated, but also that he continued his apostolic labor for some years afterward. For the historical facts mentioned in the epistles to Timothy and Titus cannot be placed in any portion of Paul's life prior to or during his first imprisonment in Rome; and that the style in which those epistles are written and the condition of the church described in them forbid the supposition of such a date. Consequently we must acknowledge that after his Roman imprisonment he was at liberty at Ephesus (1 Tim. 1: 3), Crete (Tit. 1: 5), Macedonia (1 Tim. 1: 3), Miletus (2 Tim. 4: 20); Nicopolis (Tit. 3: 12), and that he was afterwards a second time a prisoner in Rome (2 Tim. 1: 16, 17).

2. INFORMATION CONCERNING EPAPHRODITUS
2: 25-30

come shortly. 25 But I counted it necessary to send to you Epaphroditus,

---

25 But I counted it necessary to send to you Epaphroditus, —Epaphroditus was a messenger of the church at Philippi to Paul during his imprisonment at Rome, who was entrusted with their contribution for his support. He had been very ill, and it was very necessary that he should be sent, for he would hardly recover thoroughly, while longing to return to his home, nor could the Philippians be happy till they saw again their messenger, whose work in their stead had cost him a severe illness, and nearly his life. He must return at once.

[2: 25, 26.] PHILIPPIANS 195

my brother and fellow-worker and fellow-soldier, and your ³messenger and minister to my need; 26 since he longed ⁴after you all, and was sore trou-

---
³Gr. *apostle.*
⁴Many ancient authorities read *to see you all.*

---

my brother—He is called a brother as a member of the body of Christ.

and fellow-worker—He labored with Paul to spread the gospel among those who knew not the Lord. The term is used of Aquila and Priscilla (Rom. 16: 3), of Timothy (Rom. 16: 21), and of Titus (2 Cor. 8: 23).

and fellow-soldier,—[This shows how full of danger the work of the gospel was at that time to those who executed it faithfully; and that the sincere preachers of the gospel, together with the martyrs who sealed it with their blood, bring before us a noble army commanded by Christ, which was successfully warring against infidelity and other powers of darkness which were in opposition to God.]

and your messenger and minister to my need;—As Timothy was intended to be a special messenger from Paul to the Philippian church, so Epaphroditus had come as a special messenger from Philippi to Paul in prison in Rome. He was undoubtedly, personally, in sympathy with the special object of his mission—ministering to Paul's needs. As the love of Christ, as it takes possession, opens the heart to the needs of all men, so it certainly opened the heart of Epaphroditus to the need of his brother in bonds, of the founder of the Philippian church, of the truest and bravest of Christ's servants. For his sake he was willing to leave beloved brethren and sisters in Christ, and brave the dangers of the voyage. And it would be with peculiar tenderness and interest that he would deliver to Paul the loving messages of the beloved church and their fellowship in his need.

26 **since he longed after you all,**—In his sickness he longed for the friends and brethren at home, especially so since they had heard of his sickness, and doubtless manifested great interest in him.

and was sore troubled,—The strength of *sore troubled* will be recognized from its being used of Christ's agony in the garden (Matt. 26: 37; Mark 14: 33), and nowhere else in the New Testament. The strong character of the expression is not unsuited to

bled, because ye had heard that he was sick: 27 for indeed he was sick nigh unto death: but God had mercy on him; and not on him only, but on me also, that I might not have sorrow upon sorrow. 28 I have sent him there-

the feelings of one who has been very ill at a distance from all his friends, and during convalescence feels that home is the only place in which he can thoroughly recover.

because ye had heard that he was sick:—[There can be no question that a considerable time had elapsed since Paul's arrival at Rome before these words were written. The Philippians first had to learn of his need, to make their collection and send it. After the arrival of Epaphroditus in Rome he fell sick, for Paul implies that he had exerted himself and so brought on his illness. This becomes known in Philippi, and the anxiety of his friends in Philippi had been reported to Paul.]

27 for indeed he was sick nigh unto death:—[Such an illness must also have continued over an extended period of time. The words here used indicate that the report which reached the Philippians had come short of the reality.]

but God had mercy on him; and not on him only, but on me also, that I might not have sorrow upon sorrow.—God was merciful to spare the life of Epaphroditus, and it was likewise a mercy to Paul lest the sorrow for the loss of so worthy a friend should be added to the sorrow of his imprisonment and trial. The passage, over and above its interest as an example of the strong personal affection which belonged to Paul's nature, and harmonized with his deep Christian love, is noticeable in showing clearly that his power or miracle, great as it was, was not his own, to use at his own will. When it was needed to be "the signs of an apostle" (2 Cor. 12: 12), it was given; and at special times, as at Ephesus (Acts 19: 11), it was given in special fullness. [But this instance, together with the case of Trophimus, of whom Paul says: "Trophimus I left at Miletus sick" (2 Tim. 4: 20), is clear proof that the power of performing cures, and of working miracles, was a power which only was given to the apostles occasionally, and did not at all depend upon their own will. He would undoubtedly have healed Epaphroditus if he could. Nor, if the power of working cures had awaited his disposal, would he have left Trophimus at Miletus sick.]

fore the more diligently, that, when ye see him again, ye may rejoice, and that I may be the less sorrowful. 29 Receive him therefore in the Lord with all joy; and hold such in honor: 30 because for the work of ⁵Christ he came nigh unto death, hazarding his life to supply that which was lacking in your service toward me.

⁵Many ancient authorities read *the Lord.*

28 I have sent him therefore the more diligently, that, when ye see him again, ye may rejoice, and that I may be the less sorrowful.—He was the more careful, more delighted, to send him at once to them, that when they saw him, they might rejoice at his recovery, and it would lessen the sorrow of himself to know that they were relieved of anxiety for him.

29 Receive him therefore in the Lord with all joy;—Paul exhorts them because he had been zealous in sending him to them so soon as he was able to travel to receive him with joy. It would be joy of the whole church for the restoration to health and to them of the member whom they regarded so highly. It would be a joy with thanksgiving because they had in mind how gracious the Lord had been in saving his life.

and hold such in honor:—As there were not many such faithful brethren to be found, he exhorted them to set high store by Epaphroditus when he arrived.

30 because for the work of Christ—The work is a New Testament phrase for the preaching of the gospel. (Acts 15: 38.)

he came nigh unto death, hazarding his life—This bears testimony to his worth and to the truth that he came nigh to death because he risked his life to supply needed help to Paul, and in proclaiming the word.

to supply that which was lacking in your service toward me. —[This represents him as encountering the labor and danger which attended on Paul's circumstances with full free will, and an entire disregard of consequences to himself, such as only true devotion could supply.] This would naturally endear him much to one of Paul's temperament, and who showed such gratitude for all favors shown him.

[The bonds by which men are held together in Christ are strong because they are bonds in truth, righteousness, and in aspiration which take souls forward into the light and glory of God. When men are held to each other by the ties of selfishness, or some fierce hate which is cherished in common, or by vices and crimes which are cherished in common, they are liable to fly asunder at any moment. Faith and love and purity are cementing energies. Faces set alike toward heaven, and hearts set alike on the things of Christ, always insure an increasing fellowship and sympathy. If Christian men ever divide, as they sometimes do, and become alienated from each other, it is not because there is any natural tendency in "the law of the Spirit of life in Christ Jesus" to work separation of heart from heart and life from life, but for the reason that, in these instances, selfishness or prejudice or passion or inability to see clearly has been too much for the measure of Christian character that has been attained. It is not because they are Christians; it is because they are so imperfect in their character—so feebly developed, and so far from what they ought to be, that the disciples of Jesus are ever led to entertain ill feelings toward each other, and mutually to say hard things. Christ is love, and love is a bond of union. Paul and Timothy and Epaphroditus and the faithful hearts who were behind them had their oneness and sympathy in Christ.]

SECTION FIVE

WARNINGS AGAINST JUDAISTIC FALSE TEACHERS AND WICKED DECEIVERS IN CONTRAST WITH THE APOSTLE
3:1 to 4:1

1. THE SPIRIT OF FALSE TEACHERS AS DISTINGUISHED FROM THAT OF PAUL
3: 1-16

1 Finally, my brethren, rejoice in the Lord. To write the same things to you, to me indeed is not irksome, but for you it is safe. 2 Beware of the

1 Finally, my brethren, rejoice in the Lord.—He encourages them to rejoice in the Lord, despite these afflictions brought upon them.

To write the same things to you, to me indeed is not irksome, but for you it is safe.—There was no cause of sorrow to him in writing the exhortations and warnings, and it might be needful to them as a matter of safety to give them the caution that follows. The same things refer to the things he taught them when present, which doubtless were the things concerning the circumcision of the Gentile converts. His first visit to them was when he delivered the apostolic decrees given at Jerusalem on the subject. (Acts 15: 19, 20.) This question had greatly subsided at the time this epistle was written, yet he thinks it safe that he write it to them. He taught that the demand that the Gentile Christians should be circumcised was a great sin against God and wrong to the Gentiles.

2 Beware of the dogs,—It was out of harmony with Paul's usual style to apply this term to any one. The Jews called the Gentiles *dogs*, as a symbol of what was ignoble and mean, now for the same reason he calls them *dogs*. [Those persons who bark and rail at such as they hate are called *dogs*. They are inclined to abominable courses; are *dumb dogs*; they do not faithfully warn and instruct men; are *lazy dogs;* do not faithfully work; are *greedy dogs;* they never get enough of worldly things; and are given to bark at and reproach the people of God. (Isa. 56: 9-11.)]

dogs, beware of the evil workers, beware of the concision: 3 for we are the circumcision, who worship by the Spirit of God, and glory in Christ Jesus, and have no confidence in the flesh: 4 though I myself might have confidence

---

beware of the evil workers,—The evil workers were the Judaizing teachers. They were actively at work, but in the wrong direction. These Judaizers were like the Pharisees before them, of whom the Savior said: "Ye compass sea and land to make one proselyte; and when he is become so, ye make him twofold more a son of hell than yourselves." (Matt. 23: 15.)

beware of the concision:—He applies the term *concision* to those who insisted on the literal act of circumcision, but had lost its true spirit. As the literal, fleshly seed of Abraham had brought them up to, and given way to the circumcision of the heart, "the putting off of the body of the flesh, in the circumcision of Christ." (Col. 2: 11.)

3 for we are the circumcision,—Christians have put off the body of the sins, are the circumcised, "having been buried with him in baptism, wherein ye were also raised with him through faith in the working of God, who raised him from the dead." (Col. 2: 12.)

who worship by the Spirit of God, and glory in Christ Jesus, —They are the true circumcision who worship God in the Spirit, and rejoice in Christ Jesus, but have no confidence in the flesh to save. The fleshly has given way to the spiritual circumcision. That which is of the flesh is the *concision*. Jesus said: "But the hour cometh, and now is, when the true worshippers shall worship the Father in spirit and truth." (John 4: 23.) Circumcision and descent from Abraham of the flesh can no longer save.

and have no confidence in the flesh:—[*Flesh* is here the antithesis both to *Christ Jesus* and the *Spirit*. What the apostle meant by the term is explained very fully in the two following verses. It includes all that a Jew valued most, and all that was the source of his vaunted righteousness, all that led to the familiar contempt for those who stood outside the covenant, but with special emphasis on the thought that the Jewish confidence was primarily based on the fleshly act of circumcision which widened out into confidence founded on one's own effort to attain righteousness as contrasted with that rooted in the consciousness that righteousness is only at-

even in the flesh: if any other man ⁶thinketh to have confidence in the flesh, I yet more: 5 circumcised the eighth day, of the stock of Israel, of the tribe of Benjamin, a Hebrew of Hebrews; as touching the law, a Pharisee; 6 as

⁶Or, *seemeth.*

---

tainable in union with Christ and through the instrumentality of the Holy Spirit.]

4 though I myself might have confidence even in the flesh: if any other man thinketh to have confidence in the flesh, I yet more:—He here shows that he is not condemning a trust in the fleshly line of Abraham because he is deficient in this respect, for if any man had ground for trusting in his fleshly descent, he was the man. [Paul gives here his spiritual biography. The repetition of the pronoun I which occurs fifteen times in this passage shows the strong personal element running through it. He begins by a description of himself as Saul the Pharisee and gives a catalogue of the privileges and advantages which were the pride and glory of vain Pharisees and so proves that even from his opponents' own point of view, which assumes all through this passage, that he had a better claim to boast than any of them, if he were so inclined.]

5 circumcised the eighth day,—He was neither an Ishmaelite, who had been circumcised at the age of thirteen, nor a proselyte, who would have received circumcision in mature life. In his case the sacred rite, of which the Jews were always so proud, had been received in its perfection. [The parents of such a child must have been zealous for the law, and careful that their son should be made fully a partaker of the Abrahamic covenant.]

of the stock of Israel,—Born of Rachel, a legitimate wife, not of a handmaid, and therefore of good Israelitish stock. [He mentions this that it may be clear that not only he but his parents were Israelites. He was not of a father or mother who had come into the privileges of the chosen race as proselytes.]

of the tribe of Benjamin,—He was born of the tribe of great renown in the national history, a tribe which gave Israel its first king; which remained loyal to the royal line of David, and to the worship of Jehovah, and preserved its own strain with remarkable purity. The Holy City and temple stood on its soil.

touching zeal, persecuting the church; as touching the righteousness which is in the law, found blameless. 7 Howbeit what things were ⁷gain to me, these

---

⁷Gr. *gains.*

---

a Hebrew of Hebrews;—He was a son of Hebrew parents and stock. By this he would mark the purity of his descent. All his ancestors were Hebrews. He was born in Tarsus away from the Holy Land, but there was no intermixture of other blood in his veins. [We can judge that this was likely to be so when we find that the son was sent to study in Jerusalem at the feet of Gamaliel. Only those who were proud and careful for the strict Jewish character of all belonging to them would have sought to have their son placed under such a teacher away from their own home. We can see also how learned Paul was in all that concerned his own people.]

as touching the law, a Pharisee;—He observed the law with the minuteness of a Pharisee, the most scrupulous of all in the observance of every minutia of the law. [He explains this as brought up in Jerusalem "at the feet of Gamaliel, instructed according to the strict manner of the law of our fathers" (Acts 22: 3), and again he tells us "that after the straitest sect of our religion I lived a Pharisee" (Acts 26: 5). And thus far he has spoken only of those distinctions as a Jew, which depended on others. His birth, family, and education were not in his own hands, but yet he could point to them as each one marking him for a privileged member of the chosen people. He now proceeds to tell that his former zeal for Judaism did not disgrace such parentage and training.]

6 as touching zeal, persecuting the church;—His zeal for the law led him to persecute the church of Jesus Christ, to follow them to strange cities, to cast men and women into prison, and when they were put to death he gave his vote against them. (Acts 26: 10.)

as touching the righteousness which is in the law, found blameless.—Such righteousness as consisted in obedience to the legal ordinances he could claim, for he had claimed them all. It is clearly to externals that he is referring, for his words imply that it was to mean he had approved himself; none of his fellows surpassed or even equaled him in strictness of legal observance.

have I counted loss for Christ. 8 Yea verily, and I count all things to be

All his prejudices, feelings, and works led him to maintain the observance of the law. He says: "I advanced in the Jews' religion beyond many of mine own age among my countrymen, being more exceedingly zealous for the traditions of my fathers." (Gal. 1: 14.) His careful observance of the legal ordinances had brought him to be in the eyes of his fellows, one in whom no fault could be found. [The claim to *blamelessness* from a Pharisaic viewpoint was by no means uncommon as we learn from the story of the rich young ruler who came to Jesus. (Luke 18: 18-24.) There was nothing unusual or presumptuous in the assertion that in his outward conduct there had been found neither fault nor failure. There is no contradiction between his statement here and the description of his inward struggle in Rom. 7: 7-23. It was not the infraction of the outward demands of the Mosaic law in its ethical and ceremonial aspect that filled his heart with torment, but the sense of sin in his innermost being; neither is it inconsistent with the following: "I thank him that enabled me, even Christ Jesus our Lord, for that he counted me faithful, appointing me to his service; though I was before a blasphemer, and a persecutor, and injurious: howbeit I obtained mercy, because I did it ignorantly in unbelief; and the grace of our Lord abounded exceedingly with faith and love which is in Christ Jesus" (1 Tim. 1: 12-14), because there he is regarding his past in Judaism from the Christian and not from the Pharisaic viewpoint as he is doing here.]

7 Howbeit what things were gain to me,—Paul was honored because of his blamelessness and zeal in the Jews' religion, of which he was very proud. In these like the rest of his nation, he had rested his hope.

these have I counted loss for Christ.—All the profits and honors gained in the observance of the Jewish law, and in maintaining the traditions of the fathers, he counted loss—worse than nought for the sake of Christ. Instead of service to be recorded, and regarded worthy of honors, they were sins and crimes condemned, and sorrowed for through life. All gains out of Christ are losses for Christ.

8 Yea verily, and I count all things to be loss—He carries the thought further, not only were the services of the Jewish law

loss for the excellency of the knowledge of Christ Jesus my Lord: for whom I suffered the loss of all things, and do count them but refuse, that I may gain Christ, 9 and be found in him, ⁸not having a righteousness of mine own,

⁸Or, *not having* as *my righteousness that which is of the law.*

---

and the persecutions loss, but he counted blessings gained in the knowledge and service of Christ so immeasurably safer as to everything else, that all else was nothing compared with it.

for the excellency of the knowledge of Christ Jesus my Lord: —[This sets forth the idea of a business transaction, exchanging what was worthless and even ruinous for what was a treasure of surpassing worth. (Matt. 13: 45.) Knowledge here signifies his whole experience in Christ. It reaches far beyond mere intellectual knowledge, includes faith, service, sacrifice, and is analogous to the phrase "to be in Christ"—the spiritual knowledge by which the individual becomes one with Christ, so that his whole life is lived in Christ and he has no consciousness of being apart from Christ. It is a knowledge that is constantly developing as the intimacy with the Master becomes closer until it reaches the culmination when it constitutes the whole secret of the Christian life.]

for whom I suffered the loss of all things,—The threefold emphasis upon his renunciation, twice in this verse and once in the preceding verse, is very similar to the self-abnegation of Christ. (2: 7, 8.) Paul is now a man in Christ Jesus who dominates the world of manhood for him—*Christ Jesus my Lord.* [For Christ's sake Paul did suffer the loss, yea, *all things,* the sum total of his old life's values. His own family probably regarded him as a disgrace to Judaism. His Pharisaic fellow members considered him a deserter from the cause. The Jews in general regarded him as a renegade. He had paid the price for Christ's sake. But it was worth the price. He had no regrets.]

and do count them but refuse, that I may gain Christ,—For Christ he had given up all things, and counted them as refuse to be turned from, that he might gain Christ. [He was not a madman in reckless values; it was the greatest bargain of his life. He lost the Jewish world to gain Christ the Lord of all.]

9 and be found in him,—[Being found in Christ is the very crown of the Christian life. To "gain Christ" and "be found in

even that which is of the law, but that which is through faith in Christ, the righteousness which is from God, ⁹by faith: 10 that I may know him, and the

⁹Gr. *upon*.

him" are parallels, and the general trend of the passage is that he has in mind his Christian course as a whole, from the day when he came to know "the excellency of the knowledge of Christ Jesus," till "that day" (2 Tim. 4: 8), when Christ's work in him shall be consummated in final union with him.]

not having a righteousness of mine own, even that which is of the law,—He begins by describing the righteousness which he claimed to have possessed from the Pharisaic standpoint. According to the strict Jewish view he already stood in right relation to God as a member of the covenant people, and his observance of the law and its demands proclaimed him righteous in actual practice. Paul here calls the law of Moses a "righteousness of mine own," which means that the law of Moses had been nailed to the cross (Col. 2: 14), and taken out of the way. While it was in force it was God's way of making man righteous, but after its repeal to seek righteousness, through it, was to seek one's own righteousness. Then the things commanded by God at one time, or to one people, taken from them and given to a different people at a different time, bring not God's righteousness but man's righteousness.

but that which is through faith in Christ,—The righteousness which is of faith is that which is gained by doing the things to which faith in Christ leads. Faith in Christ leads man to do the things that Christ has commanded. These things ordained by God were sealed by the blood of Jesus Christ which cleanses from all sin. The righteousness thus gained is the righteousness which comes through faith in Jesus Christ.

the righteousness which is from God by faith:—That is, faith in God that changes a man's feelings, desires, and character into a likeness of God. He is led by faith to live the life that pleases God, to do the will of God, becomes righteousness according to the righteousness of God, and becomes in life and character like God. Even when a man's heart is purified by faith, and his affections all reach out towards God and seek conformity to the life of God it is imperfect. His practice of the righteousness of God

power of his resurrection, and the fellowship of his sufferings, becoming con-

---

falls far short of the divine standard. The flesh is weak, and the law of sin reigns in our members; so that we fall short of the perfect standard of divine righteousness; but if we trust God implicitly and faithfully endeavor to do his will, he knows our frame, knows our weakness, and as a father pities his children, so the Lord pities our infirmities and weaknesses, and imputes to us the righteousness of Jesus Christ. So Jesus stands as our justification and our righteousness, and our life is hid with Christ in God.

10 that I may know him,—In seeking the righteousness which comes through faith in Christ, led him to trust and obey him, to do his will, and in so doing he sought to know Christ, to trust and obey him. He longed to go deeper and know more of Christ by inner experience.

and the power of his resurrection,—To gain the presence of that Spirit by which Jesus was raised from the dead, he ever kept before his mind that his own deepest spiritual experience must correspond with the vital facts in the scheme of redemption. He must die to sin and be raised to newness of life, and the power that raised Jesus from the dead was the power to raise him from spiritual death to the new and abiding life in and through the exalted Christ. [Paul is here not thinking so much of the historical facts of the resurrection of Christ, nor of his own resurrection after death, but rather of his own experimental knowledge of the power or force in Christ's resurrection in its influence on his own inner life. He felt the grip of this truth in its appeal to sacrifice for the Lord in doing acts of kindness to others and denying self to help the poorest and stand out faithfully for the most unpopular of his teaching.] It is the heroic spirit in man that responds to this. It admires and responds to the appeal to do and sacrifice for the welfare of others. The strength and vigor of the hero is that the spirit is tested by its capacity to labor, to deny self, and to suffer for the good of others. Like many other things, this heroic spirit looks beautiful in others; but when we come to a personal test, we fail to prove our love and fidelity. We are not willing to deny self, and to suffer for the good of others. The spirit is strong to see, the spirit is weak to stand.

formed unto his death; 11 if by any means I may attain unto the resurrection from the dead. 12 Not that I have already obtained, or am already made

and the fellowship of his sufferings,—He desired to know so as to have the benefit of the fellowship in the sufferings of Christ, because he wished to share them. "If we endure, we shall also reign with him." (2 Tim. 2: 12.) [Being in Christ involves fellowship with him in all points—his obedient life, his spirit, his sufferings, his death, and his glory. He was thinking of the spiritual process which is carried on in the soul of him who is united to Christ. As he understood the power of Christ's death and resurrection, he was able to understand his sufferings and to enter into them with sympathy and spiritual blessing.]

becoming conformed unto his death;—Through these sufferings he would be brought into conformity to his death—to die for Christ's sake like that which Christ suffered for man. Paul so gloried in persecution and affliction for the sake of Jesus that he was ambitious to die for Jesus' sake. [If we are to share in the glory of Jesus, we must also share in his suffering. (Rom. 8: 17-28.) So he rejoiced to fill up on his part the sufferings of Christ. In dying on the cross Christ was regarded as *sin* (2 Cor. 5: 21), and identified himself with the sin of the world. So now we are identified with Christ's sufferings and death.]

11 if by any means I may attain unto the resurrection from the dead.—Not that he might be simply raised from the dead, but that he might enjoy the promises of the resurrection connected with conformity to his life, sufferings, and death. [This is the consummation of the whole process of redemption outlined in verses 9 and 10. The apparent distrust is not distrust, but the distrust inspired by the humility which comes from the consciousness of his own weakness as he faces the great work to be accomplished. The particular form of the phrase "the resurrection from the dead" shows that he has in view here the resurrection of the righteous only.]

12 Not that I have already obtained,—He explains that he, an apostle of Jesus Christ, who had been more abundant in labors and sufferings than all others, had not already attained to the blessedness of salvation that came to those who were raised in

perfect: but I press on, if so be that I may ¹⁰lay hold on that for which also I was laid hold on by Christ Jesus. 13 Brethren, I count not myself ¹¹yet to have laid hold: but one thing *I do,* forgetting the things which are behind,

¹⁰Or, *lay hold, seeing that also I was laid hold on*
¹¹Many ancient authorities omit *yet.*

Jesus, neither had he completed his race. He gathers up the whole past in its relation to the present.

or am already made perfect:—Jesus was made perfect through suffering the death of the cross, and became the author of eternal salvation to all them that obey him (Heb. 5: 7, 8), and Paul did not claim perfection before he suffered as did his Master. [There is a relative perfection which was true of Paul and of all who grow in grace at all and are no longer babes in Christ. (3: 15.) Concerning that he is not speaking. This wholly dissatisfaction with his spiritual attainments and eager longing for loftier heights in Christ we often see in Paul's writings. (Eph. 3: 17-19; 13-16; Col. 1: 28.)]

but I press on, if so be that I may lay hold on that for which also I was laid hold on by Christ Jesus.—Christ Jesus laid hold on Paul when he appeared to him on the Damascus road, and called him to his service, and he through the obedience and death sought to gain the crown of righteousness, which God had promised to him, and not to him "only, but also to all them that have loved his appearing." (2 Tim. 4: 8.) He did not boast of his attainments, but was humble, modest, distrustful of self, and felt what he received was of God's mercy.

13 Brethren, I count not myself yet to have laid hold:—He here repeats that he had not attained that for which he sought, but in order to attain it, he made it the one supreme end of his life. [Absolute perfection he expressly denies. He has not yet reached his goal. There is a relative perfection which was true of Paul and of all who grow in grace and are no longer babes in Christ. (1 Cor. 3: 15.) Dissatisfaction with his spiritual attainments and his longing for a closer union with Christ we often see in his epistles. (3: 17-19; 4: 13-16; Col. 1: 28.)]

but one thing I do, forgetting the things which are behind, and stretching forward to the things which are before,—Forgetting all earthly aspirations, honors, and desires, [he had no de-

and stretching forward to the things which are before, 14 I press on toward the goal unto the prize of the ¹²high calling of God in Christ Jesus. 15 Let ue therefore, as many as are ¹³perfect, be thus minded: and if in anything ye are otherwise minded, this also shall God reveal unto you: 16 only, whereunto we have attained, by that same *rule* let us walk.

¹²Or, *upward*
¹³Or, *full-grown* 1 Cor. 2. 6.

---

sire to look backward. He reached forward to grasp the goal with the forward pressing of the body.]

14 I press on toward the goal unto the prize of the high calling of God in Christ Jesus.—He made it the one supreme end of his life, and made this one thing overcome all other considerations. [He calls it "the high calling," and speaks of "the hope of his calling" (Eph. 1: 18), and "heavenly calling" (Heb. 3: 1). It is God calling and beckoning us on and upward toward himself "in Christ Jesus." (Heb. 12: 1.) The crown is laid up for all who run the race with patience and "have loved his appearing." (2 Tim. 4: 8.)]

15 Let us therefore, as many as are perfect,—In verse 12, he said he did not claim to be perfect. Here he classes himself and others as perfect. There he spoke of being perfected by reaching the mark at the end of life. He was not perfected until he reached that state. Here he speaks of those having passed from the law of Moses into complete and perfect revelation of God through Christ. [The term *perfect* is here used in the sense of relative perfection, contrasting the mature Christians with babes in Christ who lacked the experience and development which others have obtained.]

be thus minded:—To be just what he has been saying in the preceding verses—that they have not yet obtained absolute perfection. [He did not wish his readers to think they had already reached the goal because in one sense they belong to the ranks of the mature.] They were not to forget that faith is to be made manifest in the life, and that the prize is not won because they knew it to be before them at the end of the race-course. It is only bestowed on those who run to the end.

and if in anything ye are otherwise minded, this also shall God reveal unto you:—If any do not see the full truth, God will lead them to it yet, which has its full explanation in the following: "If any man willeth to do his will, he shall know of the teaching, whether it is of God, or whether I speak from myself." (John 7: 17.) That is, if any one who desires to do the will of God does not yet see as Paul does, God will lead him into the full truth, as God promises: "And let us know, let us follow on to know Jehovah: his going forth is sure as the morning; and he will come unto us as the rain, as the latter rain that watereth the earth." (Hos. 6: 3.) To those who follow these instructions there is hope, even if it takes time. Very few persons in this world attain to the state that they have no thought, or way, or preference of their own, who fully empty themselves of all their own ways and preferences and present to God hearts with no desire but to know and to do his will. A heart in that state is perfect before God. A sincere desire to know and do his will, without any wish or preference save to do God's will, will lead into the fullness of divine truth. All should seek this state.

16 **only,**—[This term evinces the great importance of what he is now saying—while we wait for God to further reveal his will unto us, let our present attainments be the rule of our conduct, and be sure to walk in the straight line and not to stand still. The one who becomes discouraged because he realizes that others have made attainments in knowledge and life far beyond his own; and who consequently decides that it is useless for him to even try to be and do, is not the one who will attain higher things. He fails to count into his power for attainment the power of God.]

whereupon we have attained, by that same rule let us walk.—[In this passage there seems to be the same double reference which pervades all Paul's practical teaching. He is anxious for two things—that they should keep on the same course, and that all should keep on together. In both senses he addresses the *perfect;* he will have them understand that they have attained only one thing—to be in the right path, and that it is for them to continue in it; he also bids them to refrain from setting themselves up above the *imperfect;* for the very fact of division would mark them as still carnal, mere "babes in Christ." (1 Cor. 3: 1-4.)]

If some have learned more than others, those who have learned the more must be patient and forbearing, striving to help all to learn more and more of the divine truth. None of us have learned the whole of that truth. Those who know least frequently assume that they know it all, and are the most dogmatic and exclusive. When one thinks he knows all of divine truth on any subject, he knows nothing as he ought to know it. The man who has most faithfully studied the word of God realizes what a mine of precious truth there is yet to be found in its sacred treasures. Let each learn all the truth he can, weigh all the difficulties, look upon every side of the question, teach to others what he learns, sacrifice no truth, but be patient and forbearing in teaching it, and the providences of God will favor the spread of the truth. In the meantime, let him not despise or reject him who is seeking and striving to learn the will of God, because he has not learned so much of the truth as we *think we have.* Let us all, at all times, labor diligently to bring men to serve and honor God, that they may be saved, and God will care for and direct us all into the oneness that existed between him and his Son Jesus Christ.

2. OPPOSITE DESTINY OF FALSE AND TRUE BELIEVERS
3: 17 to 4: 1

17 Brethren, be ye imitators together of me, and mark them that so walk

---

17 Brethren, be ye imitators together of me,—The apostle and his colaborers are examples to all others, for all time and in all countries, as to how the truth of God is to be spread abroad. In another epistle he says: "For yourselves know how ye ought to imitate us: for we behaved not ourselves disorderly among you; neither did we eat bread for nought at any man's hand, but in labor and travail, working night and day, that we might not burden any of you: not because we have not the right, but to make ourselves an ensample unto you, that ye should imitate us." (2 Thess. 3: 7-9.) He certainly intended this to be an example to the preachers as well as to others, and shows that he did not regard his inspiration as placing him on a plane that prevented his being an example to others in his life of labor in spreading the gospel. I do not understand that he intended this as an example to others, that they were not allowed to accept help in their preaching, for he here asserts his right to receive help and in other passages reproves Christians for not aiding him, and approves them for rendering assistance as a means of their own salvation, so as to place it as beyond doubt that a teacher may receive help and that it is a duty, the neglect of which imperils their salvation, laid on Christians to help him who gives his time to proclaiming the word. The example is to teach Christians the duty of industry and of personal self-denial and labor for the spread of the truth, and that no preacher (and every Christian is a preacher) is exempted from the obligation to preach, because others fail to support him.

The first necessity in preaching the gospel is a Christian, so deeply in earnest that nothing short of death will stop him from preaching. He must feel like Paul—"woe is unto me, if I preach not the gospel." (1 Cor. 9: 16.) He must be willing to preach it in want, in suffering, in hunger, and in prison. One who is willing to preach the gospel only when he can do it without inconvenience and self-denial on his part cannot preach it as it should be preached. He may recite the facts of the gospel, but there will be none of that earnest self-consuming zeal that carries the gospel with power to the hearts of others. I am sure that the inefficiency of the gospel to save today arises chiefly from the failure of Christians to present it with the intense zeal that the great truths of the gospel would and should naturally inspire in one who truly believes it. Paul says: "Even unto this present hour we both hunger, and thirst, and are naked, and are buffeted, and have no certain dwelling-place; and we toil, working with our own hands: being reviled, we bless; being persecuted, we endure; being defamed, we entreat: we are made as the filth of the world, the offscouring of all things, even until now," and notwithstanding all this he said: "Be ye imitators of me, even as I also am of Christ." (1 Cor. 4: 11-13; 11: 1). If we are not willing to deny self, and suffer loss of all things in order to serve and honor God and save men, we have not the spirit of Christ and are none of his.

and mark them that so walk even as ye have us for an ensample.—[Just as he had counseled the Romans (16: 17) to mark those that caused "divisions and occasions of stumbling, contrary to the doctrine" which they had learned, and to turn away from them, so he here instructs his readers to watch him and other faithful servants of the Lord for imitation.]

even as ye have us for an ensample. 18 For many walk, of whom I told you often, and now tell you even weeping, *that they are* the enemies of the cross of Christ: 19 whose end is perdition, whose god is the belly, and *whose* glory

18 **For many walk, of whom I told you often,**—[We hear much of such men in the epistles, how in their boastfulness of their superior knowledge they held themselves at liberty to indulge their fleshly appetites. Their wicked character is shown in its full development in 2 Pet. 2: 1-22, and in Jude 1-16, but the knowledge falsely so called was doing its pernicious work long before, and the indulgence of all the fleshly appetites was a characteristic of a class of people claiming to be Christians. Whether the frequent warnings to which Paul here alludes were needed when he first visited Philippi, or whether they had been given subsequently is uncertain, but the word *often* gives color to the suggestion that he warned them when present, and through messengers when absent.]

and now tell you even weeping,—Years had only given him new and bitter experience of the deadly results of such an evil influence. The special sorrow most likely lay in this, that the profligacy sheltered itself under his own preaching of liberty and the superiority of the gospel over the law.

that they are the enemies of the cross of Christ:—Such men are the greatest enemies of the cause of Christ. They led away the weak by the tempting promise of liberty, which appeals so powerfully to the carnal part of man; and they also give occasion to others who hate Christ's cause to blaspheme his name. Thus their injury to the cause of Jesus Christ operates two ways—within and without the church.

19 **whose end is perdition,**—The intense severity is only paralleled by such passages as 2 Tim. 2: 1-5; 2 Pet. 2: 11-22; and Jude 4, 8, 12, 13. All express the burning indignation of a true servant of Christ against those who turn "the grace of our God into lasciviousness," and "after they have escaped the defilements of the world through the knowledge of the Lord and Saviour Jesus Christ, they are again entangled therein and overcome." [Thus they suffer the loss of everything that makes life worth living—exclusion from the kingdom of God, and the glorious eternal home of the righteous. (Rev. 22: 15.)]

is in their shame, who mind earthly things. 20 For our ¹citizenship is in heaven; whence also we wait for a Saviour, the Lord Jesus Christ: 21 who

---

¹Or, *commonwealth*

---

whose god is the belly,—They are given up to the worst kind of lusts, and find their chief satisfaction in the gratification of their animal passions. "They that are such serve not our Lord Christ, but their own belly." (Rom. 16: 18.)

and whose glory is in their shame,—They pride themselves on those very sins of which as Christians they should be deeply ashamed.

who mind earthly things.—This presents the essentially earthly character of their state of mind and heart; they think of nothing but earthly matters, have no high and heavenly thoughts and aspirations, but concentrate their whole soul upon the things of time and sense. [For such persons the upward heavenly calling of God has no attraction. They are given up to what is base, the satisfaction of the momentary desires of the flesh, and therein they live entirely, groveling like the beasts. With all their talk of high thinking and their assumption of superiority their minds are essentially concerned with things of earth and their minds seldom rise above it.]

20 for our citizenship is in heaven;—This is in contrast with those who are actuated by these sordid, groveling, earthly motives. The believer is now in this present world, a citizen in the heavenly commonwealth, those who are in Christ, whose "life is hid with Christ in God" (Col. 3: 3), for whom "to live is Christ" (Phil. 1: 21), and who "have been crucified with Christ" and live their present life by faith in him (Gal. 2: 20), and are now members of the heavenly commonwealth and live and act under its laws. Their allegiance is rendered to it. They received their impulse to action and conduct from it. Their connection with it is the basis of their life of "righteousness and peace and joy in the Holy Spirit" (Rom. 14: 17), as distinguished from the life of those "whose god is the belly, and whose glory is in their shame, who mind earthly things." They are "fellow-citizens with the saints, and of the household of God." (Eph. 2: 19.) The commonwealth of believers is an actual fact on earth, because it is one with "the Jerusalem that is above." (Gal. 4: 26.)

shall fashion anew the body of our humiliation, *that it may be* conformed to

whence also we wait for a Saviour, the Lord Jesus Christ:—[The consummation of this citizenship, however, is yet to come. As members of the heavenly commonwealth they are still pressing on in obedience to the upward call (3: 14), hence they are in an attitude of earnest expectation.]

21 who shall fashion anew the body of our humiliation,—The special aspect in which the expected Savior, the Lord Jesus Christ, is viewed is that of changing the mortal body of the believer into the likeness of his own glorified body. Our earthly mortal body that goes down to the grave, he calls the body of our humiliation, the body of death, in whose members sin reigns. (Rom. 7: 23, 24.) When Jesus comes again without sin unto salvation, he will transform our bodies into the likeness of his body in the glorified state. He will change them in nature and condition so that they will be fitted to dwell with his immortalized and glorified body. "It is sown in corruption; it is raised in incorruption: it is sown in dishonor; it is raised in glory: it is sown in weakness; it is raised in power: it is sown a natural body; it is raised a spiritual body. . . . And as we have borne the image of the earthy, we shall also bear the image of the heavenly. . . . For this corruptible must put on incorruption, and this mortal must put on immortality." (1 Cor. 15: 42-53.) The apostle says: "Beloved, now are we children of God, and it is not yet made manifest what we shall be. We know that, if he shall be manifested, we shall be like him; for we shall see him even as he is." (1 John 3: 2.) He shall thus change our mortal bodies in their nature or character and appearance, into the likeness of his glorified body. The likeness of man's spiritual nature to that of Jesus Christ must begin here on earth. Jesus will use all the power in his kingdom through his laws to transform the body of our humiliation into the likeness of his glorified body that he uses to subdue all things unto himself.

that it may be conformed to the body of his glory,—He exerts all this power in his kingdom through his laws to transform our sinful, perishing bodies into the likeness of his glorified body; but this will be done only as our spirits are conformed to his spirit. Our bodies are the homes in which our spirits dwell, and God

the body of his glory, according to the working whereby he is able even to subject all things unto himself.

1 Wherefore, my brethren beloved and longed for, my joy and crown, so stand fast in the Lord, my beloved.

---

gives a home suited to the character of the spirit. While the spirit is erring and sinful, the body in which it dwells is mortal and suffering. When the spirit shall be sinless—as Paul says: "And be not fashioned according to this world: but be ye transformed by the renewing of your mind, that ye may prove what is the good and acceptable and perfect will of God" (Rom. 12: 2)—God will give it an immortal body like to the glorified body of the Lord Jesus. When the soul is given over to sin, fitted for companionship with the devil, the body will be one of suffering and woe in hell.

according to the working whereby he is able even to subject all things unto himself.—The first transformation is that of our spirits. God will give bodies suited to our spirits. The only peace, the only refuge from turmoil and strife of earth, is in submission to the laws of God, and this molds into the likeness of God, of Jesus, who was God manifest in the flesh, the temporal and fleshly suffering with Jesus here works out a far more exceeding and eternal weight of glory and honor with him in the world to come. This reward comes through the conformation of our lives to the life of Jesus. Our bodies then will be transformed into the likeness of his glorified body there. It must be attained through practicing these laws that constitute God's code of morality for the universe, and by which all spirits must be tested and justified or condemned at the last day.

4: 1 **Wherefore,**—[By this word, just as at the conclusion of the description of "the depth of the riches both of the wisdom and the knowledge of God" (Rom. 11: 33-36), and of the glorious climax of the doctrine of the resurrection (1 Cor. 15: 35-58), Paul makes the vision of future glory to be an inspiring force, giving life to the sober, practical duties of everyday Christian life and its responsibilities. For faith which comes by hearing is not only the "assurance of things hoped for," but "a conviction of things not seen." (Heb. 11: 1.)]

my brethren beloved and longed for,—[The peculiar affectionateness of this verse is very noticeable. It is strikingly coincident with the words addressed, some years before, to another Macedonian church: "For what is our hope, or joy, or crown of glorying? Are not even ye, before our Lord Jesus at his coming? For ye are our glory and our joy." (1 Thess. 2: 19, 20.) But the passage before us impresses us deeply with the apostle's sense of loss caused by his enforced separation from them. One of his severest trials as a prisoner was that his bonds prevented his freedom of movement among the churches. Because they were his *beloved* they were longed for by him.]

my joy and crown,—[Yet, though his heart goes forth to the Philippians in great tenderness, that is not his only thought with reference to them. They had given him, as a church, nothing but delight. He tells them, therefore, of his rejoicing in the memory of them, and of their love, but looking forward to the great day when the Lord shall come, he tells them, too, that in that day their faith will be his joy and crown in the presence of the Lord, into whose service he had been privileged to bring them.]

so stand fast in the Lord, my beloved.—[Christ is to be the element in which the standing fast required of them is to have its specific character, so that in no case can the spiritual life ever act apart from the fellowship of Christ. In no other epistle so much as in this has Paul multiplied the expressions of love and praise of his readers; a strong testimony certainly as to the praiseworthy condition of the church.]

SECTION SIX

FINAL EXHORTATION TO COOPERATION BETWEEN HIMSELF AND THE PHILIPPIAN CHURCH
4: 2-20

1. INDIVIDUALS EXHORTED TO HARMONY
4: 2, 3

2 I exhort Euodia, and I exhort Syntyche, to be of the same mind in the Lord. 3 Yea, I beseech thee also, true yokefellow, help these women, for they labored with me in the ²gospel, with Clement also, and the rest of my fellow-workers, whose names are in the book of life.

²Gr. *good tidings.* See ch. 1. 5.

---

2 I exhort Euodia, and I exhort Syntyche, to be of the same mind in the Lord.—These two women are mentioned only here, no doubt of prominence in the church at Philippi, who had been at variance and had disturbed the peace and harmony of the church. Paul pled with every church to which he wrote that they might be one—united in action, maintaining the unity of the Spirit in the bonds of peace. A Christian shows his selfishness and his disregard for God when he disturbs the body of Christ to gratify his own and gain his ends. He ought to be willing to bear and suffer wrong rather than defile the temple of God.

3 Yea, I beseech thee also, true yokefellow,—Who the yokefellow was it is impossible to determine at this distance. Probably it was Epaphroditus who carried this letter to the church at Philippi, and was one of them, and was an active teacher among them.

help these women, for they labored with me in the gospel,—It is uncertain as to who these women were who had labored with him in the gospel. Many think Euodias and Syntyche were they, others think he refers to other women, who had been helpers with him in the Lord's work. The language is not specific enough to determine with certainty. Women frequently accompanied Paul in his preaching tours as colaborers, and in a modest way, they could reach their own sex to make known the gospel as men could not. Much of the preaching was done in private in the apostolic labors. It would be much more effective and thoroughly done if it were so now. That it was material help appears the more probable, because he asks that the same help be extended to Clement and others of Paul's fellow laborers.

with Clement also,—Of the Clement here mentioned we have no further knowledge for certain. He may have been the same whose Epistles to the Corinthians are preserved among the writings of the Apostolic Fathers. For Philippi was a colony of Rome, and probably in close connection with Rome. But the name was far too common for this to be at all certain.

and the rest of my fellow-workers,—We might judge from this language that even before the apostle's departure from Philippi the converts had become numerous. But in such a work every member became a teacher. The youngest true believer must tell of the Lord who had redeemed him from sin, and so became a bearer of the message of life. The sentiment became prominent among the early Christians that every member of the body should be a bearer of the message of life to others. Hence, the first spreading of the gospel was done by the "lay members" as they are now called. When the great persecution rose against the church which was in Jerusalem, they were scattered abroad throughout the regions of Judea and Samaria and went about preaching the word as they went. (Acts 8: 1-8.) And "some of them, men of Cyprus and Cyrene, who, when they were come to Antioch, spake unto the Greeks also, preaching the Lord Jesus. And the hand of the Lord was with them: and a great number that believed turned unto the Lord." (11: 19-21.) This is a clear manifestation that God intended all his children, men and women, should bear a part in the work of converting the world. And that this work was not to be confined to a select few.

I do not believe that this work was even chiefly done by public sermons. Men and women as they traveled taught those they met by the way. Around the fireside where they tarried, Christ and the resurrection constituted their theme. The direct personal appeal went from man to man and from woman to woman, simply as men and women. The unpretentious simplicity and earnestness of the appeal were its striking characteristics. There was no formality or professional dignity that separated man from man. A message like this delivered because the heart was full of the theme, full to overflowing with the earnest desire that others might share the salvation they enjoyed, found ready entrance to the heart when told by simple-minded, unpretending men and women. But few of these men, none of the women, made public addresses. Men and women today, thoroughly in earnest, full of the spirit of Christ would not wait to make sermons to men and women. They would make the direct, personal appeal to their companions, their children, to their neighbors and to their neighbors' children. They would do it as they walked by the way and as they sat in the house. If the heart is full of zeal for God and man, out of this abundance the life and mouth will speak. Zeal for God and man go together. They are inseparable. No man can feel a true zeal for God's honor and glory without feeling a corresponding anxiety for the salvation of men.

Let us direct our efforts in the direction of making Christians and churches what God desires they should be. We should not seek to substitute anything else in place of this. To do this is fatal to the cause of Christ. We should seek to make every man and every woman an earnest worker to save others. The most successful way to do this is for each to go earnestly to work. The working spirit is contagious. It is a mistake to think we can do proxy work, that we can pay others to visit the sick, look after the needy, and preach the gospel to the lost. Personal service is needed for our own personal benefit. Spiritual exercise in these things is necessary for our spiritual growth. We cannot satisfy the demands of the law of God on us for effort to save our fellow man by paying others to preach. We might give every dollar we have to others to preach, it would not release us, in the sight of God, from the obligation to teach our families, neighbors, and all with whom we come in contact, the way of life. The fatal error of this age is that we attempt to work for the cause of Christ by proxy.

In all this I have kept out of view the public proclamation of the gospel. I do not mean that this could or should be dispensed with. Public preaching is a part of the divine provision for saving men. I insist on the private personal appeal of man to man to make the public preaching effective as God intended that it should be. The private appeal is the complement of the public discourse. Both are needed. The individual Christian can in no way support the public preaching so effectively as by diligently engaging in the private preaching—both by precept and example.

whose names are in the book of life.—[For passages referring to the "book of life," see Dan. 12: 1; Rev. 3: 5; 13: 8; 17: 8; 20: 12; 21: 27. From that book the names may be "blotted out" now (Rev. 3: 5), till the end fixes it forever. There is a peculiar beauty in the allusion here. The apostle does not mention his fellow laborers by name; but it matters not—the names are written before God, in the book of life. If they continue in his service, those names shall shine out hereafter when the great names of earth shall fade into nothingness.]

2. GENERAL EXHORTATION TO JOYFULNESS
4: 4-7

4 Rejoice in the Lord always: again I will say, Rejoice. 5 Let your ³forbearance be known unto all men. The Lord is at hand. 6 In nothing be

³Or, *gentleness* Comp. 2 Cor. 10. 1.

4 Rejoice in the Lord always: again I will say, Rejoice.—When we surrender self and lose ourselves in Christ, the fountains of joy are at once opened. Having yielded the heart wholly to Christ, man is at once with himself, and in this harmony begins a joy which this world can neither give nor take away. To be in Christ as the basis of all true blessedness means that the whole of our nature shall be occupied with and upon him; though turning to him, the will submitting itself in glad obedience to his supreme commandments; and all the current of our being setting toward him in earnestness of desire, and resting in him is the secret of blessedness. If thus we are joined to the Lord, and he is in us and we in him, then we have that blessedness for which we seek. They who thus dwell in Christ by faith, love, obedience, and enjoyment can look over all the fields alive with enemies, overcome unrest, and have opened to them the source of assurance, and unto such the apostle says: "Rejoice in the Lord always: again I will say, Rejoice."

5 Let your forbearance be known unto all men.—This passage is intense—practical. It deals with pressing personal needs and problems. It lays bare a trouble which is common to almost all Christian experience; it points out the means and methods of

anxious; but in everything by prayer and supplication with thanksgiving let

relief from this trouble. He exhorts them not to become embittered and alarmed; but to let all see that they can be calm and moderate, and that they control themselves in the most trying ordeals through which they were called to pass. [Exhibit in your lives that which was such a beautiful trait in your Master's character, and do not be too insistent upon what is perhaps your just due.]

The Lord is at hand.—The Lord is near to protect and shield his people. This is given as a reason why they should ever use moderation, for the promise is: "Jehovah is nigh unto all them that call upon him, to all that call upon him in truth. He will fulfil the desire of them that fear him; he also will hear their cry, and will save them." (Psalm 145: 18, 19.)

6 **In nothing be anxious;**—Do not look with fear and dread or with anxiety to the future. [The prohibition is of that painful anxiety which is inevitable in all who feel themselves alone in mere self-dependence amidst the difficulties and dangers of life. It is possible to sink below this anxiety in mere levity and thoughtlessness; it is possible to rise above it by casting care on him who careth for us, and knowing that we are but fellow workers with him. (1 Pet. 5: 7; 2 Cor. 6: 1.)

but in everything—[Everything in respect to affliction, embarrassment, and trials; everything relating to their spiritual condition. There is nothing which pertains to body and mind which they could not go and spread it all out before the Lord.]

by prayer—The Scriptures teach plainly that God is pleased with prayer from his children and that he is more ready to hear and bless them than the kindest of earthly parents are to give good things to their children; yet the prayers of Christians are not answered as they are taught to expect, and the question arises in their minds: Does God hear and answer prayer in this age? Certainly we live in the age when prayer should be offered; and if it should be offered, it will be answered. When God ceases to answer prayer, he will not expect man to pray. But there are conditions of prayer needful to its acceptance with God. One important and essential condition is that the prayer must be in earnest and

| 4: 6, 7.] | PHILIPPIANS | 223 |

your requests be made known unto God. 7 And the peace of God, which passeth all understanding, shall guard your hearts and your thoughts in Christ Jesus.

---

from the heart. When the heart earnestly desires a thing, it bends all the energies of the soul and body to the accomplishment of the end desired. Then when the heart prays for a thing the body is brought into active service to obtain it. The earnestness of the service in seeking the obedience is the measure of the desire of the heart. The thing needed to gain acceptance and favor for our prayers is earnest, self-sacrificing labor, and devotion on our part to gain that for which we pray. Then God will hear and grant our petitions. What is needed for our own good and for the good of the world is to realize that our service to God should be more earnest and devoted. We can make our prayers prevailing prayers if we will; but we cannot do it without earnest self-sacrifice, like that made by those who did prevail with God and whose examples are given for our encouragement and imitation.

and supplication—Supplications seem to be prayer continued in strong and incessant pleadings, till the evil is averted, or the good communicated. Especially was this needful when they were enduring persecution for the sake of Jesus Christ.

with thanksgiving let your requests be made known unto God.—All this must be done in connection with thanksgiving for all the blessings received. When persecuted they should think they were counted worthy to suffer shame for his name, and thank God for it.

7 And the peace of God,—The peace and composure of spirit that God gives to them that trust him. Jesus possessed it, as he did all virtues and excellencies in a perfect degree. Nothing ever excited his fear or apprehension. Amid all dangers and trials and threatening that would appall others he was quiet and composed. Only in Gethsemane did the human assert itself, and then only for a time.

which passeth all understanding, shall guard your hearts and your thoughts—God gives all who trust him that peace of mind which no one, from a human standpoint, can understand. Paul said: "And we know that to them that love God all things work together for good" (Rom. 8: 28), which brings peace to those who truly love the Lord.

in Christ Jesus.—This assurance depends upon the strength and reality of our faith. [It is only in Christ that the mind can be preserved in peace. It is not mere confidence in God, but it is by confidence in him as he is revealed through Christ Jesus, and by faith in him. True believers, abiding in Christ, realize his promise: "Peace I leave with you; my peace I give unto you: not as the world giveth, give I unto you. Let not your heart be troubled, neither let it be fearful." (John 14: 27.)]

3. GENERAL AND FINAL SUMMONS TO CHRISTIAN PROGRESS
4: 8, 9

8 Finally, brethren, whatsoever things are true, whatsoever things are

8 **Finally, brethren,**—[He now specifies six motives which all who seek Christian perfection should keep constantly in mind; and those six elements must be realized and illustrated in the life before much headway toward Christian perfection can be attained.]

whatsoever things are true,—In accord with the word of God which is the standard of truth: "Thy word is truth." (John 17: 17.) All must stand here or be false to the core. Nothing ever stood securely without truth as a basis; nothing will stand without it stands on the bedrock of truth. This requires truth in its completeness, and in all its demands. [It is not truth in speech merely; nor in discharge of social trusts merely; it is truth in itself and for its own sake, rich with all wealth and beautiful with all comeliness. It is truth as an achievement of the mind, truth as a rule of conduct, covering all possible spheres and relations in which one can stand. A man who is false to his engagements, or false in his statements and promises, is one who will always disgrace the cause of Christ.]

whatsoever things are honorable,—Whatever is honorable in the sight of God and man. [Whatsoever things are dignified, reputable, by all who esteem high standards of action, who scrupulously conform their lives to an exalted rectitude. No ideal is lofty enough; no ideal is safe to follow until it stands for what is honor-

[4: 8.] PHILIPPIANS 225

⁴honorable, whatsoever things are just, whatsoever things are pure, whatsoever things are lovely, whatsoever things are ⁵of good report; if there be

⁴Gr. *reverend*.
⁵Or, *gracious*

---

able. It is not enough to be prudent and circumspect, and hesitate in the presence of temptation to be mean and unworthy lest standing may be lost in the estimation of the community. One is to be loyal to the honorableness which has the ring of the integrity of heaven in it, and is secure of the approbation not only of good men, but of God.]

whatsoever things are just,—[This goes to the bottom of things. One may easily test the question whether he loves and reveres justice because it is justice or looks upon it simply as an instrumentality with which to further the ends of selfishness. (1 Sam. 12: 3.) Justice maintains right relations between man and man, holds the balance fairly between conflicting interests, coordinates the rights of each withal. Love of justice is the moral part of piety, as the love of truth is the intellectual part of it. Justice is peculiar in this respect, that there are no degrees of it, as there are degrees of goodness or generosity; for a man less than just is unjust. A man, again, may do a hundred kindly acts, but if he fail in one act of justice the blemish is fatal to character. There is, therefore, great need that members of the body of Christ should be just in all their acts. Their relation to Christ does not exempt them from the laws which bind men of the world.]

whatsoever things are pure,—It is chastity and self-control, and unsullied hand and speech and thought and straightforwardness and elevated aim, and a life, lifted as far as possible out of defilement.

whatsoever things are lovely,—[This suggests the kindly graces of character. There is such a thing as being dignified and venerable, but not lovely. A Christian should not be morose, unkind, or faultfinding. Nothing tends to injure the cause of Christ more than an unlovely temper, an eye severe and unkind, a brow hard and stern.]

whatsoever things are of good report;—Well spoken of among men, and so bringing a good name. Here the word denotes

any virtue, and if there be any praise, ⁶think on these things. 9 The things

⁶Gr. *take account of.*

things in their true nature so excellent that to name them is a goodly and sacred thing—*fair-sounding*. Not merely having a fair sound to the popular ear, but fair-sounding, as implying essential worthiness.

if there be any virtue,—This points to manliness, courage, and valor; but it is to be taken as inclusive of every form of moral excellence. Christians are to have the excellence that comes from the *true,* from the *honorable,* from the *just,* from the *pure,* from the *lovely;* but lest that should not cover the whole ground of excellence, he adds, "If there be any virtue."

and if there be any praise,—[He does not intend that the Philippians should follow after all that the carnal world might praise, but that they should devote themselves to the performance of good works, which merit commendation, that the wicked and those who are enemies of the gospel, while they deride Christians and cast reproach upon them, may, nevertheless, be constrained to commend their deportment.]

think on these things.—[The word think indicates the making up of a reckoning. He had just given a list of virtues as constituents of the Christian character, and the employment of this word may have been suggested by the thought that they must add virtue after virtue, and endeavor to make the reckoning as complete as they could. Count up these things, as you do so, make an earnest endeavor to cultivate the whole.] Ponder them well and practice them faithfully. We grow like our thoughts; we cannot entertain impure thoughts without becoming corrupt, and we cannot think good thoughts without becoming pure. Meditation precedes, and works follow.

9 The things—He now gives his own life, under the direction of the Spirit of God, as the examples by which they were to judge whether the *things* bore these qualities or not. His teaching and example was the standard by which they were to judge, and no one is authorized to do anything, in the service of God, save what Paul taught by precept or example.

4: 9.] PHILIPPIANS 227

which ye both learned and received and heard and saw in me, these things do: and the God of peace shall be with you.

---

which ye both learned and received—[The only difference between "learned" and "received" seems to be that in *learned* they were pointed more to the activity of the taught; in *received* more to the activity of the teacher. The fact that Paul holds up these high categories before them shows that they were in an advanced state of activity in Christ. At the same time it was not long since they had come out of heathenism. And he refers them to such simple rules as he had laid down for their conduct.]

and heard and saw in me,—They heard when he was absent, and saw when he was present. It is well when both teaching and life go together. It was a great advantage to them that, when the rules of their life were completely changed for them, these were not only presented in their particularity, but were exemplified in the life of their teacher whom they saw among them. Thus could they be led on from a state of childhood in Christ to that state of maturity in him.

these things do:—Paul urges upon them to think of and do the things set forth in his own life—to meditate upon them as characteristic of Christian living, and practice them as they had heard them presented in his teaching, or seen them exemplified in his manner of life.]

and the God of peace shall be with you.—Paul had been guided by the Holy Spirit in what he had taught and done, and his example was the explanation of his teaching to them. If they would follow as he followed Christ, the God of peace, who brings peace, would be with them. This was the assurance of good to them in the persecutions that were upon them. [Paul knew that his own pursuit of the high standard which he set before them had brought him peace, even amid the greatest afflictions, through the dwelling presence of God. And his constant feeling of joy in the Lord, even in his chains, was a telling evidence that the God of peace was with him.]

4. THANKSGIVING FOR THE GIFTS OF LOVE FROM THEM
4: 10-20

10 But I ⁷rejoice in the Lord greatly, that now at length ye have revived your thought for me; ⁸wherein ye did indeed take thought, but ye lacked opportunity. 11 Not that I speak in respect of want: for I have learned, in whatsoever state I am, therein to be content. 12 I know how to be abased,

---

⁷Gr. *rejoiced*.
⁸Or, *seeing that*

---

10 But I rejoice in the Lord greatly,—[He had not till now expressly thanked them for their generous gift which was likely the occasion of this epistle. The very fact of his accepting it from them showed his confidence in their affection. This was indeed his right, but he seldom laid claim to it. It is quite likely that the delicacy of his language here is due to the base slanders uttered against him at Corinth and in Macedonia (1 Thess. 2: 5), as making the gospel a means of livelihood (1 Cor. 9: 3-18; 2 Cor. 11: 8, 9; Gal. 6: 6).]

that now at length ye have revived your thought for me; wherein ye did indeed take thought,—He expressly guards against wounding their feelings by connecting this statement with the next clause in which he asserts, "wherein ye did indeed take thought."

but ye lacked opportunity.—Now the opportunity presented itself, they had improved it, they had helped him.

11 Not that I speak in respect of want:—He explains that he rejoiced at the help they sent him, not that he was in want, for he had schooled himself to be content in whatever state he was.

for I have learned,—[This sums up his experiences to the moment of writing and regards them as a whole. His sense of independence of material conditions was not a natural endowment.]

in whatsoever state I am,—[The reference has in view his position at that particular time.]

therein to be content.—The contentment of faith, with a face now lighted up with unspeakable joy in God, now cast down with sorrow and wet with tears for God's enemies. The Christian martyr is the final example of the memorable protest against the evils of the world.

12 I know how to be abased,—He knew how to be brought

4: 12.]   PHILIPPIANS   229

and I know also how to abound: in everything and in all things have I learned the secret both to be filled and to be hungry, both to abound and to be in want. 13 I can do all things in him that strengtheneth me. 14 How-

---

low, to suffer need, to submit to straitened circumstances. [This was the result of the lesson he had learned. The meaning attached to the word *abased* is illustrated by what Paul said to the Corinthians: "Or did I commit a sin in abasing myself that ye might be exalted, because I preached to you the gospel of God for nought?" (2 Cor. 11: 7), where the sense of "keeping myself low" could have been made with reference to his working as a tentmaker, but more probably pointing to the comparative poverty which was the result of his self-denying action. So it comes to denote any form of adversity, a going down into reproach, poverty, or sorrow.]

and I know also how to abound:—[To overflow; the very antithesis of the thought in "to be abased."] He had experienced both extremes, but had learned how to accommodate himself to both conditions and to be content with much or little. He had so exalted the spiritual and eternal interests and considerations in contrast with these temporal matters that they had become nothing to him. He bore it for the sake of Christ, and he found such spiritual riches in him that the hunger was nothing.

in everything and in all things—In every case individually, and in all cases collectively. [Every individual circumstance of life, and life as a whole.]

have I learned the secret—The original, from which our English word "mystery" is derived, denotes the act of initiation into the secrets and privileges of the "Mystery Religions" of Greece and the East. From its use in connection with the "mysteries" the term came to have the sense of "to become familiar with," which is the meaning here—"I have been initiated into, have become familiar with, the secret."

both to be filled and to be hungry, both to abound and to be in want.—The word *filled* originally denoted the feeding of animals with grass from which it came to have the meaning of to be filled *to repletion*. Jesus said: "Blessed are they that hunger and thirst after righteousness: for they shall be filled." (Matt. 5: 6.) Paul had known both lots, and was prepared for either, just as it pleased God to send.

beit ye did well that ye had fellowship with my affliction. 15 And ye yourselves also know, ye Philippians, that in the beginning of the ²gospel, when I

---

13 I can do all things in him that strengtheneth me.—His strength to do and bear all things came from Christ, whose he was. [He traces his ability to be independent of circumstances to the indwelling of Christ. There was nothing for which Paul did not feel himself adequate, in the strength that Christ imparts. To him there belonged the fullest and completest self-sufficiency which was compatible with his utter dependence upon Christ.]

14 Howbeit ye did well that ye had fellowship with my affliction.—Notwithstanding the fact that he could bear all things, he rejoiced that they had sent to his necessities [for by their practical sympathy with him they had become sharers in his imprisonment and sufferings and had taken something of his burden upon themselves. So as it had been his own aim to know "the fellowship of his sufferings" (3: 10); to be so intimately united with Christ that his sufferings and death became their own. The union of the Christians with Christ produces a similar fellowship of Christians with Christians.]

15 And ye yourselves also know,—He reminds them of their former liberality to show his love for them; he was not unwilling to receive kindness from them.

ye Philippians,—[Paul occasionally addressed his readers directly by a general term that embraced them *all* and summed them up in one class. (2 Cor. 6: 11, 12; Gal. 3: 1.) It was always a mark of deep emotion when he was impelled to make this direct appeal so that *every* reader might feel that he was *personally* addressed. In all three cases where this direct appeal occurs it follows an autobiographical sketch in which he put prominently forward his own work and the spirit in which that work was done.] The mention by name does not mark merely, but specifies them, gratefully, and earnestly, as they were remembered and acknowledged doers of the good deed.

that in the beginning of the gospel,—At the beginning of the gospel to them at Philippi, and their churches in Macedonia. [This is one of the expressions which illustrates the very considerable importance which the apostle attached to the Macedonian mis-

departed from Macedonia, no church had fellowship with me in the matter of giving and receiving but ye only; 16 for even in Thessalonica ye sent once

---

sion as the very first definite step towards bringing the gospel to Rome, the very center of the Empire, and, therefore, toward the evangelizing of the world.]

when I departed from Macedonia,—[The time to which reference is here made is that of leaving Macedonia for Athens and Corinth. (Acts 18.: 14.) At Corinth we are informed that he received offerings from Macedonia: "When I was present with you and was in want, I was not a burden on any man; for the brethren, when they came from Macedonia, supplied the measure of my want." (2 Cor. 11: 9.) His language to the Thessalonians which is as follows: "For ye remember, brethren, our labor and travail: working night and day, that we might not burden any of you, we preached unto you the gospel of God" (1 Thess. 2: 9), "neither did we eat bread for nought at any man's hand, but in labor and travail, working night and day, that we might not burden any of you" (2 Thess. 3: 8), which precludes all idea that any part of this contribution was from Thessalonica.]

no church had fellowship with me in the matter of giving and receiving but ye only;—[At Thessalonica he met with little success or sympathy, as far as we see from the history. Yet to this church was sent the first of his episles in order of time which we possess, and it was probably written before that second missionary journey, in which Paul first visited Europe, came to an end. There was, no doubt, formed the beginning of a congregation, which the labors of those left behind nursed into a greater strength. At Berea there was more sympathy exhibited for his teaching, but neither the Thessalonians nor Bereans contributed to his support.]

16 for even in Thessalonica ye sent once and again unto my need.—They did not wait to see what others would do, they gave what they could. Not only had they contributed to his aid when he departed, but they sent "once and again." [Well might he speak so favorably of this church to the Corinthians, inasmuch as they formed such a contrast with all others. Even now how sad a picture of selfishness and ingratitude does Paul draw here in the

and again unto my need. 17 Not that I seek for the gift; but I seek for the fruit that increaseth to your account. 18 But I have all things, and abound:

---

praise he bestows upon this faithful church. The example shines so brightly only by its contrast with the prevailing selfishness.] The example of the Philippian church shines luminously by the side of many churches of the present day, doling out mere pittances to those who have spent their lives in building them up.

17 Not that I seek for the gift; but I seek for the fruit that increaseth to your account.—He desired them to do these things, not that his wants might be supplied, but for their own good. To do his teaching here, it is necessary to sum up what he said to them in this epistle concerning their duty and their discharge of the same. The Philippian church enjoyed the honor of being the first to send to Paul, and I doubt not was the most faithful in the work. He addresses the epistle "to all the saints in Christ Jesus that are at Philippi, with the bishops and deacons." These constituted the church in its organized state. He further says: "I thank my God upon all my remembrance of you, always in every supplication of mine on behalf of you all making my supplication with joy, for your fellowship in furtherance of the gospel from the first day unto now; . . . even as it is right for me to be thus minded on behalf of you all, because I have you in my heart, inasmuch as, both in my bonds and in the defence and confirmation of the gospel, ye all are partakers with me of grace." (1: 3-7.) They had so helped him in his imprisonment; and when proclaiming and confirming the gospel that they all—the whole church—became partakers of whatever grace he enjoyed. They had fellowshipped him; all the saints, with the bishops and deacons, had done this, so that whatever grace he enjoyed from his work they were with him partakers of it. He informs them what he means by administering to him: "I counted it necessary to send to you Epaphroditus, my brother and fellow-worker and fellow-soldier, and your messenger and minister to my need." (2: 25.)

Those themselves not preaching may have fruit in new converts made, or in the word of God multiplied by sustaining and aiding those who are preaching, with their money and their prayers. Their prayers are an abomination unless accompanied by the free,

> I am filled, having received from Epaphroditus the things *that came* from you, an odor of a sweet smell, a sacrifice acceptable, well-pleasing to God.

cheerful, and glad use of their money to aid in the work. Each Christian is to give personal help and sympathy to the poor, the sick, the naked, in shame and imprisonment. Those having goods must distribute them with free and cheerful hands, in a word, they are to use their money freely and cheerfully, to honor God, uphold and extend his cause, and to help those who have given their lives to the extension of God's kingdom, now old and in need. We are to embrace every opportunity to do good. The measure of our labor and sacrifice is the necessity of God's cause and man's sufferings. My deliberate conviction from the study of God's instructions on this subject is that God will call it robbery of him for his professed servants to neglect those who have worn out their lives in the service of God and man, now old, sick, and in dire need.

18 But I have all things, and abound:—He had through their kindness all he needed.

I am filled, having received from Epaphroditus the things that came from you,—Epaphroditus was the messenger of the church, through whom they sent their bounty to Paul, by which they had fellowship with him in his work—bore his burdens and shared his rewards; hence he says of these gifts, "Not that I seek for the gift; but I seek for the fruit that increaseth to your account." The gifts that were sent him by them were placed to their account.

an odor of a sweet smell, a sacrifice acceptable, well-pleasing to God.—All sacrifice made in Christ's name to help those who preach the gospel goes up to God as an odor of a sweet smell, a sacrifice acceptable and well-pleasing to God. [Whatever is done to the servant is done for the Master, and whatever is done for Christ brings abundant recompense. The gift, therefore, is seed producing already a harvest of blessing for its generous donors; and a sacrifice laid upon the altar of God is a gift, therefore, is seed producing already a harvest of blessing for its generous donors; and a sacrifice laid upon the altar of God is a gift which he will receive, and with which he is pleased. The figure was very common of sacrifices in the Old Testament times. (Gen. 8: 21;

19 And my God shall supply every need of yours according to his riches in glory in Christ Jesus. 20 Now unto ⁹our God and Father *be* the glory ¹⁰for ever and ever. Amen.

⁹Or, *God and our Father*
¹⁰Gr. *unto the ages of the ages.*

Ex. 29: 18.) The gift was a spiritual sacrifice. They were not actually buying grace, but they pleased God with this proof of their love and loyalty. (Rom. 12: 1; Heb. 13: 16; 1 Pet. 2: 5.) Surely these are golden words for the loving tokens from the Philippians.]

19 **And my God shall supply every need of yours**—He assures them that his God in return for their favors to him would supply all their needs. This is a promise that God will bless abundantly and multiply the seed to those who freely give to God. No more distinct promise of earthly good was ever made to the Jews. The same promise is distinctly made to the Philippians. Some erroneously think that under the Jewish law temporal blessings alone were promised—under the Christian, the promise of temporal blessings has not been withdrawn, they are as great as under the Mosaic law, but through Christ the spiritual blessings have been added. Hence Christ says: "He shall receive a hundredfold now . . . and in the world to come eternal life." (Mark 10: 30.) [God has unlimited resources and love. The measure of his beneficence is "the unsearchable riches of Christ." (Eph. 3: 8.)]

according to his riches in glory in Christ Jesus.—This teaches the lesson frequently expressed in the New Testament, that if we will freely sacrifice for Christ, he will so bless us that we will need no good thing.

20 **Now unto our God and Father be the glory for ever and ever.**—[The glory belongs to God as our Father. Let us freely and gladly give it to him. Our glory in the end will be to see Jesus the crowned King of kings and Lord of lords, and enjoy the blessings he has in store for the faithful. That will be glory for us.]

Amen.—[This word is used for the purpose of adopting as his own what had just been said—"so it is," or "so shall it be." The word is limited to religious atmosphere, being on human lips an expression of faith that God holds the thing true, or will or can make it true. At the close of public prayers, thanksgivings, benedictions, or doxologies the people used to say, "Amen" (Neh. 8: 6), and in the service of the synagogue (Psalm 41: 13). That this custom passed over from the synagogue to the Christian assemblies we gather from 1 Cor. 14: 16, where Paul speaks of the customary, *Amen,* by the listeners at the close of the thanksgiving.]

SECTION SEVEN

SALUTATIONS AND BENEDICTION
4: 21-23

21 Salute every saint in Christ Jesus. The brethren that are with me salute you. 22 All the saints salute you, especially they that are of Cæsar's household.
23 The grace of the Lord Jesus Christ be with your spirit.

---

21 Salute every saint in Christ Jesus.—To salute is to bear assurance of love and kindness for persons. He asks those who should read the epistle to bear the assurance of his love and goodwill to every saint at Philippi. The spirit of Christian brotherhood was to prevail.

The brethren that are with me salute you.—The brethren who were with him were his companions in his imprisonment, not that they were imprisoned, but a number remained near him to render assistance in his works, to comfort and encourage him. These all sent their salutations, or assurances of love and goodwill to the saints at Philippi.

22 All the saints salute you,—The church members in Rome generally, as distinguished from the smaller circle just mentioned.

especially they that are of Caesar's household.—The saints of Cæsar's household could hardly be his own family. But he kept, as emperors did, a large number of servants, guards, and retainers. Any servant or guard would be called of his household. Some of these had become Christians, and sent brotherly salutations to the church at Philippi.

23 The grace of the Lord Jesus Christ be with your spirit.—[The normal method of closing a letter at that period was by the mere use of *farewell*, as is shown by the many *papyrus* letters, discovered in recent years, as well as by letters included in the New Testament itself. (Acts 15: 29.) Paul, however, uses a formula of his own: "The salutation of me Paul with mine own hand, which is the token in every epistle: so I write. The grace of our Lord Jesus Christ be with you all." (2 Thess. 3: 17, 18.) His signature was also different from that employed by the other apostolic writers, for Peter and John invoke *peace* and not *grace* as their parting blessings. (1 Pet. 5: 14; 3 John 14.) Paul's simplest greeting in its simplest form is: "Grace be with you" (Col. 4: 18), and reaches its highest development in: "The grace of the Lord Jesus Christ, and the love of God, and the communion of the Holy Spirit, be with you all" (2 Cor. 13: 14). But in every form, simple or elaborate, *grace* is the essential constitutent and in every instance except in Col. 4: 18 it is "the *grace* of our *Lord Jesus Christ*" that is emphasized. This is the core of the apostle's message. It is through the grace given by Christ and through the right use of it that man learns something of the love which God has for man as it is through the grace of Christ that the love of God manifests itself and is reflected in the love which man has for his fellow man. Even in the full benediction *grace* comes first, and here Paul is following the line of his own experience. It was the *grace* of our Lord Jesus Christ that revealed to him the love of the Father in all its infinite richness, it is his *grace* that made it possible for him to become partaker of the Holy Spirit, by which he became inseparably united to Christ and to whose divine influence he was indebted for all that was of value in his life.]

COMMENTARY ON THE EPISTLE
TO THE COLOSSIANS

CONTENTS

	Page
INTRODUCTION	243
I. Colossæ	243
II. Origin of the Colossian error	243
III. Time and place of writing	245

SECTION ONE

CHRIST THE HEAD OF ALL THINGS IN CREATION AND REDEMPTION (1: 1-29) 247

1. Address and greeting (1: 1, 2) 247
2. Thanksgiving for the faith and love of the Colossian Christians (1: 3-8) 249
3. Prayer for their progress in the knowledge of Christ as head of all things (1: 9-23) 253
4. The apostle's joy in his sufferings and labors for Christ (1: 24-29) 266

SECTION TWO

BE NOT LED AWAY FROM CHRIST THE HEAD (2: 1-23) 273

1. Importance of the subject (2: 1-7) 273
2. Reason why they should be steadfast and not drawn away by the influence of false teachers (2: 8-15) 276
3. Warnings against ritualistic prohibitions and against angel worship (2: 16-19) 282
4. These enforced by the fact of their having died with Christ (2: 20-23) 285

SECTION THREE

LIVE AS THOSE SHOULD LIVE WHO HAVE RISEN WITH CHRIST (3: 1 to 4: 6) 288

1. Fellowship with the exalted Christ the motive to the new life (3: 1-4) 288
2. Exhortations—negative and positive (3: 5-17) 290

	Page

3. Special precepts as to household relations (3: 18 to 4: 1) 301

4. Exhortations in relation to prayer and conduct towards those without (4: 2-6) 307

SECTION FOUR

CONCLUDING EXHORTATIONS (4: 7-18) 310

1. Personal intelligence (4: 7-9) 310
2. Salutations and messages (4: 10-17) 312
3. Farewell greeting (4: 18) 319

INTRODUCTION TO COLOSSIANS

I. COLOSSAE

Colossæ was a city of Phrygia on the Lycus River, one of the headstreams of the Maeander. It stood at the head of a gorge where the two streams unite, and on the great highway traversing the country from Ephesus to the Euphrates Valley, twelve miles from Hierapolis and ten miles from Laodicea. Its history is chiefly associated with that of the two cities. Early, according to Herodotus and Xenophon, it was a place of great importance. As the neighboring cities, Hierapolis and Laodicea, increased, the importance of Colossæ declined. Nevertheless it continued to be one of the most important meeting places of the East and the West. While its permanent population was Phrygian, with a mixture of Greeks and Jews, it was constantly visited by travelers of all nationalities, who kept it always simmering with new ideas.

II. ORIGIN OF THE COLOSSIAN ERROR

The three cities mentioned were the mission field of Epaphras, and his labors seem to have been crowned with success. These chuches were planted and grew rapidly. But it was that kind of rapidity that does not promise permanent success. It was too feverish to be healthy. Some of those who eagerly expressed their faith in Christ brought with them many of the cherished ideas of the time, partly Jewish and partly pagan, which they saw no reason to discard but which they were ready to defend as an important, indeed essential, part of God's message to man. They endeavored to prove that the old faith could live with the new; that a man might become a Christian without discarding any of his principles or prejudices. The result was that the gospel was soon in imminent danger of being submerged by a rising tide of non-Christian beliefs and practices. Epaphras became alarmed, and went the long, perilous journey to Rome to consult with Paul about the situation.

At the beginning of the Christian era, in consequence of the decay of the national and popular religions, all the permutations and combinations of beliefs new and old were being tried. The Lycus valley, a hotbed of theosophy, gnosticism, and mysticism, was the natural scene of the most striking of these experiments. The new teachers at Colossæ carefully refrained from saying anything directly opposed to the gospel. They merely called it *imperfect,* and professed to be able to supplement it. They claimed to know the way to lead the Christian beginner onward and upward to perfection; that they were able to initiate him into the mysteries of the higher life. That they could put into his hand the key of philosophy. They taught that as the flesh is the seat of sin, it must be mortified; strict dietary rules must be observed; the festivals of the Mosaic law must be observed; and in general life was to be regulated in accordance with the best human traditions from whatever quarter they may have come, and as Paul's idea of God was so one-sided, failing to explain the original relation between the supreme God and sinful matter, and so to lay the foundation for a scheme of reconciliation, it must be balanced by a doctrine of the mediation of angels, æons, or elemental spirits. And the gospel which Epaphras preached must be supplemented by the splendid visions of the mystic and meritorious practices of the ascetics. Redemption was not the function of Christ alone; the labor was divided among the whole host of God's angelic ministers, before whom men must bow in trembling adoration.

It is a well-known fact that much of the Lord's teaching was elicited by the errors of his disciples, so also was much of Paul's teaching brought forth by the errors of the churches. The doctrine of the Colossian epistle is the gospel restated in contact with the philosophy of one of the centers of Greek culture. To the doctrine of the mediation of angels Paul opposes the grandest and fullest conception of the person and work of Christ that is found in God's message to the lost and sin-cursed world. He presses three normative conceptions upon the minds of his readers—the uniqueness of Christ's personality, the completeness of his work, and the finality and perfection of his revelation. The Colossians sought a true idea of God—in Christ dwells all the fullness of the Godhead bodily, of creation—Christ is the creator of all created being, including the angelic orders; of history—all things are from Christ and unto Christ; or redemption—believers in Christ are all buried with him in baptism, and rise with him to walk in newness of life; of atonement—Jesus Christ has by the blood of the cross secured the sinner's peace. They sought a philosophy—in Christ are all the treasures of wisdom and knowledge hidden; a higher life—it "is hidden with Christ in God." They sought initiation into the mysteries of God—Christ is the open secret of the universe. They desired to obtain perfection—man is complete in Christ.

III. TIME AND PLACE OF WRITING

Colossians, Ephesians, and Philemon were evidently written from Rome, sometime in the year 62. There are many links of connection between them. Tychicus was the bearer of both Ephesians and Colossians (Eph. 6: 21, 22; Col. 4: 7, 8), and Onesimus, the subject of Philemon, was companion of Tychicus (Col. 4: 9). Greetings are sent in Colossians and Philemon to the same group of friends. (Col. 4: 10, 12, 14; Phile. 23, 24.) In Phile. 2 a message is sent to Archippus, and in Col. 4: 17 we learn that he was a very useful man in the church at Colossæ.

COMMENTARY ON THE EPISTLE TO THE COLOSSIANS

SECTION ONE

CHRIST THE HEAD OF ALL THINGS IN CREATION AND REDEMPTION
1: 1-29

1. ADDRESS AND GREETING
1: 1, 2

1 Paul, an apostle of Christ Jesus through the will of God, and Timothy ¹our brother, 2 ²to the saints and faithful brethren in Christ *that are* at Colossæ: Grace to you and peace from God our Father.

¹Gr. *the brother*
²Or, *to those that are at Colossae, holy and faithful brethren in Christ*

---

1 Paul, an apostle of Christ Jesus—Paul did not always bring his apostolic authority to mind at the beginning of his epistles. To the Thessalonians he had not then adopted the practice. In the joyous epistle to the Philippians, he had no need to urge his authority, for none among them ever questioned it. In that to Philemon, friendship is uppermost, and though he says, "I have all boldness in Christ to enjoin thee that which is befitting, yet for love's sake I rather beseech," and did not command as an apostle, but besought him as a prisoner of Jesus. In other epistles he puts his authority in the foreground as here, and its basis in the will of God is asserted with emphasis in the epistle to the Galatians, where he had to deal with more defiant opposition than elsewhere encountered.

through the will of God,—This is assertion of divine authority, a declaration of independence of all human teaching or appointment, and a disclaimer of individual merit, or personal power. The weight to be attached to his words was due entirely to their being the words which God spoke through him.

and Timothy our brother,—He associates Timothy with him in this epistle, as he usually did the faithful and prominent teachers with him.

2 to the saints—The root idea of the word, which is an Old Testament word, is not moral purity, but separation to God. The holy things of the old covenant were things apart from ordinary use to the service of God. For that reason on the high priest's mitre was written, "HOLY TO JEHOVAH." (Ex. 28: 36.) [So the solemn obligation on all Christians is to separate from the world and devote themselves to God. We are Christians if we give ourselves up to God, in the surrender of our will and practical obedience of our lives—so far and not one step further. We are not merely bound to this consecration if we are Christians, but we are not Christians unless we thus consecrate ourselves. The true consecration is the surrender of the will, which no man can do for us, and the one motive which will lead us selfish and stubborn men to bow our necks to that gentle yoke, and to come out of the misery of pleasing self into the peace of serving God, is drawn from the great love of him who devoted himself to God and man "who gave himself for us, that he might redeem us from all iniquity, and purify unto himself a people for his own possession, zealous of good works." (Tit. 2: 14.)]

and faithful—They were faithful as well as saints. We are united to Christ by faith. The church is a family of believing men and women consecrated to the service of God.

brethren—This points not merely to Christian love, but to common possession of a new life. If we are brethren, it is because we have one father, because in us all there is one life. The name proclaims that all Christians are born into the family through faith in Jesus Christ, and thereby partake of a common new life, which makes all its possessors children of God, and therefore brethren one of another. It is the expression of the real bond which gathers all believers into one family, and declares the mightiest privilege of the gospel that to "as many as received him, to them gave he the right to become children of God, even to them that believe on his name: who were born, not of blood, nor of the will of the flesh, nor of the will of man, but of God." (John 1: 12, 13.)

in Christ—They were believers in him, "baptized into Christ Jesus" (Rom. 6: 3), brethren in him. That spiritual but most real union of Christians with their Lord is never far away from Paul's thoughts, and in the Ephesian epistle it is the very burden of the whole. To be "in him" is to be "made full" (Col. 2: 10); "in him" is to be blessed "with every spiritual blessing" (Eph. 1: 3);

"in him dwelleth all the fulness of the Godhead bodily, and in him ye are made full" (Col. 2: 9, 10). If we live in him, we live in purity and joy. And John says: "I heard a voice from heaven saying, Write, Blessed are the dead who die in the Lord from henceforth; yea, saith the Spirit, that they may rest from their labors; for their works follow with them." (Rev. 14: 13.)

that are at Colossae—The epistle was addressed to the saints at Colossæ, set apart to the service of God, sanctified by receiving the word of God as the rule of their life.

Grace to you and peace from God our Father.—He gives the usual salutation in the form of a prayer. [Grace and peace are comprehensive words. In Christ grace is included in all God's gracious giving. It is the consummation of the unspeakable gift (2 Cor. 9: 15), and of all the blessings that come to man through Christ. Peace is the harmony and satisfaction which comes into a life that has accepted God's grace, is reconciled to God, and rests in assurance of the forgiveness of sins.]

2. THANKSGIVING FOR THE FAITH AND LOVE OF THE COLOSSIAN CHRISTIANS
1: 3-8

3 We give thanks to God the Father of our Lord Jesus Christ, praying

---

3 We give thanks—In all Paul's epistles to churches, with the exception of that to the Galatians, the salutation is followed by thanksgiving. [It was ever his way to appreciate before criticizing. There was much in the condition of the Colossians for which he most heartily thanked God—their faith and love, strengthened by their hope of the coming of the Lord; their personal acceptance of the world-wide gospel; their regard for Epaphras who had labored among them so faithfully for years, and who was then in Rome with a heart full of gratitude for their kindness.]

to God the Father of our Lord Jesus Christ,—He to whom Paul gives thanks is God, the divine person whom Jesus addressed as *Father*. (John 17: 1, 5, 11, 21, 24, 25.) [The usual form is "the God and Father of our Lord Jesus Christ." (Rom. 15: 6; 2 Cor. 1: 3; 11: 31.) Paul did not hesitate to use "God of our Lord Jesus Christ" as Jesus himself did to Mary Magdalene: "I ascend

always for you, 4 having heard of your faith in Christ Jesus, and of the love which ye have toward all the saints; 5 because of the hope which is laid up

---

unto my Father and your Father, and my God and your God." (John 20: 17.) The use of *Lord* with Jesus Christ shows the high sense of the term here. Jesus Christ stands on the same plane with God the Father.]

praying always for you,—Thanksgiving was a part of the apostle's prayers and doubtless both were closely united in his mind. He thanked God whenever he prayed for them, having heard of their faith and love. [It is probable that *always* belonged both to "give thanks" and to "praying."]

4 having heard of your faith—This gratitude grew out of the good report he had heard about them from Epaphras. (1: 8.) Whatever may be the force of the words, clearly here they harmonize with many indications that the Colossian church, though well known to Paul, was not known by personal knowledge.

in Christ Jesus,—Their faith in Christ denotes that it moved in the sphere of Jesus Christ. (2 Tim. 1: 13.) It was more than fidelity; it was Christ-centered faith.

and of the love which ye have toward all the saints,—Faith in Christ Jesus and love toward all the saints are inseparably connected—one produces the other. The leading truth of Christ Jesus as the Son of God was his love to man, especially to those redeemed and purchased by his blood. No one can have a living faith in Christ without it sharing itself in love for man, especially those of the household of faith. [Faith in the Lord Jesus Christ as the Messiah brings fellowship with one another and disregards all bounds of race or nations, class or set. Their love for one another grew out of their faith and love for Christ. "We know that we have passed out of death into life, because we love the brethren." (1 John 3: 14.) By this same test the Colossians had given the proof of their faith.]

5 because of the hope which is laid up for you—Paul gives thanks (connecting back with verses 3, 4) for the hope laid up in heaven of which they had learned through the gospel. The thing reserved in heaven for them, which they learned through the gospel, was eternal life, with its blessings and glories. Jesus came to

for you in the heavens, whereof ye heard before in the word of the truth of the ³gospel, 6 which is come unto you; even as it is also in all the world

³Gr. *good tidings:* and so elsewhere; see marginal note on Mt. 4. 23.

bring life and immortality to light. He died on the cross to open the future to man, showing how little this short and sorrowful life is compared with the future eternal life.

in the heavens,—The plural is a Hebrew conception, which probably originated in such language as: "Behold, unto Jehovah thy God belongeth heaven and the heaven of heavens, the earth, with all that is therein." (Deut. 10: 14.) Solomon in his prayer (1 Kings 8: 27) used the same expression. The rabbis spoke of two heavens, and Paul of the third heaven. (2 Cor. 12: 2.) It appears to be a superlative expression here, including all regions and spheres of the unseen world.]

whereof ye heard before in the word of the truth of the gospel,—[This refers to the gospel not chiefly of graciousness and mercy, but rather as the revelation of eternal truths, itself changeless as the truth it reveals. He was not teaching them anything new, but his purpose was to confirm them in the true doctrine which they had already received. The gospel was then winning its way over the hearts of sincere men and women. Hence the need of warning against the growth of the wild speculations of false teachers who had crept in among them.]

6 which is come unto you;—The gospel had reached them and was abiding with them. [The success of the gospel at Colossæ was a gratifying evidence, both of its inherent truthfulness and of its rapid progress in the Gentile world.]

even as it is also in all the world—"All the world" refers most likely to all parts of the Roman Empire. The gospel has gone into all divisions of it, yet not to every person. He says: "The gospel which ye heard, which was preached in all creation under heaven." (1: 23.) This means that it had gone into all the different parts of the known world, or the Roman Empire. [To Paul, held as a prisoner at Rome, and with his messengers coming and going, and news reaching him from time to time of the advance of the cause of Christ, the strong expression "all the world" was natural to him. From Rome "all the world" is surveyed, just as what took place at Rome seemed to be "proclaimed throughout

bearing fruit and increasing, as *it doth* in you also, since the day ye heard and knew the grace of God in truth; 7 even as ye learned of Epaphras our be-

---

the whole world." (Rom. 1: 8.) The readers then are assured that the gospel which has come to and remains with them is the same as in the whole world; they need have no fear that it was imperfect; it is the false teachers that are not in agreement with the universal gospel.]

bearing fruit and increasing,—From the day they heard the gospel and knew the grace, mercy, and love of God in reality, it brought forth fruit in manifesting love to all the saints. Knowing what God had done for them inspired their hearts to do good for others. They showed the same spirit of devotion and sacrifice for others that Christ showed for them. Believing in Christ transferred to their hearts the mind that was in him which led him to leave the Father's throne, take upon himself the form of a servant, and made subject to the death of the cross to redeem them from death. [The figure is borrowed from a fruit-bearing tree which both bears fruit and grows. (Matt. 7: 17; 13: 32; Luke 13: 9.) *Bearing* refers to the faith, the love, the Christian virtues which the gospel produces in the internal and external life; *increasing* to the extension and multiplication of its adherents. (Acts 6: 7; 12: 24; 19: 20.)]

as it doth in you also,—[This points to Colossæ as part of the field in which the gospel was fruitful and growing, furnishing a proof of its efficiency.] When a man in truth and reality understands and knows this grace of God to man, it will bear fruit in his heart and life in doing good, showing love to others.

since the day ye heard and knew the grace of God in truth; —[The Colossians had experienced the love of Christ and his gracious salvation and knew this truth not only in their reception, but as realities, but essentially different from the doctrines of the false teachers.]

7 even as ye learned of Epaphras—Epaphras was apparently the founder of the Colossian church. He had remained in connection with it (4: 12), and seems to have come to Paul to inform him of the presence of false teachers whose doctrines were threatening its welfare.

loved fellow-servant, who is a faithful minister of Christ on ⁴our behalf, 8 who also declared unto us your love in the Spirit.

⁴Many ancient authorities read *your*.

our beloved fellow-servant,—It is noticeable that he alone of all Paul's companions received the name *fellow servant,* which may perhaps point to some very special piece of service he had rendered to Paul.

who is a faithful minister of Christ—The Colossians had learned the truth of Epaphras, who had been faithful in declaring to them the gospel of Christ.

on our behalf,—In these words Paul endorses his teaching as a true representative of his own. [They further indicate that Epaphras was a messenger of Paul, sent possibly at the time when he was stationed at Ephesus, and when "all they that dwelt in Asia heard the word of the Lord, both Jews and Greeks." (Acts 19: 10.) This explains the attitude of authority toward a church which he had not seen.]

8 **who also declared unto us your love**—By this he means that Epaphras had come to Rome and there told Paul the story of the Colossian church. Consequently, from Epaphras the Colossians heard the good news of salvation, and Paul hears the report of the good work at Colossæ from Epaphras.

in the Spirit.—This implies genuine Christian love, which is "the fruit of the Spirit." (Gal. 5: 22.) The love here would seem to be especially towards Paul, a part of the love "toward all the saints." (1: 4.)

3. PRAYER FOR THEIR PROGRESS IN THE KNOWLEDGE OF CHRIST AS HEAD OF ALL THINGS
1: 9-23

9 For this cause we also, since the day we heard *it,* do not cease to pray and make request for you, that ye may be filled with the knowledge of his

9 **For this cause**—This refers to the entire preceding paragraph, because of what had been heard respecting the Colossian church.

we also, since the day we heard it,—The receipt of the intelligence produced immediate results and led to prayer.

do not cease to pray and make request for you, that ye may be filled with the knowledge of his will—[To be so filled that

will in all spiritual wisdom and understanding, 10 to walk worthily of the

every part of their being should be permeated, and thus controlled and elevated by an intelligent comprehension of the will of God.] At the time this was written the full will of God had not been revealed and collected. The preaching was done chiefly by men partially inspired, or gifted, and they were not able to teach the whole will of God. Even the apostoes did not know it all at once. Some things were revealed to one that were not to another, and Paul and Barnabas had to go up to Jerusalem to the other apostles that they might have a decision from the whole body on the question of the circumcision of the Gentiles. Then there was disputing, conferring, and hearing what had been revealed to the different ones before the decision was reached. (Acts 15: 1-29.) There was then a care and anxiety that those taught by the less gifted should be taught the whole will of God.

in all spiritual wisdom and understanding,—The combination of wisdom and understanding is what we all need, and is that for which Paul prayed on behalf of the Colossians. [One may have intellectual attainments and his mind filled with learning without being wise. In the knowledge of God's will both wisdom and insight are required. He prays that amid such wisdom and understanding they may be made full with a fullness embracing intelligent acquaintance with the will of God. The progress does not consist in leaving behind old truths, but in profounder conception of what is contained in these truths. The law of the Christian life is continuous increase in the knowledge of the depths that lie in the old truths, and of their far-reaching applications. We are to grow in knowledge of the Christ by coming ever nearer to him, and learning more of the infinite meaning of our earliest lesson that he is the Son of God who died for us.]

10 to walk—To know and do his will and to conform to the directions given is to walk worthy of him. So the principle is brought out here very distinctly, that the last result of knowledge of the divine will is an outward life regulated by the will of the Lord.

worthily of the Lord—[We are to walk in a manner corresponding to what the Lord is to us, and has done for us. There

[1: 10, 11.] COLOSSIANS 255

Lord ⁵unto all pleasing, bearing fruit in every good work, and increasing ⁶in the knowledge of God; 11 ⁷strengthened ⁸with all power, according to the

⁵Or, *unto all pleasing, in every good work, bearing fruit and increasing &c.*
⁶Or, *by*
⁷Gr. *made powerful.*
⁸Or, *in*

---

are other forms of the same thought in the following expressions: "I therefore, . . . beseech you to walk worthily of the calling wherewith ye were called" (Eph. 4: 1), "that ye receive her in the Lord, worthily of the saints" (Rom. 16: 2), "let your manner of life be worthy of the gospel of Christ" (Phil. 1: 27), and "to the end that ye should walk worthily of God" (1 Thess. 1: 12). In all these passages there is the idea of a standard to which our practical life is to be conformed.]

unto all pleasing,—To be holy, upright, truthful, full of mercy, and compassion is to please God. This ennobles and exalts life. [No thought will so spur us to diligence and make all life solemn and grand as the thought that "we make it our aim, whether at home or absent, to be well-pleasing unto him." (2 Cor. 5: 9.) Nothing will free one from being entangled with the things of this world as the ambition to "please him who enrolled him as a soldier." (2 Tim. 2: 4.)]

bearing fruit in every good work,—To be fruitful is to bear much fruit in every good work. Good works are all to be tested and proved·by the will of God as the perfect standard of all good. We grow as we learn and bear fruit. [Sometimes the loudest proclaimers of the truth are the poorest performers of it. Fruit bearing is more difficult than mere denunciation of error, but it is a more effective answer in the end. It is the best protection for those tempted by error. It is a sad situation if the "most orthodox" have a bad reputation, not to say bad character.]

and increasing in the knowledge of God;—To increase in the knowledge of God is to so increase in the knowledge of his will that we may understand better what good works are, and how they are to be performed. Everything that seems good to a man's own eyes is not good in the eyes of the Lord. Hence what God orders is the only standard of good.

11 strengthened with all power,—As one learns more of the truth and walks more faithfully in it, he is strengthened by the

might of his glory, unto all ⁹patience and longsuffering with joy; 12 giving thanks unto the Father, who made ¹⁰us meet to be partakers of the inheri-

⁹Or, *steadfastness*
¹⁰Some ancient authorities read *you*.

---

might of God. This strength from God comes through knowing and doing the will of God. Jesus said: "If a man love me, he will keep my word: and my Father will love him, and we will come unto him, and make our abode with him." (John 14: 23.) For the Father and Son to abide with him is to make him strong.

according to the might of his glory,—This strikes one as unusual, but elsewhere says: "Our light affliction, which is for the moment, worketh for us more and more exceedingly an eternal weight of glory." (2 Cor. 4: 17.)

unto all patience and longsuffering with joy;—The strength that God gives by his glorious power is strength to be patient, to suffer long with joyfulness. The one made strong by God is able to withstand temptations and trials and sufferings with patience and joyfulness. [The ground of such joy is given by the apostle in these words: "Insomuch as ye are partakers of Christ's sufferings, rejoice; that at the revelation of his glory also ye may rejoice with exceeding joy." (1 Pet. 4: 13.) This enabled the Christians to meet all their trials with a buoyant sense of mastery. Paul and Silas illustrated this at Philippi when, after having been beaten and thrust into prison, they sang praises unto God. (Acts 16: 22-25.) The possession of such power would render the Colossians impregnable against the follies and sinfulness of the false teachers.]

12 giving thanks unto the Father,—Here Paul prays that the Colossian Christians may have the grace of gratitude for what God has done for them, and for the provisions of his grace in Christ, which is a part of the worthy walk for which he prays on their behalf.

who made us meet—We have here the deepest grounds for thanksgiving, which are likewise the preparations for a true estimate of the worth of Christ who gives them. The grounds of thanksgiving are but various aspects of the one great blessing of salvation. The language points distinctly to a definite past act by which the Father at a definite time made us "meet," delivered, and translated us by a definite act in the past, but is continuously and

1: 12, 13.] COLOSSIANS 257

tance of the saints in light; 13 who delivered us out of the power of dark-

progressively possessed at present. Paul and those associated with him labored under the commission, given by the Lord after his resurrection (Matt. 28: 19, 20; Mark 16: 15, 16), which made all who heard and obeyed the gospel (Rom. 1: 16) "meet" to be partakers of the inheritance.

to be partakers of the inheritance of the saints—The word inheritance and the word *saints*, which never throws off its Old Testament reference, and which has here its usual New Testament meaning of *set apart to the service of God*, recall the division of Canaan among the Israelites. Similarly the Lord said to Saul of Tarsus: "I send thee [to the Gentiles] to open their eyes, that they may turn from darkness to light and from the power of Satan unto God that they may receive remission of sins and an inheritance among them that are sanctified by faith in me." (Acts 26: 17, 18.) Compare: "And ye shall inherit the land by lot according to your families" (Num. 33: 54), where lot is the instrument of allotment, and 32: 19; Josh. 17: 6 where it is an allotted portion of the land, and "Wherefore Levi hath no portion nor inheritance with his brethren; Jehovah is his inheritance, according as Jehovah thy God spake unto him." (Deut. 10: 9.) The inheritance of the saints includes the whole portion of spiritual blessing of God's family on earth.

in light—[Light is characteristic of everything pertaining to the inheritance of the saints. Their eternal home will be a world of light, as God is light and dwells in light. (1 John 1: 5; 1 Tim. 6: 16; Rev. 21: 24.) And the glory of that splendor will illumine their path on earth. (2 Cor. 4: 6; Eph. 5: 8.) Since the inheritance of the saints is both a present possession and a future enjoyment, the words *in light* must have the same double reference. The sons of God are already heirs (Rom. 8: 16, 17), and therefore in the light, and the light in which they walk is an *earnest* of their share of the allotment of blessing which belongs to the faithful children of God in heaven.]

13 who delivered us out of the power of darkness,—As light is of God, darkness is of the evil one. He who is under the rule of the evil one is under the power of darkness. God has delivered

ness, and translated us into the kingdom of the Son of his love; 14 in whom we have our redemption, the forgiveness of our sins: 15 who is the image of the invisible God, the firstborn of all creation; 16 for in him were all things

Christians from the power of darkness, from the service and dominion of the evil one.

and translated us into the kingdom of the Son of his love;—The kingdom of the Son of his love is the church or rule he has established here on earth. It is in contrast with the power of darkness. All out of the kingdom are under the power of darkness. To translate is to carry over or cross the line. He has carried us across the line that separates the power of darkness from the kingdom of light.

14 in whom we have our redemption,—To redeem is to rescue or deliver from enthrallment from which one cannot deliver himself. Jesus with his own blood paid the redemption and delivered those who would accept it from the enthrallment of the evil one.

the forgiveness of our sins:—The redemption is of Jesus. It can be enjoyed in him as his servant, and it is the forgiveness or deliverance from sin.

15 who is the image of the invisible God,—Those who would behold God may see him reflected in the face of the Son, for as Jesus said to Philip: "He that hath seen me hath seen the Father." (John 14: 9.) The same thought is expressed in the following: "In whom the god of this world hath blinded the minds of the unbelieving, that the light of the gospel of the glory of Christ, who is the image of God, should not dawn upon them." (2 Cor. 4: 4.) And again, man is called "the image and glory of God." (1 Cor. 11: 7.) Jesus is the idea and expression of God. God is invisible to man as even Moses learned when he asked to see the glory of God pass by. (Ex. 33: 19-23.) God dwells in the light unapproachable, whom no one has seen or can see. (1 Tim. 6: 16.) But we see God in Christ. (John 14: 9.) God is like Christ. In the face of Jesus Christ God has given the light of the knowledge of his glory. (2 Cor. 4: 6.)

the firstborn of all creation;—In respect to all creation he occupies the relation of priority. From this it follows that over all

1: 15, 16.] COLOSSIANS 259

created, in the heavens and upon the earth, things visible and things invisible,

creation he occupies the relation of supremacy, such as is according to the "firstborn," and as such as is pre-eminently due to "the firstborn of all creation," because he is in his higher nature Maker and Head of all created being, representing and revealing in this way the perception of the invisible God. From this essential conception, by a natural contrast, the thought passes on to distinction from, and priority to, all created being. Exactly in this same order of conception, it is said: "God . . . hath at the end of these days spoken unto us in his Son, whom he appointed heir of all things, through whom also he made the worlds" (Heb. 1: 1, 2), and "all things were made through him; and without him was not anything made that hath been made" (John 1: 3). [The passage before us indicates the same thought in the words "firstborn of all creation," and works it out in the verses following. In tracing the Messianic line of promise, it is always prominent that, while the Messiah is always true man, "the seed of Abraham," "the son of David," yet on him are attributed attributes too high for any created being as is indicated by the prophet: "For unto us a child is born, unto us a son is given; and the government shall be upon his shoulder: and his name shall be called Wonderful, Counsellor, Mighty God, Everlasting Father, Prince of Peace. Of the increase of his government and of peace where shall be no end, upon the throne of David, and upon his kingdom, to establish it, and to uphold it with justice and with righteousness from henceforth even for ever. The zeal of Jehovah of hosts will perform this." (Isa. 9: 6, 7.) He is declared to be Immanuel, "God with us" (Matt. 1: 23), and his kingdom a visible manifestation of God. Hence the thought contained in the word "firstborn" is not only sovereignty, "the highest of the kings of the earth" (Psalm 89: 27) but also likeness to God and priority to all created being.]

16 for in him were all things created,—This certainly means that Jesus is the Creator of the whole universe. All the laws and purposes which guide the creation and government of the universe reside in him. He stands at the head above all created things. God the Father is represented as originating and providing all

whether thrones or dominions or principalities or powers; all things have been created through him, and unto him; 17 and he is before all things, and in him all things; ¹¹consist. 18 And he is the head of the body, the church:

---

¹¹That is, *hold together*.

---

things; the Word as creating; the Spirit as organizing, giving law, and guiding forward to the accomplishment of the ends.

in the heavens and upon the earth,—The heavens refer to the material heavens around the earth. [According to this division the heavens include all the universe except the earth, and include all the heavenly bodies and their inhabitants. The declaration, then, is that all things that are in the worlds above us were the work of his creative power. The earth includes all the animals, plants, minerals, waters—in fact all the earth contains.]

things visible and things invisible,—This includes the whole under a new principle of division. The visible includes all persons and things within reach of the human eye; the invisible includes all objects beyond its reach.

whether thrones or dominions or principalities or powers;— This list is meant to be exhaustive that no portion of the celestial hierarchy may be exempted from essential dependence on Christ. Paul makes no attempt to give the real rank of these orders.

all things have been created through him,—"All things" is solemnly repeated, but beside the fact of creation we have here the permanent result—have been created and continue to be. This result has him as its end.

and unto him;—He is the end of creation, containing the reason in himself, why creation is at all, and why it is as it is. [He is the medium and instrument of the divine energy, the Alpha and the Omega, the beginning and the end. All things come from and through him, and tend to him. (Rom. 11: 36.)]

17 and he is before all things,—He and he only is; all else is created. This refers to the "I am" of eternal existence, as claimed by himself: "Verily, verily, I say unto you, Before Abraham was born, I am." (John 8: 58.)

and in him all things consist.—In him all things stand together as united parts of one whole. Just as in the bosom of the

1: 17, 18.]   COLOSSIANS   261

who is the beginning, the firstborn from the dead; ¹²that in all things he
------
¹²Or, *that among all he might have &c.*

Son all things sprang into being, so in him as their compassing element all things find their bond of union and their orderly arrangement into one whole. [The emphasis rests on the word *Head*. The fullness of Paul's statement here, taken in connection with 2: 18, 19, indicates that the Colossian church was in danger from false teaching respecting the relation of Christ to the creation, especially to the angels.]

18 **And he is the head of the body, the church:**—The church is the spiritual body of which Christ is the head. The individual Christians are members of that body, all moved and directed by the Head. [The same is taught in the following: "Now I rejoice in my sufferings for your sake, and fill up on my part that which is lacking of the afflictions of Christ in my flesh for his body's sake, which is the church." (1: 24.) The plain statement is that the church is the body of Christ. The same thing is said in the following: "And he put all things in subjection under his feet, and gave him to be head over all things to the church, which is his body, the fulness of him that filleth all in all." (Eph. 1: 22, 23.) Everyone therefore who belongs to Christ necessarily belongs to the church. To be out of the church is to be out of Christ. To be in Christ is to be in the church.]

who is the beginning,—He is the beginning of the new life to us—the first fruits from the dead. "But now hath Christ been raised from the dead, the firstfruits of them that are asleep. . . . But each in his own order: Christ the firstfruits; then they that are Christ's, at his coming" (1 Cor. 15: 20-23), and the one "who abolished death, and brought life and immortality to light through the gospel" (2 Tim. 1: 10).

the firstborn from the dead;—The same title is given him by the apostle John. (Rev. 1: 5.) He was the first raised from the dead to die no more. Some had been restored to fleshly life. "But now hath Christ been raised from the dead, the firstfruits of them that are asleep." (1 Cor. 15: 20.) He was the Head, above all, and was the leader of all. "He that descended is the same also that ascended far above all the heavens, that he might fill all

might have the preëminence. 19 ¹³For it was the good pleasure *of the Father* that in him should all the fulness dwell; 20 and through him to reconcile all things ¹⁴unto ¹⁵himself, having made peace through the blood of his

---
¹³Or, *For the whole fulness* of God *was pleased to dwell in him*
¹⁴Or, *into him*
¹⁵Or, *him*

---

things." (Eph. 4: 10.) In the Scriptures the resurrection is called a birth. Of course this and to be "born of water" and of the Spirit are both figurative births. *Birth* is the beginning of a new life and separate existence. When a child is born of his mother, it is the beginning of a new and separate life. Birth does not give life; it introduces into a new state. When a man passes out of a state of sin into the life of Jesus Christ, the beginning of this new life is called a birth; when he is raised from the dead and begins a new and separate life in eternity, it is called a birth from the grave.

that in all things he might have the preeminence.—[That he and none other, the very one who rose, might become the first in rank; the word occurring only here in the New Testament. This is God's purpose, partially fulfilled already, to be entirely fulfilled at his coming. The central place Paul assigns to the person of Christ is the proper place in all Christian thought.]

19 **For it was the good pleasure of the Father that in him should all the fulness dwell;**—After his resurrection from the dead, Jesus said to his disciples: "All authority hath been given unto me in heaven and on earth." (Matt. 28: 18.) John said: "And the Word became flesh, and dwelt among us (and we beheld his glory, glory as of the only begotten from the Father), full of grace and truth." (John 1: 14.) Paul says: "For in him dwelleth all the fulness of the Godhead bodily." (Col. 2: 9.) From these passages it is evident that God committed all authority to his Son Jesus Christ in redemption and the salvation of the world. (Matt. 28: 18-20.)

20 **and through him to reconcile all things unto himself, having made peace through the blood of his cross;**—Jesus shed his blood that God "might himself be just, and the justifier of him that hath faith in Jesus." (Rom. 3: 26.) His blood was shed for the remission of sins, as the following shows: "If we walk in the light, as he is in the light, we have fellowship one with another,

cross; through him, I say, whether things upon the earth, or things in the heavens. 21 And you, being in time past alienated and enemies in your mind

and the blood of Jesus his Son cleanseth us from all sin." (1 John 1: 7.) [It is not God who needs to be reconciled, but the universe that is alienated from God. God's attitude and plan are set forth by Jesus, who said: "For God so loved the world, that he gave his only begotten Son, that whosoever believeth on him should not perish, but have eternal life." (John 3: 16.) God gave his Son for the world of sinners while they were hostile to him. (Rom. 5: 8.) Here Paul glories in the grand scope of Christ's work of reconciliation of a universe out of harmony with God. It was God who planned the reconciliation (2 Cor. 5: 18, 19) that is carried out by the Son (Eph. 2: 16).]

through him, I say, whether things upon the earth, or things in the heavens.—By or through Jesus who reconciled everything to him by the blood shed on the cross. "But all things are of God, who reconciled us to himself through Christ, and gave unto us the ministry of reconciliation; to wit, that God was in Christ reconciling the world unto himself, not reckoning unto them their trespasses, and having committed unto us the word of reconciliation." (2 Cor. 5: 18, 19.) God invites man to enter into Christ. There they meet and are reconciled in Christ. He said this was done by Christ, even of things on the earth and in the heavens.

21 **Ask you, being in time past alienated and enemies in your mind**—He warns the Colossians not to forget their state of estrangement as heathen Gentiles. He wishes them to appreciate their sad condition when they were so long estranged from God. To the Ephesians he says: "Wherefore remember, that once ye, the Gentiles in the flesh, . . . were at that time separate from Christ, alienated from the commonwealth of Israel, and strangers from the covenants of the promise, having no hope and without God in the world." (Eph. 2: 11, 12.)

in your evil works,—Paul himself gives the best comment on these words in the following graphic description of paganism: "For the wrath of God is revealed from heaven against all ungodliness and unrighteousness of men, who hinder the truth in unrighteousness. . . . Professing themselves to be wise, they be-

in your evil works, 22 yet now [16]hath he reconciled in the body of his flesh

[16]Some ancient authorities read *ye have been reconciled.*

---

came fools, and changed the glory of the incorruptible God for the likeness of an image of corruptible man, and of birds, and four-footed beasts, and creeping things. Wherefore God gave them up in the lusts of their hearts unto uncleanness, that their bodies should be dishonored among themselves: for that they exchanged the truth of God for a lie, and worshipped and served the creature rather than the Creator, who is blessed for ever. Amen. For this cause God gave them up unto vile passions: for their women changed the natural use into that which is against nature: and likewise also the men, leaving the natural use of the woman, burned in their lust one toward another, men with men working unseemliness, and receiving in themselves that recompense of their error which was due. And even as they refused to have God in their knowledge, God gave them up unto a reprobate mind, to do those things which are not fitting; being filled with all unrighteousness, wickedness, covetousness, maliciousness; full of envy, murder, strife, deceit, malignity; whisperers, backbiters, hateful to God, insolent, haughty, boastful, inventors of evil things, disobedient to parents, without understanding, covenant-breakers, without natural affection, unmerciful: who, knowing the ordinance of God, that they that practise such things are worthy of death, not only do the same, but also consent with them that practise them." (Rom. 1: 18-32.)

22 yet now hath he reconciled—Christ came into the world in a body of flesh that he might reconcile lost man to God, and cleanse him from sin.

in the body of his flesh through death,—While Christ came in a body of flesh and blood to save man from sin, there is a definite historical event involved in the death of Christ on the cross, and though the reconciliation is not effective with any given individual till he accepts the terms of reconciliation through Christ, God has thereby laid the foundation for the complete reconciliation which becomes effective when the sinner becomes obedient to the terms of pardon.

1 : 22, 23.] COLOSSIANS 265

through death, to present you holy and without blemish and unreprovable before him: 23 if so be that ye continue in the faith, grounded and stedfast, and not moved away from the hope of the ¹gospel which ye heard, which was preached in all creation under heaven; whereof I Paul was made a minister.

¹Gr. *good tidings*; and so elsewhere; see marginal note on Mt. 4. 23.

to present you holy and without blemish and unreprovable before him:—To the end that he might bring them to such a state of holiness that they would be holy and without blame, and not deserving reproof in the sight of God. His object was to redeem man from sin and lead him to so live that in the judgment he would be held blameless before God. [As all animals offered in sacrifice to God were to be without blemish, so should those who are unreservedly devoted to God, for it is the aim of holiness which God's claim stamps on all objects claimed by him.]

23 if so be that ye continue in the faith, grounded and stedfast,—Paul wished them to take no chance with plausible false teachers who were pleading with them that the gospel which they had heard from Epaphras needed additions.

and not moved away from the hope of the gospel which ye heard,—[They had heard the gospel, hence there was no excuse for their being moved away from the hope it presented. The expression points to a possible danger threatening them, thus preparing for the warning to follow.]

which was preached in all creation under heaven;—It seems strange that at that time the gospel had been preached among all the nations, but if we consider the earnest character of the Christians, who gloried in persecution and death for Christ's sake, it will not seem so strange. The greatest hindrance to the gospel in our day is the lukewarm and indifferent character of professed Christians. Personal consecration and devotion are the great needs to spread the gospel abroad. [The motive of Paul here is at once to emphasize the universality of the gospel, which had been offered without reserve to all alike, hence he warns the Colossians not to be led by false teachers into a course contrary to the gospel. The great message of God's love in Jesus Christ commends itself to us because it can go into any part of the world, and there upon all kinds of people work its wonders, as is shown by the mission work in all parts of the world today.]

whereof I Paul was made a minister.—He did not hesitate to magnify his office as a minister of the gospel of Jesus Christ. He proclaimed unhesitatingly the universal supremacy of Christ and the subordination to him of all principalities and powers, and that all life and all powers are mediated through him and are subject to his supreme will. He claimed for him the control of life in all its manifold departments and in every sphere, visible and invisible, and places in his hand the government of the world and the direction of every power that makes for the progress of humanity. Paul's message is as modern and pertinent as when he sent it to the Colossians. [There are those today who challenge the competency of Paul as an interpreter of Christ. We should listen to no words which make Christ's dominion and sovereignty, and his sole and all sufficient work on the cross, less mighty as the only power that knits heaven and earth together.]

4. THE APOSTLE'S JOY IN HIS SUFFERINGS AND LABORS FOR CHRIST
1: 24-29

24 Now I rejoice in my sufferings for your sake, and fill up on my part that which is lacking of the afflictions of Christ in my flesh for his body's

---

24 Now I rejoice in my sufferings for your sake,—At the time of writing the epistle Paul was a prisoner in chains, and suffering much for them. Because he insisted that the Gentiles should be received into the church without circumcision the Jews persecuted him and pressed the case against him with such bitterness that he was finally sent to Rome where he suffered much affliction. Therefore he could say, "for your sake." [The opposition and affliction Paul endured for the cause of Christ were like those which Christ endured, and he submitted to them as a servant of Christ, and by faith bore them to advance the cause of Christ among men. All this was occasioned by his rendering obedience to the glorified Lord.]

and fill up on my part that which is lacking of the afflictions of Christ—Christ suffered to save men, but Paul insists that man must suffer with him for his own salvation and the salvation of his fellow men. In redeeming man Christ did for man only what could not do for himself. He could suffer persecution and

1: 24, 25.] COLOSSIANS 267

sake, which is the church; 25 whereof I was made a minister, according to

self-denial to save himself and others. Paul did this and so filled up what was lacking in the afflictions of Christ.

in my flesh for his body's sake, which is the church;—The affliction which Paul suffered was for the sake of his body, the church. When Christ breathed his last, all sufferings needful for the complete establishment of the kingdom of God on earth had not yet been endured. For the full realization of the purpose of God it was needful, not only that Christ should die for the sins of the world, but that the gospel should be preached to all nations. This involved, owing to the wickedness of men, hardships and afflictions to those who proclaimed the message. These sufferings and afflictions Paul willingly endured in order to save men. Consequently, just as the life on earth of the servants of Christ is in some sense an extension of his life on earth among men—for in them he lives (Gal. 2: 20)—so the sufferings of Paul were in a similar sense a continuation of the sufferings of Christ. This is in close harmony with, and further emphasizes, Paul's constant teaching that Christ's servants share all that Christ is and has and does. (Rom. 8: 17; 1 Cor. 1: 9; Phil. 3: 10.) But this by no means suggests that Paul's sufferings were in any sense propitiatory or that Christ's sufferings were not so. For the one point in common here mentioned and made conspicuous by repetition is suffering *on behalf of another*. We should note the infinite dignity here given to sufferings endured for the spread of the gospel. These Christ condescends to join with his own afflictions while in the body and of his mysterious agony on the cross as endured for the benefit of the church which he recognizes as his own body.

25 whereof I was made a minister,—Paul was a minister of the church according to or through the duties God laid on him to preach the gospel to the Gentiles, to fulfill the word of the Lord Jesus spoke to him at the time of his conversion, telling him the mission to which he had called him: "To this end have I appeared unto thee, to appoint thee a minister and a witness both of the things wherein thou hast seen me, and of the things wherein I will appear unto thee; delivering thee from the people, and from the Gentiles, unto whom I send thee, to open their eyes, that they may

the ²dispensation of God which was given me to you-ward, to fulfil the word of God, 26 *even* the mystery which hath been hid ³for ages and generations: but now hath it been manifested to his saints, 27 to whom God was pleased to make known what is the riches of the glory of this mystery among the

²Or, *stewardship* See 1 Cor. 9. 17.
³Or, *from all ages &c.* Gr. *from the ages and from the generations.*

turn from darksess to light and from the power of Satan unto God, that they may receive remission of sins and an inheritance among them that are sanctified by faith in me." (Acts 26: 16-18.)

according to the dispensation of God which was given me to you-ward,—[This clause is explanatory of Paul's position as a minister of Christ and of his church. For that reason he had a spiritual function in it committed to him by God, and because of that very fact it was a joy for him to suffer for its welfare.]

to fulfil the word of God,—To achieve the full aim of the gospel, by proclaiming everywhere to Jew and Gentile salvation through faith in Christ, and by leading man to accept it on Christ's own terms. (Matt. 28: 18-20; Mark 16: 15, 16.)

26 even the mystery which hath been hid—The hidden purpose of God in the gospel, which could not have become known without his revelation. Being revealed it is no longer a mystery, in the sense of a secret or even a difficult thing, but only as a matter which required a revelation from God to make it known. It is God's eternal purpose to save men through Christ without reference to whether Jew or Gentile, on the condition of faith, in the manner described in the gospel.

for ages and generations:—Besides the ages of the world, the generations of men living in them are brought into special prominence and thus the concealment from the beginning of human history until the gospel was proclaimed through Christ.

but now hath it been manifested to his saints,—It was made known by Paul and others who proclaimed the gospel.

27 to whom God was pleased to make known—It was God's will and grace, through no merits of the saints, to make known to them the riches of his glorious mystery among the Gentiles.

what is the riches of the glory of this mystery among the Gentiles,—God was minded to make known how abundant is

Gentiles, which is Christ in you, the hope of glory: 28 whom we proclaim, admonishing every man and teaching every man in all wisdom, that we may

the splendor with which, in the great day, those initiated on earth into the gospel privileges and blessings will be enriched. [The conception of the inclusion of all Gentile people of the whole world in the hitherto undisclosed plan of God was so inspiring to Paul that he accumulates phrase on phrase to enhance the greatness of the blessings in Christ bestowed by God on the Gentiles.]

which is Christ in you, the hope of glory:—Christ within man is the only hope of glory. This alone qualifies him for the glory that is with God. Without being fitted and qualified in character for that glory none can attain to it, none could enjoy it if it were attained. Christ Jesus as he lived here on earth is the perfect pattern of the life fitted to attain and enjoy that glory with God. Christ within us makes us like Christ in life, like him in fidelity to God and his will. Like him in cherishing humilty, love, goodwill, and kindness to man. Like him in seeking happiness by denying self to make others happy. Like him in repressing evil thoughts and desires within our own souls, and cherishing those who are pure and true and good. Like him in practicing the principles that dwelt in his own breast. Faith is the means given us by which to lift our souls up to Christ that he may dwell in and work through us. But unless he dwells in our heart through faith, reproducing in our lives the life of the Son of God, our faith is vain, we are yet in our sins, we are without God and without hope in the world.

28 whom we proclaim,—He declared the whole counsel of God that he might be free from the blood of all men. To the Ephesian elders he said: "Wherefore I testify unto you this day, that I am pure from the blood of all men. For I shrank not from declaring unto you the whole counsel of God." (Acts 20: 26, 27.)

admonishing every man and teaching every man—[This solemn emphasis has reference to the universality of the gospel, whose counsels of perfection are not, as the false teachers would have it, for a privileged inner circle of votaries, but for every one without exception who comes to Jesus Christ; and to the fact that in this universality the individual is never lost sight of or merged

present every man perfect in Christ; 29 whereunto I labor also, striving according to his working, which worketh in me ⁴mightily.

⁴Or, *in power*

---

in the community; *each soul, each life*, as if there were no others, is to be perfect in Christ.]

in all wisdom,—[In the whole field of that wisdom which is not a mere mass of knowledge, but the principles and secrets of a life of faith and love. The point is that every believer may and should learn every secret of grace. There are no spiritual secrets behind the gospel.]

that we may present every man perfect in Christ;—Paul gave them all the teachings God gave him, that he might purify and perfect their hearts and present every man, at the judgment, perfect in Christ Jesus; but I do not believe the emotion and temptation to sin can be purged out of any one without suffering in the flesh unto death. Christ was not made perfect until he had suffered. Of him it is said: "Though he was a Son, yet learned obedience by the things which he suffered; and having been made perfect, he became unto all them that obey him the author of eternal salvation." (Heb. 5: 8, 9; see also 2: 9, 10.) If it required the sufferings of the cross that Jesus the Son of God might learn obedience and be made perfect, that he might become the author of eternal salvation, it does not seem possible that man, frail and sinful, should be made perfect without suffering. The apostle says: "Forasmuch then as Christ suffered in the flesh, arm ye yourselves also with the same mind; for he that hath suffered in the flesh hath ceased from sin." (1 Pet. 4: 1.) Jesus possessed the sinful emotions within him until they were purged out by suffering. I do not believe the emotion and temptation to sin is purged out without suffering in the flesh unto death. A person who claims that he is equal or surpasses Jesus in the elements of his character that lead to freedom from sinful desires and impulses is hardly worthy of notice. Yet there was a perfection to which Jesus attained and cherished during his life—his heart was perfect toward God. He desired with a perfect heart to do the will of God, which was sufficiently strong to hold in check the sinful emotions of the flesh, so that he committed no sin. Man may approximate this perfection of heart. The heart may be brought to sincerely desire to do the will of God, but does not attain the degree of power over the flesh so as never to sin in thought, word, or deed. To do this would be for man in human nature to equal Jesus with his divine nature. The thought and claim of sinless perfection in human beings savors of presumption, the worst of all sins before God. The claim of being sinless by those who really know very little of what constitutes true Christianity is well calculated to bring the religion of Jesus Christ into contempt with thinking people.

While this is true, it is right for every Christian to keep before him the example of the sinless life of Jesus, and the perfection of the heart in its sincere and earnest desire to do the will of God, and strive to emulate them. The passage under consideration brings before us the diligent effort on the part of Paul to so admonish and teach believers in Christ that they will finally be so perfect in Christ that they will be accepted of God. A perfection of heart—a sincere desire to do the will of God in all things—is to be cultivated and striven for. Its attainment is gradual, and it is doubtful if it can ever be said to be perfect while in the flesh. As the heart approximates this perfection, it seeks to bring the flesh in subjection, but the sinful emotions and desires are purged out only through the suffering and weakness that end in death. [The emphatic repetition, *every man . . . every man . . . every man*, makes conspicuous the universality of Paul's aim. Every one he meets is to him a possibility of another fully-developed trophy presented in the final triumph. Consequently, *every man* is an object for the discipline and teaching needed to make this possibility actual. It also carries a solemn individual appeal to those thus warned and taught.]

29 whereunto I labor also, striving according to his working,—[Paul underwent labor, like an athlete in the contest for masteries, even to the point of weariness, in order to present every man perfect in Christ. He often referred to the difficulties of his work as the following show: "We waxed bold in our God to speak unto you the gospel of God in much conflict." (1 Thess. 2: 2.) "For to this end we labor and strive, because we have our hope set on the living God, who is the Saviour of all men, specially of them that believe." (1 Tim. 4: 10.) "I have fought the good fight, I have finished the course, I have kept the faith." (2 Tim. 4: 7.)]

which worketh in me mightily.—[The power worked in him mightily because Christ was his life. (Eph. 6: 10.) This power is accessible to all who surrender themselves unreservedly to Christ. He did not always have his own way, but he had learned to do without his way, so that no one could rob him of his glory in Christ. He led the victorious life because he let Christ rule and reign in his heart. The power of Christ in Paul was not because he walked in his own wisdom, but because of his conforming his will to the will of Christ. In a real sense, therefore, the Christian is a reproduction of Christ. A small dynamo can retain its energy if continually replenished. Christians themselves are spiritual dynamos, but they must be in constant union with Christ the source of life and energy. The constant inflow of power from Christ enabled Paul to be a continuous supply of energy for others.]

SECTION TWO

BE NOT LED AWAY FROM CHRIST THE HEAD
2: 1-23

1. IMPORTANCE OF THE SUBJECT
2: 1-7

1 For I would have you know how greatly I strive for you, and for them at Laodicea, and for as many as have not seen my face in the flesh; 2 that their hearts may be comforted, they being knit together in love, and unto all

1 For I would have you know how greatly I strive for you, —This conflict for those he had not seen was mental conflict, one of the heart. Possibly a striving in prayer (4: 12) to God for them, that they might know the full truth of God, and be faithful to it. This epistle to them to encourage them to be faithful was a result of that struggle and anxiety in their behalf.

and for them at Laodicea, —All the Christians in the Lycus Valley, in which Laodicea was located, were exposed to the vicious influences of the false teachers.

and for as many as have not seen my face in the flesh; —The disciples at Colossæ and Laodicea knew of Paul and his work, but had never seen his "face in the flesh." He had never visited the churches in that locality. He only knew those individuals who had visited him.

2 that their hearts may be comforted, —His anxiety in behalf of all who had not seen his face arose from the fear that they might not receive the full teaching of the word of God. The only teaching they had received was yet verbal. The scriptures had not been completed and collected. Paul was the only apostle who had labored in that section of the country; and the other teachers, if inspired at all, were only partially gifted. So there was great danger that where the apostles did not go the teaching would be imperfect and partial. [He regards the danger to which they were exposed and the afflictions which they endured and by mention of these prepares them for his exhortation.]

they being knit together in love, —This describes the manner in which the comforting should take place. The light and service secured by the full knowledge of the gospel would bring additional comfort, would more favorably unite and cement them together in

riches of the [5]full assurance of understanding, that they may know the mystery of God, [6]even Christ, 3 in whom are all the treasures of wisdom and knowledge hidden. 4 This I say, that no one may delude you with persuasiveness of speech. 5 For though I am absent in the flesh, yet am I with you

---

[5]Or, *fulness*
[6]The ancient authorities vary much in the text of this passage.

---

love. The increase in knowledge and the more complete conformity of the life to the will of God is always laid down as the condition of fuller comfort and more perfect union in love.

and unto all riches of the full assurance of understanding,—This refers to the spiritual riches, and it comes through practicing what is known. The knowledge is of Christ, and in him all the treasures of the knowledge and wisdom are hidden.

that they may know the mystery of God, even Christ,—To learn Christ is to learn the mystery of God. [Christ in whom the inscrutable nature of God, rich in the hidden treasure of wisdom and knowledge, is revealed to us.]

3 **in whom are all the treasures of wisdom and knowledge hidden.**—Christ as the Mediator is the great treasure house, so to speak, where is found all the wisdom and knowledge needful for the Christian. Christ is what abundant treasures are in reference to the supply of our wants.

4 **This I say, that no one may delude you with persuasiveness of speech.**—He gives them this knowledge that they may not to be turned away from Christ by enticing words. He gives the following warning concerning false teachers. "For they that are such serve not our Lord Christ, but their own belly; and by their smooth and fair speech they beguile the hearts of the innocent." (Rom. 16: 18.) And again he warns: "Be no longer children, tossed and to and fro and carried about with every wind of doctrine, by the sleight of men, in cratiness, after the wiles of error." (Eph. 4: 14.) The protection against this being carried away by error given in enticing words is a full knowledge of God's will as delivered in Christ. The Colossian church was steadfast in faith and true to the word of God, though not taught by an apostle.

5 **For though I am absent in the flesh, yet am I with you in the spirit,**—Paul's heart was really with the Colossian Christians, from whom he was absent, and whom he had never seen.

in in the spirit, joying and beholding your order, and the stedfastness of your faith in Christ.

6 As therefore ye received Christ Jesus the Lord, *so* walk in him, 7 rooted and builded up in him, and established [7]in your faith, even as ye were taught abounding [8]in thanksgiving.

---

[7]Or, *by*
[8]Some ancient authorities insert *in it.*

---

joying and beholding your order, and the stedfastness of your faith in Christ.—Through the reports of Epahras he could see and enjoy their order and the steadfastness of their faith as though he was present with them and saw it. [They held their position as good soldiers of Christ, and their faith in him enabled them to present to every enemy an immovable line of battle. The tone of this verse suggests that looseness of faith exposes Christians to disastrous results.]

6 **As therefore ye received Christ Jesus the Lord,**—[They who welcomed the good news of salvation through Christ Jesus thereby receive Christ himself to be their Lord and their life. Where the message of his love is welcomed, he himself comes in spiritual and real presence, and dwells in the spirit.]

so walk in him,—Live your life, regulate your whole conduct in accordance with the way you learned Christ, and in union with him.

7 **rooted and builded up in him,**—This suggests stability and nourishment and life derived from inward contact with Christ. It calls attention to the foundation on which the character is builded up in him. The root, the foundation, is faith in Christ.

and established in your faith, even as ye were taught—The completing the life and forming the character must be by obedience to him, by a continued walk in Christ, and this fixes or establishes the faith. [A progressive increase of faith is the condition of all Christian progress. The faith which is already the firmest is still capable of and needs strengthening. Its range can be enlarged, its tenacity increased, and its power over heart and life reinforced. The eye of faith is never so keen but that it may become more long-sighted; its grasp never so close that it may not be tightened; its realization never so solid but that it may be made more substantial; this continued strengthening of faith is the most essential form of a Christan's effort at self-improvement. Strengthen your faith and you strengthen all graces; for it measures our reception of divine help.]

abounding in thanksgiving.—[They should abound in thanksgiving because they had received the knowledge of the great truths and blessings through the Lord Jesus Christ.]

2. REASON WHY THEY SHOULD BE STEADFAST AND NOT DRAWN AWAY BY THE INFLUENCE OF FALSE TEACHERS
2: 8-15

8 ⁹Take heed lest there shall be any one that maketh spoil of you through his philosophy and vain deceit, after the tradition of men, after the

---

⁹Or, *See whether*

---

8 **Take heed lest there shall be any one that maketh spoil of you through his philosophy and vain deceit,**—He warns them that they must not let any one pervert them from the faith in Christ by their human reasonings and theories that are vain and deceptive. The Spirit recognized that no salvation could come to man through human philosophies, or the deductions of human reason, through the vain deceit of man's experience as developed in society, in history, or in any worldly experiences or wisdom can teach. All efforts to find righeousness in any of these spoil men, deprive them of the only true righteousness that is found in Christ, and that comes from God through Christ Jesus. All the philosophies of men, all the deceits of human wisdom, and all the rudiments of the world discovered by human reason spoil men, ruin their souls, lead them to everlasting death by leading them away from God and his salvation.

after the tradition of men—[This so-called philosophy was a man-made scheme. God has nothing to do with it. It was originated entirely by men and is handed along from men to men. "The stream rises no higher than its source."]

after the rudiments of the world,—[As to their subject matter, it concerns itself with what is of the world. This marks the chief point of contact with the earlier Judaism, in the stress still laid on matters of ritual law, ascetic observance, and the like. The phrase suggests more than Jewish ritualistic observances, since "world" includes the whole sphere of material things, and Paul is

⁹ʳᵘdiments of the world, and not after Christ: 9 for in him dwelleth all the fulness of the Godhead bodily, 10 and in him ye are made full, who is the

---
¹⁰Or, *elements* See Gal. 4. 3 marg.

---

giving the category to which the false teaching belonged. To go back to rudiments was to show themselves children. (Gal. 4: 3.)]

and not after Christ:—[This is in contrast with all that precedes—Christ is the source, substance, and the end of the plan of salvation. What is not after Christ is rudimentary; all teaching that does not make him the center only serves to lead men captive. All culture apart from him is an illusion and deceit.]

9 for in him dwelleth—Not a mere emanation of the Supreme Being, but *dwelleth* and remains forever—not dwelling in him for a time and leaving him again.

all the fulness—The whole is an extension and enforcement of "for it was the good pleasure of the Father that in him should all the fulness dwell." (1: 19.)

of the Godhead bodily,—[The false teachers claimed to be in horror of all that was material, as having in it the seed of evil, and for that reason they denied either the reality of our Lord's body or its inseparable connection with the Godhead in him. Hence Paul's emphasis here; as John also in the following: "And the Word became flesh, and dwelt among us (and we beheld his glory, glory as of the only begotten from the Father), full of grace and truth." (John 1: 14.) And he gave the following warning: "Beloved, believe not every spirit, but prove the spirits, whether they are of God; because many false prophets are gone out into the world. Hereby know ye the Spirit of God: every spirit that confesseth that Jesus Christ is come in the flesh is of God: and every spirit that confesseth not Jesus is not of God: and this is the spirit of the antichrist, whereof ye have heard that it cometh; and now it is in the world already." (1 John 4: 1-3.)]

All the wisdom, power, and goodness of the Godhead for uplifting and saving men is embodied in the person of Jesus Christ. And in his provisions are found the only source and righteousness and life for man. Whosoever looks away from him and his teachings turns his back upon God and upon all his provisions for the salvation of man. "But of him are ye in Christ Jesus, who was

head of all principality and power: in whom ye were also circumcised with a circumcision not made with hands, in the putting off of the body of the flesh,

---

made unto us wisdom from God, and righteousness and sanctification, and redemption: that, according as it is written, He that glorieth, let him glory in the Lord." (1 Cor. 1: 30, 31.) In the way of redemption provided by God, man must walk, that his righteousness and salvation may be of God and not stand in the wisdom of man. In the bodily form of Jesus Christ dwells the full power and excellence of the Godhead. For after his resurrection from the dead, Jesus said: "All authority hath been given unto me in heaven and on earth." (Matt. 28: 18.)

10 and in him ye are made full,—By entering into Christ, and living up to his requirements, they were completed and perfected in work and in character. [The divine gifts thus obtained are ample, hence they ought not to seek to supplement this sufficient supply by looking to other sources.]

who is the head of all principality and power:—The repetition of these terms indicates that the false teachers presented the angels as mediators, or in a manner which detracted from the sufficiency of Christ. This affirmation of the absolute supremacy of Christ to the angelic world meets this error. Nor is this superiority simply one of position, since the head is in vital connection with the members, who derive their life from it. [To partake of the divine fullness is not the special privilege of the initiated; it belongs to all who are united to the Lord Jesus Christ.]

11 in whom ye were also circumcised with a circumcision not made with hands,—There was a literal circumcision of the flesh in the Jewish dispensation; there is a spiritual circumcision in the church of Christ.

in the putting off—As we take off and put away clothes. The readers are said to "have put off the old man with his doings" (3: 9), and to "have put on the new man" (3: 10); and again, "put on therefore, as God's elect, holy and beloved, a heart of compassion, kindness, lowliness, meekness, longsuffering" (3: 12).

of the body of the flesh,—[The human body looked upon in its material construction, in view of the truth ever to the mind of Paul (Rom. 6: 12) that through the needs and desires arising

in the circumcision of Christ; 12 having been buried with him in baptism, wherein ye were also raised with him through faith in the working of God,

---

from the constitution of our body sin rules all those who have not become obedient to the Lord Jesus Christ. For in the man of the world the flesh, although in its self good, has come under the dominion of sin and has become the weapon with which sin enslaves its victims. Hence apart from Christ, man's flesh is "sinful flesh" (Rom. 8: 2), and his body a "body of sin" (Rom. 6: 6). Circumcision is only the outward removal, by human hands, of a small part of that body which to so many is an instrument by which sin holds them captive. But the servants of Christ have stripped off from themselves and laid aside their entire body of flesh, inasmuch they have been completely rescued from its deadly dominion. Henceforth they stand in a new relation to their own bodies—these are no longer the throne of sin but the temple of God. The apostle says: "Or know ye not that your body is a temple of the Holy Spirit which is in you, which ye have from God? and ye are not your own; for ye were bought with a price: glorify God therefore in your body." (1 Cor. 6: 19, 20.)]

in the circumcision of Christ;—In entering into Christ, they received the true spiritual circumcision made without hands, of which the circumcision of the flesh was a type. That true circumcision was the putting off the body of the sins of the flesh by that circumcision or cutting off of the sins which Christ does for us when we enter into him.

12 having been buried with him in baptism,—The putting off the body of the flesh or the true spiritual circumcision was effected by being buried with him in baptism. This implies that they were dead to sin through faith in Christ.

wherein ye were also raised with him—They were also raised with him in baptism. In this act the sins were removed, as by circumcision the flesh was cut off. [The language is taken from the coming up out of the water which is associated with the fact of Christ's resurrection, which is clearly referred to. Christ went down into the grave, but came up again. So the believer disappears under the waters of baptism. This is a side not presented in circumcision. In baptism there is an impressive exhibition of the fact that we are born anew. This new life we get in union

who raised him from the dead. 13 And you, being dead through your trespasses and the uncircumcision of your flesh, you, *I say,* did he make alive together with him, having forgiven us all our trespasses; 14 having blotted

with Christ. The working of God is signally displayed in raising Christ from the dead. It is to be taken in connection with the removal of sin which operated in Christ's death. Christ rose from the dead possessor of a new and endless life. If we take as the object of our faith the working which raised Christ from the dead, we shall become sharers with him in the same new and endless life.]

through faith in the working of God,—They were both buried and raised with Christ in baptism, by the working of faith in God. Baptism avails nothing without faith. It is only as faith recognizes a risen Savior that the act of baptism becomes of spiritual significance, and rising with Christ becomes an actual spiritual experience.

who raised him from the dead.—God's working is here set forth as the object of the believing, not as the cause. In this connection it was natural to characterize God as the one "who raised him from the dead." Only through faith in such a God as able and willing to raise us up spiritiually can we partake in this new life.

13 **And you, being dead through your trespasses and the uncircumcision of your flesh,**—They were Gentiles, as such uncircumcised; this external condition fitly indicates their depraved and carnal condition. Their uncircumcision was once the sign of their fleshly condition, but now they had received the circumcision of the heart.

you, I say, did he make alive together with him,—Now he had made them alive, brought them together with himself, when they had been buried and raised with Christ.

having forgiven us all our trespasses;—The Lord's resurrection was the expression of the fact of his acceptance by the Father; our entrance on union with him as the Risen One was the expression of our acceptance in him. [This is the most beautiful allusion to circumcision imaginable. There were those who had accepted the gospel, who through the influence of false teachers were led to think they needed to be circumcised in order to secure the remission of sin. To them the apostle said: You are complete in

out ¹¹the bond written in ordinances that was against us, which was contrary to us: and he hath taken it out of the way, nailing it to the cross; 15

¹¹Or, *the bond that was against us by its ordinances*

Christ; you need not be circumcised with a circumcision made with hands. The fleshly circumcision only took off a small portion of flesh; but spiritual circumcision, which we have in being crucified with Christ, in being buried with him in baptism, cuts off without a knife, and without a hand, the whole body of the sins of the flesh. This is Christ's way of circumcising. So we have a circumcision of all sins, the mighty mass is now cut off through our faith and baptism into Christ, with whom we have risen through the faith of the mighty operation of God, who raised him from the dead.]

14 Having blotted out the bond written in ordinances that was against us,—Not a soul was ever saved by the law of Moses, because none ever kept it, save Jesus Christ who fulfilled it completely; and he was not lost, to need salvation. Persons under the law of Moses were saved, but it was by and through Christ. No man could be justified by the law, because all sinned and violated the law; and law condemns, and does not justify, or purge from sin. All Jews and Gentiles have sinned, or broken the law, so cannot be saved by law. The law was given to train and prepare men for the reception of Jesus Christ, the promised seed, in whom all nations of the earth should be blessed.

which was contrary to us:—The Mosaic law condemned, but could not save, so it "was contrary to us."

and he hath taken it out of the way,—The whole of the Mosaic law, including the commandments written on stones (2 Cor. 3:7), was taken out of the way, nailed to the cross, and is no longer in force as a law in any of its parts. In the new covenant many laws that were in the old covenant were re-enacted and are to be obeyed not because they were in the old, but because they are a part of the new.

nailing it to the cross;—It was taken out of the way when Jesus Christ was nailed to the cross. [This is a very graphic way of saying that the obstacle to forgiveness which lay in the law—in the justice of God of which the law is an embodiment—was re-

¹²having despoiled the principalities and the powers, he made a show of them openly, triumphing over them in it.

¹²Or, *having put off from himself the principalities &c.*

moved by the death of Christ. Practically the nails which fastened to the cross the hands and the feet of Jesus, and thus slew him, pierced and invalidated the law which pronounced the just condemnation of sinners. Hence Paul could say: "There is therefore now no condemnation to them that are in Christ Jesus." (Rom. 8: 1.) By the cross of Christ Paul could truthfully affirm that "the world hath been crucified unto me, and I unto the world." (Gal. 6: 14.)

15 having despoiled the principalities and the powers,—This is a figure from the treatment of enemies when conquered. Jesus was condemned and put to death by the principalities and powers of earthly governments—Jewish and Roman.

he made a show of them openly, triumphing over them in it. —He struggled with death, overcame it and them, and in his resurrection and ascension made a show openly of his triumph over them.

3. WARNINGS AGAINST RITUALISTIC PROHIBITIONS AND AGAINST ANGEL WORSHIP
2: 16-19

16 Let no man therefore judge you in meat, or in drink, or in respect of a feast day or a new moon or a sabbath day: 17 which are a shadow of the

16 Let no man therefore judge you—Since the old covenant was nailed to the cross of Christ, and was thus made invalid, its written decrees, he tells them, are not binding on the saints, and they were not to be judged for neglecting them.

in meat, or in drink,—This refers to ceremonial, and, doubtless, extremely rigid requirements as to clean and unclean articles of food and drink. Whether a man eats or drinks or not his conduct in this respect supplies no fit ground for a judgment of him.

or in respect of a feast day or a new moon—Christians should not permit themselves to be bound to Jewish festivals in their worship of God; neither to the great annual feasts. The claims of these observances were, no doubt, greatly exaggerated, and, possibly made tests of fellowship.

things to come; but the body is Christ's. 18 Let no man rob you of your prize [13]by a voluntary humility and [14]worshipping of the angels, [15]dwelling

---

[13]Or, *of his own mere will, by humility &c.*
[14]The Greek word denotes an act of reverence, whether paid to a creature, or to the Creator.
[15]Or, *taking his stand upon*

---

or a sabbath day:—[The sabbath means rest, and was a shadow of the rest which believers have in Christ. "For we who have believed do enter into that rest. . . . There remaineth therefore a sabbath rest for the people of God. . . . Let us therefore give diligence to enter into that rest, that no man fall after the same example of disobedience." (Heb. 4: 3-11.) The seventh day was the Sabbath or rest of God in creation, and was afterwards given to the Israelites, and formed part of their economy of types. But since Christ has come, this typical rest cannot be kept without ignoring him as our rest. The Sabbath of the Israelites is past, and the first day of the week has begun in life and liberty. It is not physical rest that is to be sought, but praise and adoration to him who has brought life and immortality to light. On the first day of the week the believer ceases his daily labor, but it is that he may honor Christ by his spiritual service. The first day of the week should never be called a Sabbath, because it is neither true nor appropriate to so name his resurrection day.]

17 which are a shadow of the things to come; but the body is Christ's.—The whole system and prohibitions of the Mosaic dispensation had a typical significance, pointing to the coming of Christ. They were only a shadow of the realities which came through him.

18 Let no man rob you of your prize—The reward they were to obtain through fidelity to Christ was eternal life. There was danger that the false teachers would so beguile them that they would turn aside from their faithfulness to Christ and lose their reward.

by a voluntary humility—Self-imposed act of mortification of the body, as service to God, was the outward evidence of false humility, and points to something blameworthy; a false and perverted lowliness, which deemed that God was so inaccessible that he could only be approached through the mediation of inferior beings.

in the things which he hath ¹⁶seen, vainly puffed up by his fleshly mind, 19 and not holding fast the Head, from whom all the body, being supplied and knit together through the joints and bands, increaseth with the increase of God.

¹⁶Many authorities, some ancient, insert *not*.

and worshipping of the angels,—This was the outward evidence of false humility, and carries the idea that no man can invent methods of worship of his own, he cannot worship angels. The Lord Jesus when tempted by Satan, said: "It is written, Thou shall worship the Lord thy God, and him only shalt thou serve." (Matt. 4:10.)

dwelling in the things which he hath seen, vainly puffed up by his fleshly mind,—[This refers to the false teachers who had sprung up among the Colossians, claiming supernatural knowledge by which the mind is said to be "puffed up." The supernatural knowledge to which the pretensions were made was that favorite knowledge claimed by the mystics of the secrets of the heavenly places and especially of the grades and functions of the hierarchy of heaven. Paul brands it as belonging to the mind, not of the spirit, but to the flesh, for indeed it was really superstition, resting not on faith, but on supposed visions and supernatural manifestations. He casts no reflection on the use of one's mind, but on the gullibility and foolish pride of the ignorant victims of the charlatans.]

19 and not holding fast the Head,—Those thus puffed up with their own wisdom, and adopting their own ways of service, failed to hold Jesus as Head, and sought to act independently of him. [In this lay the fatal error. All these speculations and superstitions interfered with the direct hold of the soul on the mediation of Christ as Head, from whom alone, as being the image of the invisible God, comes all spiritual life and growth.]

from whom—This refers to Christ personally. In the parallel passage (Eph. 4:16), *whom points* to Christ as Head.

all the body,—As every part of the whole body depends for life and efficiency on its being in connection with the head, just so absolutely does every member of the spiritual body depend on Christ.

being supplied and knit together through the joints and

bands,—Through the nourishment administered to every part by each member performing his proper part under the direction of the head. The welfare and development of the whole body is dependent upon the proper working of each and every member.

increaseth with the increase of God.—By every member working effectually in his sphere, they all make the increase of the body unto the building up of itself. By this joint and harmonious working of all the parts, the body grows into the well proportioned body of Christ, all moved and governed by him. These bodies of men, controlled by the Spirit of God, are the only manifestations of the church visible to men in the flesh. This shows the close relation that every individual member sustains to Christ the Head. This relation is spiritual and is regulated by the Spirit permeating all the members of the body. The Spirit does this through the truths revealed through the apostles. (Luke 24: 48, 49; John 16: 13, 14.) Spiritual influences are directed to the spirit of man that thinks, considers, wills, purposes, and acts in accord with that will.

4. THESE ENFORCED BY THE FACT OF THEIR HAVING DIED WITH CHRIST
2: 20-23

20 If ye died with Christ from the [1]rudiments of the world, why, as though living in the world, do ye subject yourselves to ordinances, 21 Handle

[1]Or, *elements* See Gal. 4. 3 marg.

---

20 If ye died with Christ—When they were buried with Christ in baptism their death with Christ was signified and sealed. (2: 12.) They entered into that real and vital union with him which makes his death, as a complete renunciation of the old life of sin. (2 Cor. 5: 14, 15; Gal. 2: 19, 20; 6: 14.)

from the rudiments of the world,—From the ends, ways, and manners of the world.

why, as though living in the world,—If you are no longer moved by worldly rewards, honors, and ends; if you are dead with Christ to earthly conditions; since you put off at your baptism your old ways of life.

do ye subject yourselves to ordinances,—The ordinances here mean the law of Moses first, to which the Jews were disposed to cling, and teach that the Gentiles should observe; but they em-

not, nor taste, nor touch 22 (all which things are to perish with the using), after the precepts and doctrines of men? 23 Which things have indeed a

---

braced all the observances and appointments which human philosophies and reasonings could command.

21 **Handle not, nor taste, nor touch**—This is an admonition to wholly abstain from the inventions and devices of men in the worship and services of God. God has taught from the beginning that it is a fearful thing to change or in any way to modify his appointments. He has taught by precept and example, that that is the greatest sin. The expulsion of Adam and Eve from the Garden of Eden (Gen. 2: 16, 17; 3: 6-24), and the death and the woes that came upon them and the whole world, is a fearful example, warning man for all time what a fearful sin it is to add to or take from the commandments of God. He said to Moses: "Ye shall not add unto the word which I command you, neither shall ye diminish from it, that ye may keep the commandments of Jehovah your God which I command you." (Deut. 4: 2.) Indeed, the whole history of God's dealing with the human family is a condemnation of adding to or taking from the word of God. This is the presumptuous sin. The same is true of every word sealed by the blood of Christ. Every precept and every example of Jesus was given to impress the necessity of accepting the will of God, without taking from or adding to his commandments. He said: "Not every one that saith unto me, Lord, Lord, shall enter into the kingdom of heaven; but he that doeth the will of my Father who is in heaven." (Matt. 7: 21.) This plainly teaches that all worship is vain that adds to or takes from the word of God. The great end of the Bible is to lead man to give up his own ways and follow God's commandments without any modification whatever. That is the sum and substance of all true religion, as taught from the first chapter of Genesis to the last verse of Revelation.

22 **(all which things are to perish with the using), after the precepts and doctrines of men?**—The prohibitions are specific in form, and refer to certain kinds of food and drink. The Essenes taught the avoidance of oil, flesh, marriage, and of contact with strangers. Jesus had made the same point against the Pharisees who contended that in order to be saved one must wash his hands before eating. (Mark 7: 14-19.) Monks and nuns practice asceti-

show of wisdom in well-worship, and humility, and severity to the body; *but are* not of any ²value against the indulgence of the flesh.

²Or, *honor*

cism for the sake of supposed pietistic effect on themselves. The idea of poverty being essential to piety springs from the same contention.

23 Which things have indeed a show of wisdom—The inventions of men make a great show of wisdom, and worship after man's will much greater show than the commandments of God.

in will-worship,—Will-worship is after our own will. It is self-chosen; and for this single reason is a departure from allegiance to God. [However plausible and specious such worship may appear, however much of show of wisdom it may exhibit, the Holy Spirit has written its folly and emptiness so plainly that none but the willingly blind can fail to see it. Loyalty to the divine government requires hearty obedience to divine law. Whatever God commands, therefore, we must do. To hesitate is to falter, is to forsake our allegiance. To set up any "commandment of men," and honor it as a command of God, is treason. God's will is expressed in his commandments. Every commandment, even the least, is an expression of his will, and an embodiment of his authority as the monarch of the universe. To obey his commandment, to do his will, is therefore, the very essence of true piety. Everything else is mere will-worship.]

and humility,—This is a studied and affected humility, not resting on a basis of faith and love, but consciously cultivated, and therefore not inconsistent with pride. In this way false teachers would become really more dangerous—for no false teachers are so dangerous as those who assume the aspect of great humility and claim great reverence for divine things.

and severity to the body; but are not of any value against the indulgence of the flesh.—These things may have a show of humility and wisdom, so far as self-imposed worship and humility and severity of the body are concerned; but they are of no value or worth whatever as a safeguard against any real temptation to bodily indulgence. Ascetic observances do not make a man pure or shield him against fleshly temptations and indulgences.

SECTION THREE

LIVE AS THOSE SHOULD LIVE WHO HAVE RISEN WITH CHRIST
3: 1 to 4: 6

1. FELLOWSHIP WITH THE EXALTED CHRIST THE MOTIVE TO THE NEW LIFE
3: 1-4

1 If then ye were raised together with Christ, seek the things that are above, where Christ is, seated on the right hand of God. 2 Set your mind on the things that are above, not on the things that are upon the earth. 3 For

---

1 If then ye were raised together with Christ,—In these words Paul refers to what took place when they entered into Christ. "Having been buried with him in baptism, wherein ye were also raised with him through faith in the working of God, who raised him from the dead." (2: 12.) Since then they had put off the old man of sin in baptism, and had been raised with Christ, and in Christ, carry forward this begun work of conformity to the life of Christ.

seek the things that are above, where Christ is,—We seek that heavenly things by recognizing Jesus, who is in heaven, as our Head, and as members of his body, doing his will in all things. [These are the reward of faithful service on earth, and are within reach of present human effort and its noblest aim. Indeed, every effort to please Christ and to advance his kingdom may be looked upon as an effort to gain the things at his right hand, for these are an inevitable and known result of such effort. (Rom. 2: 7.)]

seated on the right hand of God.—[The life in Christ is the elevation of our whole manhood into a divine realm of thought and action. This figuratively expresses the union of Christ with God in the possession of divine power and authority, and in peace, a further reason for seeking heavenly things.]

2 Set your mind on the things that are above,—To set the mind upon him in the affections is to direct the thoughts, desires, and affections toward the things that are in heaven, cultivate an earnest desire for them, and follow the path that leads to them.

not on the things that are upon the earth.—Do not seek after the worldly, fleshly ends and aims—the gratification of the

ye died, and your life is hid with Christ in God. 4 When Christ, *who is*

flesh—wordly ambition, or earthly riches. [We may use the world without abusing it. But it must be secondary, and made subservient to the higher and heavenly interests of the soul.]

3 For ye died,—You are dead with Christ to the world, and your life is swallowed up in the life of Jesus Christ. Paul said: "I have been crucified with Christ; and it is no longer I that live, but Christ liveth in me: and that life which I now live in the flesh I live in faith, the faith which is in the Son of God, who loved me, and gave himself up for me." (Gal. 2: 20.) [This represents a distince element in Christian experience; it means that the soul passes through a death to earthly things—sin and its allurements of the flesh, just as the Lord died upon the cross. The crucifixion must have its counterpart within us. We die to the attractions of the world. The dead know not nor care for anything of this world. Their love and hatred and envy are wholly wiped out. A dead man is as cold and motionless as a stone to all things about which the living make ado. How perfectly then, how entirely, ought we to be free from sin, in order to be dead to it! It is not enough from outward acts of sin, but if the heart cherishes any liking for it. This is not dying to it. Before we can attain to that perfect sinlessness, our hearts must be completely closed against the temptation as if we were nailed down in our coffin; our ears must be deaf to his voice; our eyes must be blind to his charms. We must not only give up every evil practice; we must also stifle every evil desire. Nothing less can deserve the name of being dead to sin. This, then, is the perfection of devotion after which we are to diligently strive.]

and your life is hid with Christ in God.—By faith we are crucified to ourselves, die to our own life, and appropriate the life of Jesus and live his life, reproduces the life of the Son of God in our own bodies and lives. [Christ is our life now as well as hereafter. This is simply a summary of two truths: "Christ liveth in me" (Gal. 2: 20) as the source of life; and "for to me to live—as the actual condition of life—is Christ" (Phil. 1: 21). It is but a brief expression of faith in the truth which Jesus declared in these words: "I am the resurrection, and the life: . . . and whosoever

ᵃour life, shall be manifested, then shall ye also with him be manifested in glory.

ᵃMany ancient authorities read *your*.

. . . believeth on me shall never die." (John 11: 25, 26.) Hence our spiritual life is not only a being "with Christ"; it is also unity with Christ in the bosom of the Father.]

4 **When Christ, who is our life, shall be manifested,**—The reference is to the second coming of Christ, which was a blessed hope to Paul as it is to us. He looked for his personal coming again as a glorious hope. Christ is our life here and now, for "he that hath the Son hath the life." (1 John 5: 12.)

then shall ye also with him be manifested in glory.—It will be in glory and we shall share in that glory. "We know that, if he shall be manifested, we shall be like him; for we shall see him even as he is." (1 John 3: 2.) The glory will come as the crown of the hidden life.

2. EXHORTATIONS—NEGATIVE AND POSITIVE
3: 5-17

5 Put to death therefore your members which are upon the earth: forni-

---

5 **Put to death therefore your members which are upon the earth:**—These members are those which seek only fleshly and sensual gratification, and pertain only to the flesh. They are those of the fleshly body in contrast with the faculties and desires of the spiritual body. The exhortation is to put them to death. Hold them in restraint, check them. Unrestrained they lead to the sins enumerated.

fornication,—Strictly speaking, fornication is illicit intercourse between the sexes, whether married or unmarried. Adultery is a violation of the marriage bed, or unlawful sexual intercourse with another person, whether married or unmarried. Fornication sometimes signifies adultery. (Matt. 19: 9.) [The church of Christ should wage such a relentless warfare against all such wickedness that all such characters would either come to repentance or learn that the church has no fellowship for them.]

uncleanness,—Every manifestation in word or look or deed

cation, uncleanness, passion, evil desires, and covetousness, which is idolatry;

of the impure spirit, and so is wider and subtler than the gross physical act. It includes self-abuse, bestiality, and sodomy.

passion, evil desire,—[The source of evil deeds. More inward and more general than the preceding. They inclue not only the lusts and longings which give rise to the special sins just denounced, but to all forms of hungry appetite and desire after the "members which are upon the earth." If we desire to draw a distinction between the two, probably *passion* is somewhat narrower than *desire,* and the former represents the evil emotion as an affection which the mind suffers, while the latter represents it as a longing which it actually puts forth. The lusts of the flesh are in the one aspect kindled by the outward temptations which come with terrible force and carry the unstable captive, acting almost irresistibly on the animal nature. In the one the evil comes into the heart; in the other the heart goes out to the evil.]

and covetousness,—Covetousness is such an overmastering desire for what belongs to another that the laws of right and justice are violated to obtain it. It is closely allied to the grosser forms of sensuality, and but another form of evil desire going out to the things "which are upon the earth." The ordinary worldly nature flies for solace either to the pleasures of appetite or to the passion of acquiring. And not only are they closely connected in root, but covetousness often follows lust in the history of a life just as it does in this catalogue. When the former evil spirit loses its hold, the letter often takes its place. Many men are now mainly devoted to making money, whose youth was foul with sensual indulgence. When that palled, this came to titillate the jaded desires with a new form of gratification. In that case, covetousness is promoted vice, lust superannuated.

which is idolatry;—Those who reject the God of the Bible formulate a god from their own imagination and desires. Such a god is of necessity the deification of their own reason, desires, appetites, and lusts. The heathen embody them in idols of wood, stone, and metal which are visible objects of worship; but these images are all representatives of certain qualities which they cherish and seek to attain. They are the embodiment of their ideas of

6 for which things' sake cometh the wrath of God [4]upon the sons of disobedience: 7 [5]wherein ye also once walked, when ye lived in these things; 8 but now do ye also put them all away: anger, wrath, malice, railing, shameful

---

[4]Some ancient authorities omit *upon the sons of disobedience.* See Eph. 5. 6.
[5]Or, *amongst whom*

---

the highest good. A man really worships that on which his heart is most earnestly set, which is the chief end of his labor in life. That which man most ardently desires, he worships; and the service he renders in obtaining it is worship. Hence the Holy Spirit defines covetousness to be idolatry. The man that is covetous unduly desires and seeks money, worships it, and becomes sordid, heartless, selfish, and his whole soul is absorbed in the one end of gaining money. When a man desires, above all things, to gratify his lusts and fleshly appetites, and finds happiness only in this, he worships the god of lust; becomes licentious, sensual; loses all ennobling spiritual aspirations; and abandons himself to the gratification of his lusts, and the same is true of covetousness.

6 for which things' sake cometh the wrath of God upon the sons of disobedience:—Man left without restraint which the worship of God lays on him, controlled by his fleshly lusts alone, falls into these degrading sins; the wrath of God rests upon them to destroy them. It was for sins of this kind that God destroyed Sodom and Gomorrah, and the inhabitants of Canaan. Faith in God is the only power on earth that can hold in restraint the evil passions and lusts of man to live the life God desires he should live. All the appetites, desires, and lusts of the body, restrained and guided by the law of God, promote man's happiness and his well-being. Unrestrained, they work degradation, sink him below the brute, and bring him to ruin.

7 wherein ye also once walked, when ye lived in these things;—He reminds them that they walked in these things while they knew not God, and were given over to idolatry. [They formerly lived in the sins just mentioned. They then went along a path trodden by those whose character was derived from and determined by the principle of rebellion against God.]

8 but now do ye also put them all away:—Since they had died with Christ to the world, they were to put away the sins he now mentions.

speaking out of your mouth: 9 lie not one to another; seeing that ye have put off the old man with his doings, 10 and have put on the new man, that is

anger,—The natural passion or emotion of displeasure aroused by injury or insult, real or imagined, and directed against the cause thereof; sudden and strong displeasure. The apostle requires that this feeling be controlled.

wrath,—Deep, determined, and lasting anger; extreme and uncontrolled passion, and if not quickly subdued it grows violent and works malice.

malice,—This is a disposition or intent to injure others for the gratification of anger, jealousy, hatred; active malevolence. It is always sinful.

railing,—Scornful, insolent, or derisive language; to blame with bitterness, and may be directed either against God or man. It is sinful in either case.

shameful speaking—Obscene and filthy talk, calculated to excite the appetite, lusts, and passion which are all wrong in the sight of God.

out of your mouth:—This adds to the prohibition graphic definiteness. "Let no corrupt speech proceed out of your mouth, but such as is good for edifying as the need may be, that it may give grace to them that hear." (Eph. 4: 29.) All that comes out of the mouth that injures the hearer works yet greater injury to the speaker. These are all to be put away by Christians as unworthy of their high calling in Christ.

9 lie not one to another;—To lie is to deceive. Intentional deception is lying, no matter whether done by deed or act, whether by opening or closing the mouth. Do not deceive or take advantage of one another. To deceive in order that one may get advantage is dishonest, is to steal. Lying, deception, and dishonesty belong to the old man—the man of sin that was put off in baptism.

seeing that ye have put off the old man with his doings,—When we put off the old man of sin, we put off his deeds, cease the course of life in which we walked when following the flesh. [So complete is the change that the man himself as he formerly was is spoken of as an old garment laid aside, as though personality itself were changed.]

being renewed unto knowledge after the image of him that created him: 11 where there cannot be Greek and Jew, circumcision and uncircumcision, barbarian, Scythian, bondman, freeman; but Christ is all, and in all.

---

10 and have put on the new man,—This is the new life into which they were led by faith in Christ Jesus. Faith in Christ leads man to seek to conform his spirit and life to the life of Christ.

that is being renewed unto knowledge after the image of him that created him:—Jesus Christ created him. By obtaining a knowledge of Christ and his will, our spiritual being is changed into the likeness of Christ. That is, we learn to think, feel, purpose, and act like Christ. So the heart, the inner man, is made into his image or likeness, and through this the body is brought to obey his will. [Knowledge is the aim of the renewal and the creator is its pattern: therefore the knowledge aimed at must be a human counterpart of the creator's infinite knowledge. As the renewal makes progress, we shall in greater measure share God's knowledge of all that he has made and done. In other words, spiritual growth is growth in intelligence of spiritual things.]

11 where there cannot be Greek and Jew, circumcision and uncircumcision, barbarian, Scythian, bondman, freeman;—In Christ there are no distinctions of the flesh—no distinct nationalities or states. By the law of Moses, all had to be circumcised, and become as children of Abraham or Jews, to become the people of God.

but Christ is all, and in all.—This does not mean that those of different states and sexes do not have different duties to perform, suited to their different faculties and conditions, but all shall be the children of God without reference to these conditions. [To have Christ is to have *all things*—for he is himself all that his servants need. *And in all* his servants, as himself all things to them, *Christ is.* In the slave Christ is his liberty; in the Scythian, as his civilization and culture. And since Christ includes in himself the whole world of man's need, and dwells in all his servants, all human distinctions have in the new life passed utterly away. National and social barriers there cannot be where Christ is.]

12 Put on therefore, as God's elect, holy and beloved, a heart of compassion, kindness, lowliness, meekness, longsuffering; 13 forbearing one another,

12 Put on therefore, as God's elect,—The Christians at Colossæ, Gentiles who had believed and been baptized into Christ, are called God's elect. The Jews had been the elect of God, now both Jews and Gentiles who believed in and obeyed Jesus Christ are equally God's elect. And as his elect or chosen people Paul beseeches them to clothe themselves with the qualities that become the children of God.

holy and beloved,—As God's chosen people, he beseeches them to clothe themselves with the qualities that become the children of God. [*Beloved* describes the position of those who, carrying out by their present holiness the purpose of their election, are the objects of God's abiding love. (1 Thess. 1: 4.) This love brought about their election and set at work the means by which it was accomplished. (Eph. 1: 3, 4; 2: 4; 1 John 3: 1; 4: 9, 10.)]

a heart of compassion,—Inasmuch as we have put on Christ as members of his body, we ought to drink into his spirit—a spirit of compassion for those who have done wrong. When we were sinners against God, he showed his compassion, his love for us, by giving his Son to die for us that we might escape death.

kindness,—If we are led by the Spirit of God, we must show the same spirit—a heart of kindness to all. [The objects of compassion are the suffering and miserable; of kindness to the needy and dependent.]

lowliness,—Not proud, haughty, not thinking highly of self. [This word here means lowliness of mind and not the mock humility of 2:18. Jesus exalted lowliness and pointed out the perils of self-conceit in a number of parables and applied it to himself. (Matt. 11: 29.) This grace is opposed to haughtiness.]

meekness,—Gentile and forbearing under ill-treatment and provocation, but firm and unyielding in devotion to right. It goes far deeper down than any attitude towards man. It lays hold on the will of God as the supreme good, and delights in absolutely and perfectly conforming itself to it.

longsuffering;—Gentle and unresenting while suffering under ill-treatment. It finds its pattern in God's dealing with the un-

and forgiving each other, if any man have a complaint against any; even as ⁶the Lord forgave you, so also do ye: 14 and above all these things *put on*

⁶Many authorities read *Christ*.

---

thankful and the evil. (Luke 6: 35.) It is so natural for us when falsely accused to feel that we must defend ourselves, or to resent such treatment; but of our Lord we read that when false witnesses had risen up against him "he gave him no answer, not even to one word." (Matt. 27: 14.)

13 forbearing one another, and forgiving each other,—In differences in which we feel that we are right and our brethren wrong, we should be gentle and patient, not quick to assert our rights, or to avenge the wrongs others committed against us.

if any man have a complaint against any; even as the Lord forgave you, so also do ye:—Here Christ and his course are held up as an example to us. We are to treat others and forgive others as Christ treated and forgave us. How did Christ treat us? When we were sinners he forbore to execute justice upon us. He suffered long, treated us kindly, gave us health, sent the sunshine and rain, gave us food and raiment; and died to save us because he loved us, and desired not the death of any, but that all might repent that he might forgive them that they might live. Christ does not forgive us until we repent and turn from our sins against him. We cannot forgive those who sin against us until they repent. But Christ did love us, forbore with us, did good to us, and died for us to induce us to repent that he might save us. While those who have wronged us refuse to repent we are to be kind, and show our love for them—do good to them, return good for evil—that they may be brought to repent of their sins that we may forgive them. We cannot forgive those who sin against us till they repent.

14 and above all these things put on love,—As a bond above all the virtues, feelings, and acts, put on love, as a bond to bind all these special qualities together into one godly character—a character like that of God. Jesus said: "Love your enemies, and pray for them that persecute you; that ye may be sons of your Father who is in heaven: for he maketh his sun to rise on the evil and the good, and sendeth rain on the just and the unjust." (Matt. 5: 44, 45.) Many of us have indefinite and incorrect conceptions of what

love, which is the bond of perfectness. 15 And let the peace of Christ [7]rule in your hearts, to the which also ye were called in one body; and be ye thankful. 16 Let the word of [8]Christ dwell in you [9]richly; in all wisdom

[7]Gr. *arbitrate.*
[8]Gr. Some ancient authorities read *the Lord:* others, *God.*
[9]Or, *richly in all wisdom; teaching &c.*

---

love is. It is not an emotion, or a fleshly feeling, or a magnetic attraction, or a mere sentiment. The apostle defines it: "For this is the love of God, that we keep his commandments." (1 John 5: 3.)

which is the bond of perfectness.—We so trust and confide in God that we take his direction as our guide in all good, and do all that he directs, that we may do the greatest possible good. It, then, accepts God as the standard and inspiration of right and the source of all good; and so in discharging the obligations of love we do all that his law directs—what God would have us do to them. So love is the one thing that includes, binds in one, all that goes to make up perfection.

15 And let the peace of Christ rule in your hearts,—The heart is the inner spiritual man. The peace of God is the peace he bestows on those who love and obey him. It arises from the consciousness of union and harmony with him. If we are in union and harmony with him, who rules the world, we can bear with quiet and complacency all the minor ills, trials, and troubles that spring up in our pathway here. [It is the test of everything; by it everything is to be determined.]

to the which also ye were called in one body;—In the body of Christ the peace of God reigns. All in Christ are time and again exhorted to cherish the peace that is the fruit of trusting obedience to the Lord.

and be ye thankful.—They were called by the gospel of the Lord Jesus Christ, into the peace, and for this they should be truly thankful.

16 Let the word of Christ dwell in you richly;—The word or teachnig of Christ dwells in us richly, when we know and understand it, and it fills our hearts, moulds our thoughts and feelings, and guides our lives, accepting it as the fullness and completeness of all wisdom. [*Richly* suggests abundance. The spoken word of

teaching and admonishing [10]one another with psalms *and* hymns *and* spiritual
[10]Or, *yourselves*

Christ is to have a permanent and abundant place in the church, and on the lips and thoughts of its members, thus making them truly rich.]

in all wisdom teaching and admonishing one another with psalms and hymns and spiritual songs,—Singing is one means of getting the word of Christ into the heart of the hearers. By speaking in songs they are to teach and admonish one another, by bringing the thoughts and feelings of the heart into harmony with the sentiment of the songs. These are the ends and purposes of the worship of the song service. To present the sentiment in song helps to carry the impression to the heart. The thoughts contained in the words do the teaching and admonishing; the song is the vehicle by which the sentiments are conveyed to the heart of those who hear and understand.

Instrumental accompaniment does not aid in conveying the thoughts and sentiments to the heart of those who hear. It hinders, rather than helps. The words must be heard and distinctly understood and the sentiments apprehended to effect this end. The instrumental service hinders and diverts the mind from, instead of aiding in, this work. If it aids at all, it is in the execution of the musical performance. This is the danger point and the bane of the song service—that it be diverted to a musical performance to entertain, instead of service to God. The instrumental performance helps to corrupt it at its weakest point, and really hinders it in the main end and purpose for which God ordained it. This, I conclude, would be the case, else God would have connected the instrumental with song service. He knew what is in man, and knew exactly what would be best to effect his purpose. He did not ordain instrumental music in his service. For man to bring it in is at once to impugn the wisdom of the Almighty and to corrupt his service and pervert the end of his appointment. As a musical performance it cannot be called an aid to the singing. An aid or helper is less conspicuous and important than the thing aided. The principal occupies the chief and leading place; the aid the secondary position. The mechanical instrument occupies the leading,

songs, singing with grace in your hearts unto God. 17 And whatsoever ye do, in word or in deed, *do* all in the name of the Lord Jesus, giving thanks to God the Father through him.

---

not the secondary, part in *time* and *sound,* in the service where it is used. It usurps the chief or principal place, and the singing is done as a mere accompaniment of the instrumental service. The attention and thoughts are diverted from the sentiment of the song to the symphonies of the mechanical instrument. It defeats the chief end of the song, the moral and spiritual impression on the heart, and in the musical performance is not an aid, but a hindrance, to the leading end, and makes the singing a minor accompaniment to the instrumental performance. It defeats and perverts the service ordained by God, both in the aim and in the performance.

singing with grace in your hearts unto God.—We are to sing in the sunshine of the favor of God, our song being prompted by his great goodness to us. The melody of the lips coming from and filling the heart. Whatever goes up to God must fill the heart. In the parallel passage it is said: "And . . . be filled with the Spirit; speaking one to another in psalms and hymns and spiritual songs, singing and making melody with your heart to the Lord." (Eph. 5: 18, 19.) These passages mean exactly the same. To "be filled with the Spirit" and to have the "word of Christ dwell in you richly" are one and the same thing; to sing and make melody in the heart to the Lord and to sing with grace in the heart are one and the same thing, and mean to bring the thoughts and feelings into harmony with the sentiment sung. It is the sentiment that is sung that constitutes the worship; there is no acceptable worship in music distinct from the sentiment sung. The music of the song is only the means of impressing the sentiment sung more deeply on the hearts of both singer and hearer. What is sung must be the outgrowth of the rich indwelling of the word of Christ in the heart. The purpose is to praise God and teach the word of Christ.

17 And whatsoever ye do, in word or in deed, do all in the name of the Lord Jesus,—To do a thing in the name of the Lord Jesus is to do it for him and as he directs. Do it by his authority; do it as his servant, for his honor and glory. He is the only meditator between God and man. Does any one believe if

Christ were here in person as we are that he would go into any human society and do things as they require? We are required to give and do all we do as the servants of God. Jesus, when on earth, did nothing save what God required. He had no will of his own, no wish or desire to do anything save the will of God. If we are his disciples and do his will, we will not enter or remain in any society that Jesus did not appoint or command. God and his institutions are entitled to the whole undivided service of man in carrying out the will of God. He has nothing to divide with others. God cannot reward for what a man does as a member of another body, and to divide his time and service with that of others is to vitiate all the service rendered. God will not accept a divided or mutilated service. "Thou shalt worship the Lord thy God, and him only shalt thou serve." (Matt. 4: 10.) "But in vain do they worship me, teaching as their doctrines the precepts of men." (Matt. 15: 9.) God demands our whole time and service in his church. We need it all there to make us loyal and true citizens of that kingdom.

[Our eating and drinking—acts which seem remote from the interests and sentiments of the spiritual life—these are to be "sanctified through the word of God and prayer" (1 Tim. 4: 5), by the mention of Christ's name in thanksgiving to the Father, who through him sends us all life's blessings. And if our mere physical necessities of life are capable of being thus hallowed, there is nothing in family relations, or secular employments, or social duties, which may not receive and does not demand the same consideration. We should associate Christ with everything we do, doing all as his servants and under his eye, and in such a way that, in every part of our work, he may be glorified in us, and this will be a safeguard to the Christian. If he is to do everything in Christ's name, he must do nothing unworthy of that name, nothing with which he cannot associate it. Nowhere, in any company or in any business, must he forget, "whatsoever ye do, in word or in deed," that this worthy name is the name which he bears, and whose honor is in his keeping. This is the seal which every true Christian wears upon his heart: "Let every one that nameth the name of the Lord depart from unrighteousness." (2 Tim. 2: 19.)]

giving thanks to God the Father through him.—By living a life of constant gratitude to God the Father in the manner all is done in the name of the Lord Jesus Christ. Both in his gifts and in his chastisements, praise him. Such gratitude is through him since what he is and what he has done as our Redeemer not only makes us grateful, but gives us a Mediator for the expression of our thanksgiving. The first human motive in the Christian life is gratitude for redemption, and it does not lose its power as we feel more and more how great a Redeemer the Lord Jesus is.

3. SPECIAL PRECEPTS AS TO HOUSEHOLD RELATIONS
3: 18 to 4: 1

18 Wives, be in subjection to your husbands, as is fitting in the Lord. 19

18 **Wives, be in subjection to your husbands,**—It is fit or proper that the wife submit herself to her husband so far as she can do it in the Lord, or without disobedience to God. God ordained from the beginning that the husband should be the head of the household. The Holy Spirit says: "In like manner, ye wives, be in subjection to your own husbands; that, even if any obey not the word, they may without the word be gained by the behavior of their wives; beholding your chaste behavior coupled with fear." (1 Pet. 3: 1, 2.) It is proper for the wife to show what she regards as right, then to submit to his decisions. She may influence, but not control him.

as is fitting in the Lord.—This is what God has ordained, and it is fitting that those who are in the Lord should observe his order. [The holy and mysterious union of man and woman in marriage is fashioned in the likeness of the only union which is closer and more mysterious than itself—that between Christ and the church. (Eph. 5: 32, 33.) Such then as is the subjection of the church to Christ, such will be the nature of the wife's subjection to the husband—a subjection of which love is the very soul and animating principle. In a true marriage, as in loving obedience to a loving soul to Christ, the wife submits not because she has found a master, but because her heart has found its rest. For its full satisfaction, a woman's heart needs to look up where it loves. Since then a woman's love is in general nobler, purer, more unselfish than a man's and therein, quite as much as in physical constitution, is laid the foundation of the divine ideal of marriage, which

Husbands, love your wives, and be not bitter against them. 20 Children obey

places the wife's delight and dignity in sweet loving subjection. Of course the subjection has its limitations, for it is bound by: "We must obey God rather than men." (Acts 5:29.)]

Where the husband and wife are both earnest Christians seeking to do the will of God, in whose hearts there is real mutual affection and esteem, there will be no difficulty whatever in regard to such an admonition as this; but it will require grace to yield loving obedience when perhaps the husband is a carnal, worldly, and unreasonable man, and yet we need to remember that the marriage relationship is divinely ordained, and for the Christian woman, this relation once formed, there is no other position in conformity with the will of God than that of godly submission to the husband whom she herself has chosen. The present loose ideas in regard to easy divorce and remarriage to another are bearing fearful fruit which will increase unto more ungodliness, until there will be duplicated the corruption and vileness of the days before the flood and the unspeakable vileness and immoralities of the cities of Sodom and Gomorrah. Of all this the Lord Jesus had warned us most solemnly. For one to seek to dissolve the marriage relationship because of incompatability of temperament is to trample under foot the instructions of the Lord Jesus Christ. *Death*, or what is equivalent to it, *adultery* of husband or wife, is the only scriptural ground for the termination of the marriage contract, leaving the innocent party free to remarry. (Matt. 19:9.)

19 **Husbands, love your wives,**—In the beginning it was said: "Therefore shall a man leave his father and his mother, and shall cleave unto his wife: and they shall be one flesh." (Gen. 2:24.) Husbands must love and cherish their wives, promote their good, happiness and welfare. The apostle says: "Even so ought husbands also to love their own wives as their own bodies. He that loveth his own wife loveth himself: for no man ever hated his own flesh; but nourisheth and cherisheth it, even as Christ also the church. . . . Nevertheless do ye also severally love each one his own wife even as himself; and let the wife see that she fear her husband." (Eph. 5:28-33.) [The Christian husband is to accept his place of headship as a sacred responsibility put upon him

your parents in all things, for this is well-pleasing in the Lord. 21 Fathers, provoke not your children, that they be not discouraged. 22 ⁱⁱServants, obey

by God himself, and is to exercise authority for the blessing of his home in the love of Christ. And just as some wives may be united to tyrannical and unreasonable men, so there are husbands who, after marriage, find that the one who in the days of courtship seemed so affectionate is a veritable termagant, and as unreasonable as it is possible to be. But still the husband is to love and care for her, showing all consideration, as the apostle says: "Giving honor unto the woman, as unto the weaker vessel, as being also joint-heirs of the grace of life; to the end that your prayers be not hindered." (1 Pet. 3: 7.)]

and be not bitter against them.—[God knew how petty and trying some women's ways would be when he said this. In the power of the new life one may manifest patience and grace under the most trying circumstances, and not suffer himself to become exasperated.]

20 Children, obey your parents in all things,—In the early years of the child life, the parents stand as God unto them. They should be taught implicit obedience. When they come to know and understand their relation to God, then the first and highest duty is to teach, and the command is: "Children, obey your parents in the Lord: for this is right." (Eph. 6: 1.) Obey them in all things compatible with their obedience to God.

for this is well-pleasing in the Lord.—[There is something especially pleasing in the behavior of a lovingly obedient child, that wins "favor with God and men." (Luke 2: 52.) The law of filial obedience has its creative ground "in him" (1: 16), and is an essential part of the Christian order of life, which is the natural order restored and perfected. It is a pleasing thing to see children subjecting their impulses, their wishes, their plans, to the better judgment, and riper experience, of their parents. It is a pleasing thing to see them rendering prompt obedience. This is not only pleasing in itself, but it is well-pleasing in the Lord.]

21 Fathers, provoke not your children,—Parents ought not to be hard to please, severe, and harsh. It disheartens them, and makes them bitter and rebellious. No more sacred or important

in all things them that are your [12]masters according to the flesh; not with eye-service, as men-pleasers, but in singleness of heart, fearing the Lord: 23

---

[11]Gr. *Bondservants.*
[12]Gr. *lords.*

---

duty was ever committed to mortals than that of nurturing and training children to the Lord. Parents owe it to the children and their everlasting well-being to train them for the Lord. In no point of duty are Christians more negligent than in training them in the nurture and admonition of the Lord. They should be trained from the beginning to obey, but with love. Sympathy and encouragement should be shown.

that they be not discouraged.—Under protracted irritation the child is likely to become despondent, hopeless, sullen, losing all courage and spirit and giving up all effort to obey, and finally become reckless. They should not be fretted, but they should be encouraged and commended when they do well. [They should be so trained as to make them feel that the approbation of parents is a desirable thing, and when they act so as to deserve that approbation, it encourages them to know it. He who always finds fault with a child, who is never satisfied with what he does, who scolds, and frets, and complains, let him do what he will, breaks the spirit, and even destroys all desire of doing well. The child, in despair, soon gives up every effort to please.]

22 Servants, obey in all things them that are your masters according to the flesh;—Slavery existed in the days of the apostles by political authority; and was recognized and regulated among Christians with reference to both master and slave. God did not break and destroy the relationships fixed by political governments suddenly. He breathed into them a spirit which softened their harsh features, and gradually prepared men to see the evils of such relations and that influence finally destroyed it. Christians are to obey their masters in all things.

not with eye-service,—[Service that must be watched to see that it was done at all, or properly done. The aim of the service was to seem faithful.]

as men-pleasers,—Solely desirous of pleasing men without reference to the right or wrong of the thing done. [To please men is their aim—and therefore their work is only such as falls

whatsoever ye do, work [13]heartily, as unto the Lord, and not unto men; 24 knowing that from the Lord ye shall receive the recompense of the inheritance: ye serve the Lord Christ. 25 For he that doeth wrong shall

[13]Gr. *from the soul*.

within the range of human observation. Such merely external service is utterly unworthy of Christians. For it brings him down to the level of those whose well-being depends on the smiles of their fellows.]

but in singleness of heart, fearing the Lord:—With the desire to do right for its own sake, or rather for the sake of the Lord Jesus as their divine Master; as against the selfish aim of men-pleasers. The principles here laid down as to slaves apply to all cases where one is entitled to the service of another, whether he be slave or hired servant; and all men who work for wages, from the president down, are in the good sense of the term hired servants. The admonition is, when one is entitled to your service, render it heartily and faithfully, knowing that God will take account of your faithfulness. God will hold to accountability as unworthy the man who is not as diligent and faithful in the absence of the employer as in his presence.

23 whatsoever ye do, work heartily, as unto the Lord,—Render service to the earthly master earnestly, faithfully, from the heart, as service rendered to the Lord and not unto man.

and not unto men;—The service the Christian servant renders to the earthly master must be from the heart, and with a view to what the Lord thinks of it. [For everything should be done for Christ, as service rendered for him, in view of the relation to him. And the relation to the human master should not, in this method of regarding it, be taken into account at all, on the principle of not serving two masters.]

24 knowing that from the Lord ye shall receive the recompense of the inheritance:—The Christian slave will receive of the Lord the reward for his fidelity in the service to the earthly master. Paul says: "For he that was called in the Lord being a bondservant, is the Lord's freedman: likewise he that was called being free, is Christ's bondservant." (1 Cor. 7: 22.) When another is entitled to the service of a Christian he cannot give the

¹⁴receive again for the wrong that he hath done: and there is no respect of persons.

1 ¹²Masters, render unto your ¹¹servants that which is just and ¹⁵equal; knowing that ye also have a Master in heaven.

¹⁴Gr. *receive again the wrong.*
¹⁵Gr. *equality.*

---

time and service to God that he would were he free; so the Lord releases him from that constant service to which he holds the freeman. But if the Christian servant will serve his earthly master faithfully, the Lord will accept it as service rendered to him, and will so reward him, for such service adorns "the doctrine of God our Saviour." (Tit. 2: 10.)

ye serve the Lord Christ.—In faithfully serving the earthly master, they served Christ.

25 For he that doeth wrong shall receive again for the wrong that he hath done:—He who does not serve the earthly master with fidelity wrongs him—is not diligent in his absence as in his presence, does not faithfully look after his interests, is not faithful unto God—God will punish for the wrong he does the earthly master, certainly, God demands that his children must be trustworthy and faithful in all relations of life.

and there is no respect of persons.—God does not reward a man for being a slave or a freeman, for being rich or poor; but requires fidelity of his servants in all the relations in which they stand.

4:1 Masters, render unto your servants that which is just and equal; knowing that ye also have a Master in heaven.—He reminds them that the Master had said: "All things therefore whatsoever ye would that men should do unto you, even so do ye also unto them: for this is the law and the prophets." (Matt. 7: 12.) If masters treated their servants with severity, so would God deal with them. The condition of slaves among the Greeks and Romans was indeed wretched in the extreme. They could expect neither justice nor equity. They could not appeal to the civil courts. The Holy Spirit gave them, through Paul, a law of justice and equity to govern Christian masters.

4. EXHORTATIONS IN RELATION TO PRAYER AND CONDUCT TOWARDS THOSE WITHOUT
4: 2-6

2 Continue stedfastly in prayer, watching therein with thanksgiving; 3 withal praying for us also, that God may open unto us a door for the word, to speak the mystery of Christ, for which I am also in bonds; 4 that I may

2 Continue stedfastly in prayer,—Paul takes it for granted that they do pray and he tells them that "with prayer and supplication praying at all seasons in the Spirit, and watching thereunto in all perseverance and supplication for all saints." (Eph. 6: 18.) "Pray without ceasing." (1 Thess. 5: 17.) He was not urging long prayers, but the continuance of the habit of prayer.

watching therein—In our persistent prayers our spiritual faculties must be in active exercise. We must, while we pray, be keenly alive to our own needs and dangers and the promises of God. [To be awake is to be alive in the fullest sense, to have all the powers of perception and action in readiness. The activity of the soul in prayer is to be both energetic and incessant.]

with thanksgiving;—[This is a most appropriate accompaniment, or surrounding element, of these watchful prayers. Ceaseless prayers combined with ceaseless praise was the atmosphere of Paul's spiritual life, and should be ours.]

3 withal praying for us also,—He craved a place in their prayers as he had expressed his in their behalf. (1: 9.) He had been a prisoner for years. He had hopes of ultimate freedom, and he believed in prayer for that object. (Phil. 1: 19.)

that God may open unto us a door for the word,—"The word" is the word of God which Paul preached; and a door was wanted, in his present difficulties, through which that word may freely pass. (1 Cor. 16: 9; 2 Cor. 2: 12.) With compassionate eagerness did he desire an open door, and even if it was for a time barred and bolted in his face, he never despaired. He desired not prayer for his personal benefit or comfort, but for the removal of all external impediments to his preaching.

to speak the mystery of Christ,—Were the door once opened, he would be able freely to preach the gospel to the Gentiles.

for which I am also in bonds;—His preaching to the Gentiles was the real casue which led to his imprisonment. He was

make it manifest, as I ought to speak. 5 Walk in wisdom toward them that are without ¹redeeming the time. 6 Let your speech be always with grace, seasoned with salt, that ye may know how ye ought to answer each one.

¹Gr. *buying up the opportunity.*

---

now in the strange position of an "ambassador in chains." (Eph. 6: 19, 20; Phile. 9, 10.)

4 that I may make it manifest, as I ought to speak.—Sometimes Paul felt that he might be affrighted so that he would not faithfully declare the truth in the way that he should. [The needs of the world and the grandeur of the gospel were to Paul an imperative necessity, leaving him no choice but compelling him as if by main force to preach the word wherever he could and at all cost. This felt necessity forced him to make this appeal for the help of their prayers.]

5 Walk in wisdom toward them that are without,—Walk with wisdom and prudence towards those who are not believers. [Those not members of the church keenly watch the conduct of those claiming to be Christians. It has always been so, and is true today. They watch our walk more than our talk, and judge and measure our talk by our walk. To benefit others spiritually, the chief qualification is not gifts, but character. The lives of Christians are the Bible the world reads. (2 Cor. 3: 2, 3.) We should see that the text is not corrupted or illegible. Live so that the more you are known the more you will be esteemed, so that those who are without and anxious would naturally seek you for help and guidance, and your judgment or reproof would carry with it the weight of a consecrated character.]

redeeming the time.—Every Christian should seize and use well every opportunity to do good and promote the glory of Christ.

6 Let your speech be always with grace,—In conversation and discourse, be absolutely, at all times, and under all circumstances, kind and gracious. Evil, vicious conversation, that excites the lusts, passions, evil desires, often does more harm than many sinful deeds, and God forewarns that for all this men will be held to strict account.

seasoned with salt,—Having force and character; not insipid, but pointed. There may be reference also to the preservative and purifying power of salt. Let your speech be wholesome, not corruptive. [As food is seasoned with salt and made pleasant and palatable, so let your speech, especialy to those who are without, be not insipid nor coarse, but pleasant, pure, wholesome, and salutary.]

that ye may know how ye ought to answer each one.—Paul wished the Colossians to know how to answer the false teachers in their disputes as well as how to win people to Christ by means of grace. It is a rare gift, but a needful one. Not only must our conversation be opportune as regards the time; it must also be appropriate as regards the person. The context shows that unbelievers are meant, although the rule holds good in all social intercourse. Kindness and point, and adaptation to the hearers—these characteristics of Christian speech—when supported by a wise walk and watchfulness for proper opportunities, will give power to the humblest believer.

SECTION FOUR

CONCLUDING EXHORTATIONS
4: 7-18

1. PERSONAL INTELLIGENCE
4: 7-9

7 All my affairs shall Tychicus make known unto you, the beloved brother and faithful minister and fellow-servant in the Lord: 8 whom I have

---

7 All my affairs shall Tychicus make known unto you,— Paul was a prisoner in Rome, dependent upon the churches to render assistance unto him to live. They sent relief by messengers, each church sending its own messenger. Paul sent in turn messengers to the churches to let them know his condition, how the word of truth prospered, and to instruct the churches in the truth, and bring him word as to their condition. [The association of Tychicus with Paul in his last journey to Jerusalem, attended with so many affecting circumstances and terminating in his long imprisonment, led to a devoted attachment on the part of Tychicus to Paul. At the time this epistle was written he was with Paul in his imprisonment at Rome, about to be sent home, in charge of Onesimus, on whose account the apostle sends a letter to Philemon. In the interval between the first imprisonment in Rome and the second (2 Timothy), Paul revisits the Asiastic churches—so it is inferred from 1 Timothy (1: 3)—and Tychicus rejoins him; for we find Paul proposing to send him to Titus in Crete (Tit. 3: 12), and finally sending him from Rome once more to Ephesus (2 Tim. 6: 12).

the beloved brother and faithful minister and fellow-servant in the Lord:—It is evident that he was one in whom Paul had implicit confidence. He speaks of him here and in Ephesians (6: 22, 23) as a faithful brother and minister. Tychicus is "minister" not to Paul himself (Acts 19: 22; 13: 5), but of Christ (1 Thess. 3: 2), as Paul himself (Col. 1: 23, 25). He was the beloved and faithful minister and fellow servant in the Lord. [He was undoubtedly a lovable man because of his gracious demeanor and his tender solicitude for the welfare of the saints, and at the same time he was faithful in ministering the word of God, rebuking iniquity and comforting the penitent. Such men are rare. In

sent unto you for this very purpose, that ye may know our state, and that he may comfort your hearts; 9 together with Onesimus, the faithful and beloved brother, who is one of you. They shall make known unto you all things that *are done* here.

---

them we see the delightful combination of loyalty to the word of God and seeking the comfort and blessing of the people of God.]

8 whom I have sent unto you for this very purpose, that ye may know our state,—Paul sent them, not only to tell them of his condition and of the success of the gospel in Rome, but to learn all about their fidelity, their knowledge of the truth, and their condition.

and that he may comfort your hearts;—He would comfort their hearts by teaching them the word of God, as well as favorably reporting Paul's condition. [The Colossians did not need consolation, but courage to stand against the wiles of the false teachers and be faithful to Christ and the gospel message.]

9 together with Onesimus,—Onesimus was a slave of Philemon, of Colossæ. He had run away from his master. Paul met him in Rome, converted him to Christ, and returned him to Philemon in company with Tychicus.

the faithful and beloved brother,—Paul had learned to love and trust him, as "my child, whom I have begotten in my bonds" as his "very heart" for his goodness and his proved fidelity and helpful service to himself. (Phile. 10-13.) Greatly had he wished to retain him, but it was the servant's duty to return to his master.

who is one of you.—It was a natural and kindly feeling that prompted this reference. Ties of neighborhood and early association, as well as those of kindred, are formed, and belong to the constituted framework of human life. (Acts 17: 26.) This claim of Onesimus is not destroyed by his being a slave, at the very bottom of the social scale; nor was it forfeited by his conduct. Now that he has repented and returned, he was to be received by his fellow Christians as one of themselves.

They shall make known unto you all things that are done here.—They would make known the work done by Paul and his companions in Rome, as well as what was done to him, and what was his condition and need. [There was, therefore, no need for any detailed account of Paul's circumstances. The solicitude of which he assumes these Colossian Christians (1: 8; 2: 1) feel in his behalf shows how commanding and how great his influence over the Gentile churches had become.]

2. SALUTATIONS AND MESSAGES
4: 10-17

10 Aristarchus my fellow-prisoner saluteth you, and Mark, the cousin of

10 **Aristarchus my fellow-prisoner saluteth you,**—Aristarchus was a Macedonian, had accompanied Paul in his return from Macedonia. (Acts 19: 29.) He accompanied Paul on his return to Jerusalem, as one chosen to go with him to carry the bounty of the Macedonian churches to the poor saints in Judea. (Acts 20: 4.) He was with Paul when taken prisoner, and was either himself sent as a prisoner, or voluntarily accompanied him to Rome and remained with him during his imprisonment. (Acts 27: 2.) He was with Paul in his imprisonment, and sent salutations and expressions of good will to the Colossian brethren. [We know nothing more of his services in behalf of the cause of Christ beyond this record of his assiduous and self-sacrificing attendance on Paul. How much Paul, with his physical infirmities, owed to such friendship, and how much the church owes on his account, we cannot tell. Those who may not have great gifts for public service may serve Christ most effectually oftentime by serving his servants, by their private friendship and aid cheering the hearts and strengthening the hands of those on whom fall the heavier responsibilities of the churches' care and strife, and who but for such timely assistance mighty haply sink beneath their burdens.]

and Mark,—Mark, like Onesimus, "who once was unprofitable" to his master (Phile. 11), had been aforetime unfaithful to Paul (Acts 13: 13; 15: 36-41); which caused a serious breach between Paul and Barnabas. But now, and again at a later time, he is marked out by Paul as useful "for ministering." (2 Tim. 4: 11.) Paul's firmness and fidelity in refusing, at whatever cost, to take with him an untrustworthy man, had, we may presume, helped to arouse Mark to a better spirit. [Notwithstanding all Paul's uncompromising sternness and the intenseness of his passionate nature, there was no bitterness or suspiciousness, no cherishing re-

4: 10, 11.] COLOSSIANS 313

Barnabas (touching whom ye received commandments; if he come unto you, receive him), 11 and Jesus that is called Justus, who are of the circumci-

sentment in his heart. Some men will never trust again a friend or servant who once, under any circumstances, had failed them. But Paul shows a more Christian and wiser disposition. As he bids others do, so he acts himself, "forbearing one another, and forgiving each other." (3: 13.) As "the Lord forgave" Peter who denied him, so Paul forgave Mark who had deserted him. And by the way in which he commends him to the Colossian church, he shows how entirely Mark now has his approval and confidence.]

the cousin of Barnabas—Mark is called the cousin of Barnabas by way of commendation. (1 Cor. 9: 6; Gal. 2: 1, 9, 13.) Mary the mother of John Mark was highly esteemed in the church at Jerusalem (Acts 12: 12), and through her he may have been related to Barnabas.]

(touching whom ye received commandments; if he come unto you, receive him),—[The formal charge to the Colossian church to "receive him"—a kind of letter of commendation (2 Cor. 3: 1)—evidently shows that they had known of him as under Paul's displeasure, and were now to learn that he had seen reason to restore him to his confidence. In the epistle to Philemon, Mark is named, as of course, among his "fellow-workers." (Verse 24.) In Paul's last epistle, written just a short while before his death, there is a touch of peculiar pathos in the charge to Timothy: "Only Luke is with me. Take Mark, and bring him with thee; for he is useful to me for ministering" (2 Tim. 4: 11), from which he had once rejected him.]

11 and Jesus that is called Justus,—This is the only mention of him. He was most likely a Jew of Rome, who had become a Christian, and the fact that he was found at this time by Paul's side says a great deal for his courage and faith, as well as for his largeness of heart. [If for no other reason, then, it was fitting that his name should be honorably mentioned. His cognomen *Justus* attests his reputation among his fellow citizens for legal strictness and uprightness would make his attachment for Paul the more valuable. The surname Justus is found in Acts (1: 23; 18: 7);

sion: these only *are my* fellow-workers unto the kingdom of God, men that have been a comfort unto me. 12 Epaphras, who is one of you, a ²servant of Christ Jesus, saluteth you, always striving for you in his prayers, that ye

²Gr. *bondservant.*

---

and we learn from tradition that by it James the Lord's brother was known.]

who are of the circumcision: these only are my fellow-workers unto the kingdom of God, men that have been a comfort unto me.—The juxtaposition of the two notices seems to indicate—what is itself likely—that the brethren who held aloof from Paul in "envy and strife" (Phil. 1: 15-20) were of the circumcision. Out of them only Aristarchus, Mark, and Justus, as converts from Judaism, and as the only Jewish Christians in Rome of any prominence who stood by him as fellow workers and rendered him much encouragement and comfort in the Lord's work.

12 Epaphras,—All we know of Epaphras, we learn from the brief notices in this epistle. He has first preached the gospel to the Colossians, and perhaps to Laodicea and Hierapolis. He had come to Paul, apparently, to consult with him about the false teaching which threatened the peace of the church. He had informed him, too, of their love. It was his report which led to the writing of the epistle.

who is one of you,—He was a native of Colossæ.

a servant of Christ Jesus, saluteth you,—[This title, which Paul uses several times of himself, is not elsewhere conferred on any other individual, except once on Timothy (1: 1), and probably points to an exceptional service in the cause of Christ on the part of Epaphras.]

always striving for you in his prayers,—[The striving in prayer was due to the zeal of Epaphras and the danger of the Colossians. The appropriateness of this phase is felt by all to whom prayer is a reality, and to Epaphras this intense effort was ceaseless.]

that ye may stand—This was the purpose and purport of the prayers. *Stand* points to maturity fully assured. It appears that they needed a deeper spiritual insight and well-grounded conviction respecting the truth "as in Jesus."

4: 12-14.]　　　　　　　　COLOSSIANS　　　　　　　　315

may stand perfect and fully assured in all the will of God. 13 For I bear him witness, that he hath much labor for you, and for them in Laodicea, and for them in Hierapolis. 14 Luke, the beloved physician, and Demas salute

---

perfect and fully assured—Perfect points to maturity; fully assured to permanent state of confident persuasion.

in all the will of God.—[In everything that is the will of God, and indicates the sphere of completeness and confidence. The tone of Epaphras' prayer takes the tone from the errors which endangered the church he had founded.]

13 For I bear him witness, that he hath much labor for you, and for them in Laodicea, and for them in Hierapolis.—Paul testifies that Epaphras had great zeal in behalf of the disciples at Colossæ, Laodicea, and Hierapolis. These cities were of the Lycus Valley. Laodicea and Hierapolis were on opposite sides of the valley about twelve miles from Colossæ. At all these places Epaphras had most likely preached, and was acquainted with them. His zeal for them was shown in the constant, earnest prayer he offered continually in their behalf. We ought to strive in prayer in behalf of those we would help. "The supplication of a righteous man availeth much in its working." (James 5: 16.) The rationalism of this age, that has permeated the church, has well nigh destroyed faith in prayer. But it is the effective instrumentality to which Christians must come before they convert the world, or be fully blessed themselves.

14 Luke,—[This name occurs three times in the New Testament. (Here; 2 Tim. 4: 11; Phile. 24.) As there is every reason to believe that the man of these passages is the author of the Gospel of Luke and of Acts of Apostles, it is natural to seek the evidence in the book itself some traces of the connection with Paul, which these passages assume to exist; and although the name Luke does not occur in Acts, there is reason to believe that under the pronoun *we*, several references to Luke are to be added to the three already mentioned. Combining the traditional with the scriptural, we are able to trace the following outline of his life. He was born at Antioch in Syria, not of Jewish parents, for he is not reckoned among those "who are of the circumcision" by Paul. (Col. 4: 11.) The date of his conversion to Christ is uncertain. He was not among those "who from the beginning were eyewitnesses and ministers of the word" (Luke 1: 1, 2), or he would have rested his claim upon that ground. The ray of historical light falls on him as a follower of Jesus Christ when he joined Paul at Troas and shared his journey into Macedonia. The sudden transition to the first person plural (we) in Acts 16: 10 is most naturally explained that the writer of Acts formed one of the company from this point. His conversion had taken place before, since he silently assumes his place in Paul's company without any hint that this was his first admission to the knowledge of the ministry of Christ. As far as Philippi he journeyed with Paul and his company. The resumption of the third person (they) on Paul's departure from Philippi (17: 1) shows that Luke was left behind. During the remainder of Paul's second missionary journey no further mention of Luke is made. But on the third journey the same indication reminds us that Luke is again in the company (Acts 20: 5), having joined it at Philippi, where he had been left. With Paul he passed on to Jerusalem. (20: 5, 6; 21: 18.) Between the two visits to Philippi, seven years elapsed (A.D. 51 to 58), which Luke may have spent in Philippi, preaching the gospel. There is one passage which, if it refers to Luke, must belong to this period: "And we have sent together with him (Titus) the brother whose praise in the gospel is spread through all the churches." (2 Cor. 8: 18.) It is an opinion among some expositors that Luke was the companion of Titus on this mission. If this be so, we are to suppose that during the three months of Paul's sojourn at Philippi (Acts 20: 6) Luke was sent from that place on this mission; and the words whose praise is in all the churches enable us to form an estimate of his activity during the interval in which he has not been otherwise mentioned. The praise lay in the activity with which he preached the gospel. He again appears in the company of Paul in the journey to Rome. (Acts 27: 1.) He remained at his side during his first imprisonment (Col. 4: 14; Phile. 24); then during his second Roman imprisonment, the Second Epistle to Timothy (4: 11) shows that he continued faithful to Paul, and remained with him to the end of his affliction. After the death of Paul the acts of Luke are hopelessly obscure. It is perhaps as Luke wished it to be. We only know while he stood faithfully by the side of his beloved Paul; when he departed the history of his

you. 15 Salute the brethren that are in Laodicea and ³Nymphas, and the church that is in ⁴their house. 16 And when ⁵this epistle hath been read

³The Greek may represent *Nympha.*
⁴Some ancient authorities read *her.*
⁵Gr. *the*

---

faithful companion becomes hopelessly confused. It is enough for us, so far as regards the Gospel of Luke, to know that the writer was the tried and constant friend of Paul, who shared his labors, and was not driven from his side by danger.]

the beloved physician,—Of all Paul's friends none was dearer to him or more serviceable than Luke. [This suggests a lovable man, tender and true; a character profoundly welcome to the aching heart of the apostle.]

and Demas salute you.—From the fact that Demas is mentioned here without a word of praise while the others received commendations in various ways, many interpreters have concluded that already his true character was beginning to appear, and that Paul did not have full confidence in him. [During Paul's second Roman imprisonment, when troubles multiplied, and danger was imminent, Paul says: "Demas forsook me, having loved this present world, and went to Thessalonica." (2 Tim. 4: 10.) His departure and that of the others on whom Paul relied while in prison was one of the severest trials which he was called upon to endure.]

15 Salute the brethren that are in Laodicea,—Laodicea was the capital of Phrygia, in Asia Minor, and a little south of Colossæ. Being near Colossæ, the church would be exposed to the same perils.

and Nymphas,—Of Nymphas we know nothing, except from this passage. He was obviously a man of influence in the community and a worthy servant of the Lord.

and the church that is in their house.—"Their" evidently refers to Nymphas and his family. It was common enough for the church to meet in a private house since there were as yet no separate houses of worship. It is said that Priscilla and Aquila had such both in their house in Rome (Rom. 16: 5) and in Ephesus (1 Cor. 16: 19), and that Philemon had such in his house at Colossæ (Phile. 2). It was customary for the brethren who had large

among you, cause that it be read also in the church of the Laodiceans; and that ye also read the epistle from Laodicea. 17 And say to Archippus, Take

---

and convenient houses to gather portions of the whole community in these.

16 **And when this epistle hath been read among you, cause that it be read also in the church of the Laodiceans; and that ye also read the epistle from Laodicea.**—The present epistle was to be read in the assembly of the church at Colossæ and a copy sent to Laodicea and similarly read there. Compare the instruction to the Corinthians (2 Cor. 1: 1), which implies the sending of copies to neighboring churches. [It is generally believed among Biblical scholars that Ephesians was designed also for the other churches in the same province. This conclusion is based on the belief that, although it is addressed "to the saints that are at Ephesus," the metropolis of the Roman province of Asia which included Laodicea and Colossæ, it was probably designed for other churches in the same province—"the faithful in Christ Jesus." If so, it is quite conceivable that Paul gave orders to Tychicus to leave at Laodicea for the church there a copy of the epistle to the Ephesians. And this copy would be "the epistle *from Laodicea*" which Paul desired the Colossians to *read*. This desire grew out of the fact that the two epistles, though closely related in thought and phraseology, are quite distinct. Each supports the other. The one to the Ephesians deals chiefly with the church; that to the Colossians expounds the dignity and work of Christ, and rebuts certain special errors. This suggestion is so free from objection, and meets so well all the facts of the case, that with our scanty information we may accept it as probable.]

17 **And say to Archippus,**—Archippus is mentioned elsewhere only in Philemon. (2.) The words "say to" suggest that he was close at hand to hear what was said; and was therefore probably a member of the church at Colossæ. And this agrees with his relation to Philemon, who also seems to have been a Colossian. Archippus was called a "fellow-soldier" (Phile. 2) of Paul, which suggests that he had shared with Paul the perils of Christian work. And this agrees with the work "in the Lord" mentioned here.

heed to the ministry which thou hast received in the Lord, that thou fulfil it.

Take heed to the ministry which thou hast received in the Lord, that thou fulfil it.—He sends this caution to Archippus, who seems to have been sent on a mission to them, and warns him to be careful that he fulfil it. Do faithfully and well what the Lord had sent him to do.

3. FAREWELL GREETINGS
4: 18

18 The salutation of me Paul with mine own hand. Remember my bonds. Grace be with you.

18 The salutation of me Paul with mine own hand.—It was customary for Paul to have an amanuensis to write for him. He placed the signature himself and thereby conveyed a salutation written by his own hand. This appears to have been his usual practice, for of it he says: "which is the token in every epistle; so I write." (2 Thess. 3: 17.) It was the evidence that each was the expression of his mind as guided by the Holy Spirit. The endorsement with his name is followed by a request singularly pathetic in its abrupt brevity.

Remember my bonds.—To remember his bonds was to pray for him in his bonds. [The petition helps us to conceive how heavy a trial Paul felt in his imprisonment, to be as little as he said about it, and bravely as he bore it. He wished their remembrance, too, because his bonds added weight to his words. His sufferings gave him a right to speak. He wished their remembrance because his bonds might encourage them to steadfast endurance if need for it should arise. He points to his own sufferings, and would have them take heart to bear their lighter crosses and fight their easier battles.]

Grace be with you.—There is no richer word than grace, for it carries in it all of God's love as seen in the gift of his Son for us. [We began with grace, we are kept by grace, and it is grace that will bring us home at last.]

[The personal details of 4: 7-17 link the doctrinal and practical teaching of this epistle with the actual life of Paul. They remind us that the gospel is not a mere abstract truth, but touches the everyday life of actual men. This historic setting of the gospel, which we find in many casual notices in Paul's epistles and in the narrative of the book of Acts, furnishes proof of the historic truth of the statements on which the gospel rests. It also helps us, by reproducing surroundings and the inner and outer life of Paul, to understand and better appreciate the thought embodied in the doctrinal parts of his epistles. Time spent in bringing together, and endeavoring to interpret, these scanty notices will bear abundant fruit in a clearer conception of his inner thought and of the gospel which permeated and moulded and ennobled his entire inner and outer life.]

INDEX TO EPHESIANS

A

Adoption, unto, as sons, 19.
Air, according to the powers of the, 39.
Angels, the, minister to the church, 61.
Angry, be, and sin not, 89.
Apostle, Paul an, of Jesus Christ, 15.
Apostles, he gave some to be, 77.
Apprehend, it takes strong faith to, the love of Christ, 65.
Armor, put on the whole, of God, 125, 129.
Ascended, he, 76.

B

Baptism, there is one, 73.
Body, there is one, 72; unto the building up of the, of Christ, 79; all the, fitly framed together, 82; members of the same, 88, 115.

C

Calling, hope of his, 33.
Captivity, led, captive, 74.
Child, the, must obey parents, 117.
Children, that we be no longer, 80; obey your parents in the Lord, 118.
Chosen in Christ before the foundation of the world, 18.
Christ, in, 17; chosen in before the foundation of the world, 18; to sum up all things in, 25; we who had before hoped in, 26; is head of all things to the church, 36; all the blessings of heaven come through, 42; in his death abolished the law, 48; that, may dwell in the heart through faith, 63; glory to, in the church, 69; unto the stature of the fulness of, 80; may grow up in, in all things, 81; called into existence and formed a new world, 83; ye did not so learn, 85; was God manifest in the flesh, 87; forgive as, forgave you, 96; gave himself for us, 97; in the fear of, 110.
Christians, God the Father of all, 16; are builded together in Christ, 53; must confine their labor to that which is good, 91.
Church, Christ is the head of all things to the, 37, 112; the, is one, 53; to God be glory in the, 68; the only manifestation of the, is where the Spirit controls the bodies of men, 82; in the early, there were many imperfectly taught, 86; Christ cleansed the, by the washing of water, 113; the, should be holy and without blemish, 114.
Circumcision, the Jews called the, 46.
Clamor, 95.
Cornerstone, Jesus Christ the chief, 53.
Corrupt, let no, speech proceed out of your mouth, 92.
Courage, a lack of, to speak at all times the full truth is a besetting sin of some preachers, 135.
Covetousness, 98.
Cross, Jesus died on the, to reconcile man to God, 49.

D

Darkness, have no fellowship with, 101.
Death is the prison house for sinners, 75.
Depth, the love of Christ goes far beyond, the, of sin, 76.
Desires, doing the, of the flesh and mind, 40.
Devil, give no place to the, 89; the wiles of the, 126; at the head of the ranks of the wicked spirits, 128.
Disobedience, the spirit works in the sons of, 40.
Dispensation, unto a, 23.
Doctrine, carried about with every wind of, 80.
Drunken, be not, 105.

E

Earnest, the gift of the Holy Spirit an, of the inheritance, 28.
Ephesus, the city of, 9; origin of the church at, 10.
Eternal purpose, God's, 61.

Evangelists, he gave some to be, 77.
Eyes of the heart, the, 31.
Eyeservice, not in the way of, 122.

F

Faith, Christ dwells in the heart through, 64; there is one, 73; unto the unity of the, 79; taking the shield of, 132.
False teaching, the dishonesty of, 81.
Falsehood, put away all, 88.
Feet, having your, shod, 131.
Flesh, the works of the, 40.
Foolish, be not, 105.
Foreordained, having, us, 18, 26; God, the provisions of salvation, 19.
Forgive, as God forgave, 95.
Foundation, built upon the, of the apostles and prophets, 52.
Framed, each building fitly, together, 53.
Fullness, the, of the time, 24; to be filled with the, of God, 67; unto the stature of the, of Christ, 89.

G

Gentiles, the inclusion of the, in the church, 23; the condition of the, deplorable, 46; made nigh by the blood of Christ, 47.
God, the, of our Lord Jesus Christ, 30; raised Christ to his right hand, 36; raised those dead in trespasses and sin, 38; is a, of grace, 41; is rich in mercy, 41; dwells in each separate congregation through the spirit, 54; there is one, 73; be imitators of, 96.
Godhead, in Christ all the fulness of the, dwells, 37.
Goodness, in all, 100.
Gospel-hardened preacher, the, 32.
Grace, no peace without, 16; the riches of his, 21; by, have ye been saved, 42; special, bestowed on Paul to preach to the Gentiles, 59; to all that love the Lord, 139.
Grieve not the Spirit, 93.

H

Heart, having the eyes of your, enlightened, 31.
Heavenly places, blessings in the, 17; Christ sits at the right hand of God in the, 35; he calls the church, 42; those occupied by angels, 60; the hosts of wickedness in the, 127.
Heavens, to sum up all things in the, 25.
Height, Christ's love reaches to the, of his glory, 66.
Helmet, the, of salvation, 133.
Heritage, a, in Christ, 26.
Holiness, God does not allow us to be satisfied with anything less than perfect, 66.
Holy Spirit, the, of promise, 27.
Honor father and mother, children must, 119.
Hope, what is the, of his calling? 33.
Hoped, we who had before, in Christ, 26.
Household, the, of God, 51.
Husband, the, is head of the wife, 111; should love his wife as he loveth himself, 115.
Hymns, 107.

I

Indwelling, the, of Christ is through faith, 64.
Inheritance, the gift of the Holy Spirit an earnest of the, 28; the, of the saints, 34.

L

Lasciviousness, 85.
Law of Moses, the, abolished, 22; Christ in his death abolished the, 48.
Length, the love of Christ goes to any, necessary to save man, 66.
Light, walk in the, 100; all made manifest by the, 103.
Long-suffering, with, 71.
Lord, there is one, 72; in the name of the, 109; children to obey parents in the, 118.

INDEX

Love, in, is the condition under which growth takes place, 65; the, of Christ is as broad as the necessities of the world, 66; is all inclusive, 71; speaking the truth in, 81.
Lowliness, with all, 70.

M

Malice, 95.
Marriage, the most sacred of all ties, 116.
Masters, instruction to, 123.
Meekness, with all, 70.
Members, we are, of the same body, 88.
Mind, the spirit of the, 86.
Ministering, unto the, 78.
Mystery, the, of his will, 22; acceptance of the Gentiles on an equality with the Jews, a, 57; dispensation of the, 60.

O

Old man, the, 86.

P

Parents' duty to their children, 119.
Pastors and teachers, some to be, 78.
Paul, the prisoner of Jesus Christ, 55; constituted an apostle to the Gentiles, 56; an ambassador in chains, 136.
Paul's prayer for the Ephesians, 55, 62.
Peace, there is no, without grace, 16; Christ is our, 47; could not be preached till after the resurrection of Jesus, 50; in the bond of, 72; peace to the brethren, 138.
Power, greatness of God's, to those who believe, 34, 68.
Powers, according to the, of the air, 39.
Prayer, Paul's, for the Ephesians, 62; and supplication, 134.
Preparedness is the important thing, 130.
Principalities and powers, 127.

Prophets, the, were a distinct class of inspired teachers, 52; he gave some to be, 77.
Psalms, speaking to one another in, 107.
Psallo, 107.

R

Railing, 95.
Redemption, Christ our, 20; unto the, of God's own possession, 29; the day of, 94.
Remission, Jesus shed his blood for the, of our sins, 20.
Resurrection, the, was an act of Christ's own will, 35; it is a, power that turns death into life, 38.
Revelation, a spirit of wisdom and, 31.
Riches, the, of his inheritance of the saints, 34.
Righteousness, in all, 101; the breastplate of, 130.
Rooted, to take Christ into the heart is to be, in him, 64.

S

Saints, all Christians are called, 15, 51; glory of his inheritance in the, 34; for the perfecting of the, 78.
Sealed, ye are, in the Spirit, 94.
Servants to be obedient to masters, 121.
Singing and making melody in the heart to the Lord, 108.
Spirit, in one, 50; in the, 58; through the, in the inward man, 63; give diligence to keep the unity of the, 71; there is one, 72; grieve not the, 93; sealed by the, 94; be filled with the, 106.
Spiritual, gifts, 74; hosts of, wickedness, 127.
Stealing, 90.
Strong, be, in the Lord, 125.
Sword, the, of the Spirit, 133.

T

Thanks, giving, 109.
Time, how redeem? 104.
Times, the fulness of the, 24.

Truth, be men of, 101; gird the loins with, 130.
Tychicus, 137.

U

Uncircumcision, the Gentiles called the, 46.
Uncleanness, to work all, 85.
Union, to be in, with God we must be in union with all in union with him, 49.
Unity, the, of the faith, 70.

V

Voice, the human, 107.

W

Walk, the term, denotes the habitual tenor of life, 45, 70; no longer as the Gentiles, 83; do not, as fools, 104.
War between the people of God and the powers of darkness, 135.
We and *us*, and *ye* and *you* as used in chapters one to three, 17.
Well-pleasing to the Lord, 101.
Wisdom and prudence, the apostles were endowed with, 21.
Wives to be subject to husbands, 111.
Word of God, all the teaching the Spirit gives is found in the, 50; Christ cleansed the church with the, 113.
Work, every member has his, to do, 82.
Workmanship, the, of God saves, 44.
Works, the, that save, 43.
World, according to the course of this, 39.
Wrath, the children of, 41; let not the sun go down upon your, 89.
Wrestling, our, not against flesh and blood, 126.

INDEX TO PHILIPPIANS

A

Abased, I know how to be, 228.
Abound, how to, 229.
Adversaries, their undaunted bearing in the face of their, was a token of their destruction, 174.
Affliction, thinking to add, 164.
Affrighted, in nothing, 173.
All, the frequent use of, springs from deep affection, 156.

B

Baptism, an act of faith, 187.
Benjamin, of the tribe of, 201.
Bishops and deacons, 156.
Blemish, without, 188.
Body, the, is the spirit's vehicle of action, 168; conformed to the, of his glory, 215.
Boldness, the peculiar, was freedom of speech, 167.
Bonds, his, became manifest, 162; which hold men together, 197.

C

Choose, what I shall, I know not, 160.
Christ, for me to live is, 168; Christians must become like, in character, 180; that I may gain, 204; righteousness through faith in, 205.
Christ Jesus, in the tender mercies of, 160, 224.
Church, the Philippian, 151.
Circumcision, Christians are the, 200.
Circumcised the eighth day, 201.
Citizenship, our, is in heaven, 214.
Concision, beware of the, 200.
Confess, the lost shall, Christ as Lord, 185.
Cross, the death of the, 183.

D

Day, the, of Jesus Christ, 159, 189.
Death, whether by life or, 168; becoming obedient to, 183; conformed to the, of Christ, 207.
Depart, to, and be with Christ, 170.
Die, to, is gain, 169.

Disputings, do all things without, 187.
Dogs, beware of, 199.

E

Emptied himself of all his glories, 181.
End, perfection is only bestowed on those who run to the, 209.
Enemies of the cross, 213.
Envy, some preached Christ of, 163.
Epaphroditus, 194, 233.
Euodia and Syntiche, 218.
Evil workers, beware of, 200.
Exalted, God highly, him, 184.
Existing, who, in the form of God, 181.
Expectation, according to my, and hope, 167.

F

Faction, some preach the gospel of, 164.
Factious, there is no greater foe to unity than the, spirit, 179.
Faith, according to your, 167; righteousness through, 205.
Fashion, being found in, as a man, 182.
Fellowship, your, 157; means to share with, 158; people are said to be in, when what is true of one is true of the other, 177; the, of his sufferings, 207; in my sufferings, 230.
Fellow soldier, 195.
Fellow workers, my, 219.
Fidelity, their, was a token of their deliverance, 174.
Flesh, if he continued in the, his effort would be to magnify Christ, 169; no confidence in the, 200.
Forbearance, 221.

G

Gift, not that I seek the, 232.
Glorying, that your, may abound, 171.

God, how does, work in man to will and do? 186; of peace, 227; my, shall supply needs, 234.
Good report, 225.
Good will, some preach the gospel of, 164.
Good work, God began the, at Philippi, 158.
Gospel, the things that happened to Paul aided the progress of the, 162.
Grasped, a thing to be, 181.

H

Harmless is to be internally pure, 188.
Harmony, the law of, runs through all God's dealings with man, 166.
Heart, I have you in my, 159; acceptable service to God springs from the, 167.
Hebrew, a, of Hebrews, 201.
Honorable, whatsoever things are, 224.
Humbled, he, himself, 182.
Humiliation, body of our, 215.

I

Imitators, be, of me, 211.
Israel, the stock of, 201.

J

Joy, I, and rejoice, 190.
Just, whatsoever things are, 225.

K

Know, that I may, him, 206.
Knowledge, their growth in, enabled them to more fully obey God, 160; for the excellency of the, of Christ, 204.

L

Labor, did not, in vain, 190.
Learned of me, 227.
Lights, shine as, 188.
Like-minded, be, 177.
Likeness, made in the, of men, 182.
Longed for, beloved and, 217.
Lord, the, is at hand, 222.
Loss, Paul counted all gains under the law, for Christ, 203, 204.

Love, consolation of, 176.
Lowliness, all should cultivate a spirit of, 179.

M

Macedonia, when I departed from, 231.
Magnified, that Christ may be, 168.
Man, being found in the fashion as a, 182.
Mercies and compassions, if any tender, 177.
Miracles, not used for the good of those who wrought them, 196.
Murmurings, do all things without, 187.

N

Name, his, above every name, 184.
Needful, to abide in the flesh is more, 170.

O

Obeyed, they, not only in his presence, 185.
Odor of a sweet smell, 233.
Offence, void of, 160.
Only, 210.

P

Paul, why, did not call himself an apostle in this epistle, 155.
Paul's defense consisted in his preaching Christ, 161.
Perdition, whose end is, 213.
Perfect, Paul did not claim to be, before suffering as did Christ, 208.
Perfection, he had not attained, the he sought, 208.
Pharisee, touching the law, a, 202.
Philippi, 145.
Philippian, origin of the, church, 146; the, church the most faithful of apostolic churches, 157.
Praise, if there be any, 226.
Prayer and supplication, 222.
Preach, some, the gospel of good will, 164.
Providences, God's, are the results of his laws, 166.
Pure, whatsoever things are, 225.

R

Rejoice, therein I, 165; in the Lord always, 221; I, greatly, 228.
Resurrection, the power of his, 206; that I may attain unto the, from the dead, 207.
Righteousness, the fruits of, 161; as touching, in the law, blameless, 202; not having a, of mine own, 205.

S

Sacrifice, willing to, his life, 190.
Saints, all disciples are, 156.
Salvation, work out your own, 186.
Seek, they all, their own, 192.
Shame, the, that comes from hopes disappointed, 167.
Shortly, I hope to come, 193.
Sincere desire, a, to know and do God's will, without any wish or preference, save to do his will, will lead into the fulness of divine truth, 209, 210.
Sincerity denotes truth and uprightness, 160.
Sonship, Jesus could not give up his essentials of, 181.
Soul, the, is the emotional part of man, 172.
Spirit, the, of Christ, excludes turning from the commands of God, 167; stand fast in one, 172.
Spirits, God will give bodies suited to our, 216.
Stand, that ye, fast, 172.
Strait, this refers to the alternative between life and death, 169.
Suffer, a privilege to, for Christ, 174.

Supplication, Paul remembered the Philippians in every, 167; through your, 166.

T

Things, let each look to the, of others, 180; think on these, 226; the, 226.
Timothy, 155, 191, 194, 195.
Trembling, work out salvation with fear and, 186.
True, whatsoever things are, 224.
Trust, I, in the Lord, 193.

U

Unity, on, too much stress cannot be laid, 172; Paul pled for, among all disciples of Christ, 178.

V

Vainglory, do nothing through, 179.
Virtue, if there be any, 226.

W

Walk, whereupon we have attained, by that rule let us, 210; mark them that so, 212; many, of whom I told you, 213.
Wolves, grievous, 194.
Word of life, the, 189.
Work out your own salvation, 186.

Z

Zeal, as to, persecuting the church, 202.

INDEX TO COLOSSIANS

A

Afflictions, the, which Paul suffered were for the church, 267.
Alienated, being, in time past, and enemies, 263.
Angels, false teachers presented, as mediators, 278; worshiping of, 284.
Anger, 292.
Answer, that ye may know how to, each one, 309.
Archippus, 318.
Aristarchus, 312.

B

Baptism, buried with Christ in, 279; avails nothing without faith, 280.
Birth is the beginning of a new life, 262.
Blemish and unreprovable, without, in his sight, 265.
Body of his flesh, in the, through death, 264.
Bond of perfectness, put on the, 297.
Brethren, faithful, 248.

C

Children obey your parents, in all things, 303.
Christ, in, 248; all things have been created through, 260; in him all things stand together, 260; in him all fulness dwells, 262; fill up that which was lacking in the afflictions of, 266; the only hope of glory is, in man, 269; to learn, is to learn the mystery of God, 274; to be made full is to be in, 278; the head of all principality and power, 278; complete in, 280; if ye died with, 285; if you were raised together with, 288; your life is hid with, in God, 289; when, shall be manifested, 290; in, no distinction of flesh, 294; is all and in all, 294; let the peace of, rule in your hearts, 297.
Church, Christ is the head of the, 261.
Circumcision, the, of Christ, 278; spiritual, not made with hands, 279.
Colossæ, 243.
Colossian, origin of the, error, 243; time and place of writing the, epistle, 245.
Comforted, that their hearts may be, 273.
Compassion, put on a heart of, 295.
Covetousness is idolatry, 291.
Creator, is the, of all things, 259.

D

Darkness, all out of the kingdom are under the power of, 258.
Demas, 317.
Died, you, with Christ to the world, 289.

E

Epaphras, even as ye heard of, 252, 314.
Evil works in your, 263.

F

Faith, having heard of your, 250; established in, 275.
Fathers provoke not your children, 303.
First-born, the, of all creation, 258; from the dead, 261.
Forbearing one another, 296.
Forgave, as the Lord, you so do you, 296.
Fornication, 290.
Fruit, bearing, and increasing, 252.
Full, in Christ are you made, 278.

G

God, through the will of, 247; the Father, 249; the Father of our Lord Jesus Christ, 249; Jesus is the expression of the invisible, 258.
Godhead, of the, bodily, 277.
Gospel, not moved away from the hope of the, 265; the, was preached to all creation under heaven, 265.

INDEX

Grounded and stedfast, if ye continue, in the faith, 265.

H

Head, not holding up the, 284.
Heart, the circumcision of the, 280; in singleness of, fearing the Lord, 305.
Heartily, whatsoever you do, work, 305.
Heavens, in the, 251; the, 260.
Hope, for the, laid up, 250.
Humility, let no man rob you by a voluntary, 283; studies and affected, 287.
Husbands, love your wives, 302.

I

Idolatry, covetousness is, 291.
Instrumental accompaniment in the song service, 298.
Inventions and devices of men, abstain from the, 286.

Kindness, 295.

J

Jesus that is called Justus, 313.
Joy, long-suffering with, 256.
Judge, let no man, you, 282.

K

Knit together in love, 273.
Knowledge, filled with the, of his will, 253; increasing in the, of God, 255; renewed in, 294.

L

Laodicea, epistle from, 318.
Law of Moses, no one could be justified by the, 281; the, a shadow of good things to come, 283.
Lie not one to another, 293.
Light, in, 257.
Long-suffering, 295; with joy, 256.
Love, above all things put on, 296.
Lowliness, 295.
Luke, the physician, 315.

M

Malice, 293.
Mark the cousin of Barnabas, 313.
Masters, render unto your servants that which is just and equal, 306.
Meekness, 295.
Meet, who made us, 256.
Member, by every, working effectually in his sphere, 285.
Members, put to death your, which are upon the earth, 290.
Mind, set your, on things above, 288.
Minister, Paul was made a, of the gospel, 266.
Mouth, let no corrupt speech proceed out of your, 293.
Mystery, the, which has been hid for ages and generations, 268.

N

Nailed to the cross, the law of Moses was, 281.
Name of the Lord Jesus, do all in the, 299.
New man, put on the, 294.
Nymphas, 317.

O

Old man, put off the, with his doings, 293.
Onesimus, 311.
Ordinances, having blotted out the bond of, 281; if you died with Christ, why are you subject to? 285.

P

Passion and evil desire, 291.
Patience, unto all, 256.
Paul, an apostle of Christ Jesus, 247; was a minister of the church through the duties God laid on him, 267.
Perfect, Jesus Christ as he lived on earth is the, pattern, 269; every man, in Christ, 270.
Philosophy, no salvation comes through, 176.
Pleasing, unto all, bearing fruit, 255.
Power, strengthened with all, 255; is accessible to all, 272.
Precept and doctrines of men, the, all perish with the using, 286.
Prayer, continue steadfastly in, 307.

Pre-eminence, that he might have the, 262.
Principalities and powers, Christ despoiled, 282.
Progressive, a, increase of faith is the condition of Christian progress, 275.
Puffed up, vainly, 284.
Psalms, hymns, and spiritual songs, 298.

R

Railing, 293.
Recompense, from the Lord ye receive the, of the inheritance, 305.
Resurrection, the Lord's, expressed the fact of God's acceptance, 280.
Rob, let no man, you of your prize, 284.
Rooted and built up in Christ, 275.
Rudiments, the, of the world, 276.

S

Sabbath day, or a, 283.
Saints, to the, 247; love towards all, 250; inheritance of the, 257.
Salt, seasoned with, 308.
Seek things above, 288.
Servants obey your masters, 304.
Shameful speaking, 293.
Singing with grace in your hearts, 299.
Sinless life, all should strive for the, 271.
Speech, let your, be always with grace, 308.
Spiritual, all, wisdom and understanding, 254.

Stedfastness, the, of faith, 275.
Sufferings, Paul rejoiced in his, for Christ's sake, 266.

T

Thanks, we give, 249; giving, unto God, 256, 300.
Tradition, after the, of men, 276.
Tychicus, the beloved brother, 310.

U

Uncleanness, 290.
Universality, the, of the gospel is not for a privileged circle, 269.

V

Visible, things, and invisible, 260.

W

Walk, to, worthily of the Lord, 254; in wisdom toward them that are without, 308.
Well-pleasing unto the Lord, 303.
Word, the, of truth, 251; let the, dwell in you richly, 297.
World, all the, 251.
Will, filled with the knowledge of his, 254.
Will-worship, 287.
Wisdom, all spiritual, 254, 270.
Wives be in subjection to your husbands, 301.
Work, bearing fruit in every good, 255.
Wrath, the, of God comes on sons of disobedience, 292, 293.

www.ingramcontent.com/pod-product-compliance
Lightning Source LLC
Chambersburg PA
CBHW032033150426
43194CB00006B/258